Nigel Yates is the foremost authority on the relationship between the liturgy and the ordering of church buildings in the post reformation world. Building on his earlier book, Buildings, Faith and Worship*, which explored the liturgical arrangement of Anglican churches between 1600 and 1900, Professor Yates has provided a well researched and entertaining account of the interplay between the liturgies of the various denominations and the way church buildings, old and new, have been ordered. Professor Yates is an acknowledged expert in this field, and serious students and amateur church crawlers alike will enjoy his eye for quirky detail as well as the scholarly erudition that underpins this splendid volume.*

The Right Reverend David Stancliffe, Bishop of Salisbury, UK

This is a masterly overview of the continual process down the centuries by which the Church responds to a renewed vision of God by revisiting the church building and reshaping it to better reflect the hopes and aspirations of the community of faith. Both scholar and worshipper will be enriched by it.

The Very Reverend Richard Giles, Dean of Philadelphia Cathedral, USA

No liturgical historian or indeed anyone who has any kind of responsibility for liturgy can afford to be without this book, dealing as it does with how theology and worship affect the use of liturgical space. This book shows how different theological and liturgical insights impact on how churches have been re-ordered for worship at different times and across all the denominations, and is therefore invaluable for those responsible for modern day worship.

The Most Reverend Dr Barry C. Morgan, The Archbishop of Wales

Interesting and attractive in equal measure, and much more than a handbook or introductory overview, Liturgical Space *is comprehensive, authoritative, and suggestive in its interweaving of architecture, theology, ecclesiology, and history.*

Professor Clyde Binfield, UK

Nigel Yates is Professor of Ecclesiastical History at the University of Wales, Lampeter. As well as having written extensively on church buildings over the past twenty years, he was between 1981 and 1991 a member of the Executive Committee of the Council for the Care of Churches, advising the Church of England on reordering schemes as part of the faculty jurisdiction process, and has since spoken at major conferences on church buildings and their furnishings.

LITURGY, WORSHIP AND SOCIETY

SERIES EDITORS

Dave Leal, Brasenose College, Oxford, UK
Bryan Spinks, Yale Divinity School, USA
Paul Bradshaw, University of Notre Dame, UK and USA
Gregory Woolfenden, St Mary's Orthodox Church, USA
Phillip Tovey, Ripon College Cuddesdon, UK

The Ashgate *Liturgy, Worship and Society* series forms an important new 'library' on liturgical theory at a time of great change in the liturgy and much debate concerning traditional and new forms of worship, suitability and use of places of worship, and wider issues concerning interaction of liturgy, worship and contemporary society. Offering a thorough grounding in the historical and theological foundations of liturgy, this series explores and challenges many key issues of worship and liturgical theology, currently in hot debate within academe and within Christian churches worldwide – issues central to the future of the liturgy, to public and private worship, and set to make a significant impact on changing patterns of worship and the place of the church in contemporary society.

Other titles in the series include

Liturgy and Architecture
From the Early Church to the Middle Ages
Allan Doig

The Baptismal Liturgy of Jerusalem
Fourth- and Fifth-Century Evidence from Palestine, Syria and Egypt
Juliette Day

First Communion
Ritual, Church and Popular Religious Identity
Peter McGrail

Early and Medieval Rituals and Theologies of Baptism
From the New Testament to the Council of Trent
Bryan D. Spinks

Reformation and Modern Rituals and Theologies of Baptism
From Luther to Contemporary Practices
Bryan D. Spinks

Liturgical Space

Christian Worship and Church Buildings in Western Europe 1500-2000

NIGEL YATES

University of Wales, Lampeter, UK

ASHGATE

Published by
Ashgate Publishing Limited
Gower House
Croft Road
Aldershot
Hampshire GU11 3HR
England

Ashgate Publishing Company
Suite 420
101 Cherry Street
Burlington, VT 05401-4405
USA

Ashgate website: http://www.ashgate.com

British Library Cataloguing in Publication Data
Yates, Nigel
  Liturgical space : Christian worship and church buildings
  in Western Europe, 1500-2000. – (Liturgy, worship and society)
  1. Public worship – Europe – History 2. Church buildings – Europe – History
  I. Title
  264'.0094'0903

Library of Congress Cataloging-in-Publication Data
Yates, Nigel.
  Liturgical space : Christian worship and church buildings in western Europe, 1500-2000 /
Nigel Yates.
    p. cm. – (Liturgy, worship & society series)
  Includes bibliographical references (p.   ) and index.
   ISBN 978-0-7546-5795-8 (hardcover : alk. paper) – ISBN 978-0-7546-5797-2 (pbk. : alk.
paper) 1. Public worship–Europe–History. 2. Church buildings–Europe–History. I. Title.

  BV5.Y38 2008
  264.0094'0903–dc22

                                                                                2007042394

ISBN 978-0-7546-5795-8 (Hbk)
ISBN 978-0-7546-5797-2 (Pbk)

Printed and bound in Great Britain by MPG Books Ltd, Bodmin, Cornwall.

Contents

List of Figures

List of Illustrations

Introduction

This book has arisen from, and follows very much the outline, of the module I have taught at the University of Wales, Lampeter, in alternate years since 2001. I am extremely grateful to the groups of enthusiastic students I have taught on those occasions, and who have helped me to improve both the content and the presentation of the module over the years, and I should like to dedicate this book to all of them, but especially to Laura Jarvis and Ruth Russell-Jones, who now both hold positions within the university and still enjoy visiting churches.

This book is primarily designed for four groups of people: practitioners of church history, at both undergraduate and postgraduate level, who need to know more about the history of worship and church buildings as an adjunct to their other academic studies; clergy and other church officers and their architects who have to care for church buildings and ensure that they meet the needs of worshipping congregations; members of conservation bodies and planning authorities who have an overall responsibility for the built environment and the protection of Europe's architectural heritage; and finally for the growing band of church tourists, to enable them to put the buildings they visit into a historical and liturgical context. I am encouraged in the last of these aims by the knowledge that several of my students have told me that they now, as a result of having followed the module, visit churches looking out for things that they had previously never noticed or had not realised the significance of. I hope this book will have a similar impact on its readers.

Although I have been visiting churches, fairly assiduously, for the last fifty years, this book has grown out of a growing professional involvement in the history of church building and furnishing over the last twenty years. In 1981 I was invited to serve on the Executive Committee of the Council for the Care of Churches, the body that acts for the Church of England as its principal adviser in architectural and artistic matters. During the course of my ten-years' service on this body, I represented the Council on a number of occasions as its expert witness at consistory courts convened to consider some of the more complicated cases of church reordering. The research required on these occasions led to the publication of the first edition of my *Buildings, Faith and Worship* in 1991. Since then I have looked more widely at the contextualisation of Anglican church furnishing and liturgical arrangement and endeavoured to find interesting comparisons in the arrangement and furnishing of churches in the Anglican, Lutheran, Reformed and Roman Catholic liturgical traditions. Some of this research has already appeared in print. More will do so in the near future, including a new guide to Welsh churches and chapels and a more academic study of Scottish church interiors since the Reformation. Much of it, however, has been incorporated into this book. The very diligent reader will be able to work out, from the examples cited, those parts of Europe with which I am most familiar and I must apologise to those readers who feel that other parts of Europe have been unduly neglected. However, I should be doubtful as to whether more detailed coverage of these areas would have made much, if any, difference to the overall thesis that I have put forward in the pages that follow.

In the researches that have led to the production of this volume I have incurred many debts over the years: Peter Burman, Thomas Cocke, David Williams and the late Donald Findlay, former officers of the Council for the Care of Churches; John Hume, formerly of Historic Scotland; Tony Parkinson, formerly of the Royal Commission on Ancient Monuments and Historic Buildings in Wales; the Venerable Professor W.M. Jacob and the late Professor George Yule, with whom I have had frequent discussions about ecclesiastical buildings over the years; the Cambrian Archaeological Association, the Cromarty Trust, the Marc Fitch Fund and the Scouloudi Foundation, who have made generous grants to the costs of research; Penny Brook, Michael Carter and, especially, Abi Hyde, who have drawn the church plans reproduced in this volume; my son David for typing the text of this volume so competently; Canon Brendan O'Malley, who read and commented on the text; and last, but by no means least, my wife Paula, who has both driven me to many of the buildings described in the text and has, as always, been a source of encouragement and support at every stage of the project.

I should also like to acknowledge with gratitude those bodies that have permitted the reproduction of illustrations in this volume: National Museum, Copenhagen (Illustration 1.1); University of Wales, Lampeter (Illustrations 2.1, 3.2, 3.7, 4.2, 5.1); Rijksmuseum Het Catharijneconvent, Utrecht (Illustration 3.1); Westfries Museum, Hoorn (Illustration 3.3); Geemente Archief, Haarlem (Illustration 3.4); Museum Amstelkring, Amsterdam (Illustration 5.3); Milton House, Oxfordshire (Illustration 5.4); Diocesan Archives, Dublin (Illustration 5.5); and Ulster Folk and Transport Museum, Belfast (Illustration 5.6).

Nigel Yates
University of Wales Lampeter
February 2008

Chapter 1

The Legacy of the Pre-Reformation Church and the Impact of the Reformation

The aim of this introductory chapter is to set the scene for the core of this book, a discussion of the ways in which Christian worship and church buildings have changed between the Reformation of the sixteenth century and the present day. It will begin with a brief survey of the development of Christian worship and church buildings from the days of the Early Church to the late Middle Ages in Western Europe, and then look, in a comparative context, at the way in which the different forms of Protestant worship before the end of the sixteenth century impacted on the liturgical arrangement of church buildings and the consequences this had for the preservation or otherwise of pre-Reformation furnishings. Consideration will also be given to the changes in the appearance of Roman Catholic churches as a result of their own response to the ideas of the Protestant reformers and the new devotional culture of the Counter-Reformation.

The Origins of Christian Architecture

The first Christian churches were rooms in large private houses. Examples of such churches, dating from the third and fourth centuries, have been excavated at Dura Europas in Syria and at Lullingstone Roman Villa in Kent. When separate church buildings began to be erected after the adoption of Christianity as the state religion of the Roman Empire in the fourth century, they were based on the secular basilica, an aisled hall with an apse at each end. This was adapted so that there was only one apse, at the end opposite the entrance, and this was used as the seat of the bishop, who would have been surrounded by his presbyters, sitting on benches. The altar would have stood in front of the apse so that people could gather around it for the eucharist. The font, for the baptism of new Christians, was usually placed in a separate baptistry adjacent to the main church. The altar was usually covered by a canopy or *ciborium* and surrounded by a low screen or *cancelli*. The liturgical action at the altar was, however, fully visible. In front of this sanctuary area there was usually an *ambo*, for reading and preaching. A good example of this early basilica style of church is Santa Maria Maggiore in Rome, built in 432-40 (Figure 1.1), though it has been wholly refurnished in the centuries thereafter.

Figure 1.1   Ground plan of Santa Maria Maggiore, Rome

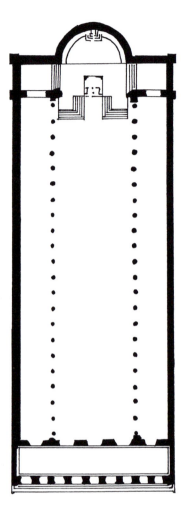

In the eastern part of the Roman Empire a slightly different type of church began to emerge from the sixth century. This was a square or cruciform building with shallow arms, the principal feature of which was a central lantern or dome. As the liturgy became more complex much of it began to take place behind a screen or iconostasis, which separated the clergy from the laity (Figure 1.2). This type of church, with only a single altar and in which the eucharist only took place on Sundays and festivals, has remained the norm among Eastern Orthodox Christians, but within the western church, under the jurisdiction of the Bishop of Rome, two major developments took place which have had a major impact on the design of church buildings. The first was the development of two distinct types of eucharistic liturgy, the sung High Mass with priest, deacon and sub-deacon for Sundays and festivals, and the more simple Low Mass, which was said by a priest alone. The medieval western church also began to develop a doctrine of purgatory, in which the prayers of the living could relieve the sufferings of the departed as they were purified before their entrance into heaven. Many people endowed special altars and chapels in churches in which Mass could be said for the repose of the souls of members of their families. A second, and equally important, development in the medieval western church was that of the sermon as a means of encouraging popular piety, delivered outside the Mass and sometimes associated with special, non-eucharistic, services or extra-liturgical devotions such as Benediction of the Blessed Sacrament, in which the people were blessed with a consecrated host displayed in a monstrance.

Figure 1.2   Ground plan of eighth-century Eastern Orthodox church

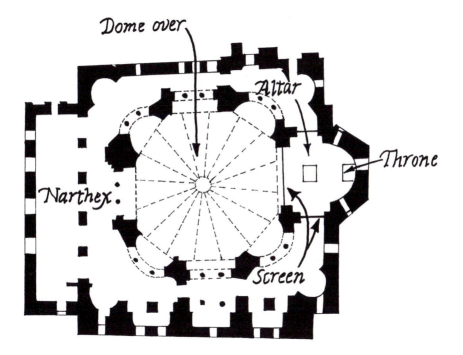

These developments in the medieval western church were to lead to the building of a very different type of ecclesiastical building, one in which the large central space with the closed-off sanctuary area was replaced by a much longer building, divided into a series of compartments. Churches that had begun as simple two-cell structures, the nave for the people and the chancel for the clergy, were extended in a variety of ways. Towers were erected at one end, or over the central part of the building, to house a peel of bells to summon people to church. The nave, and frequently the chancel, were given aisles and sometimes both outer and inner aisles. Transepts were added to make the church cruciform. In cathedrals and other large churches a separate chapel, dedicated to the Blessed Virgin Mary, was frequently added beyond the high altar. Instead of only one altar, there would be several; in the aisles or the transepts, wherever they could be accommodated, or in separate chapels added to the church by wealthy benefactors who wished to endow chantries in which priests would celebrate Mass for them and other members of their families. Before the Reformation the church of St Alphege at Solihull (Figure 1.3) had as many as ten side altars in addition to the high altar. Chancels were lengthened so that they did not just contain the high altar but stalls in which the clergy could sing the offices of Matins, Lauds, Prime, Terce, Sext, Nones, Vespers and Compline. In theory these should have been sung separately every third hour of the day and night, but in practice they were usually grouped so that they could be sung early in the morning before Mass, in the middle of the day and in the evening. The clergy in the chancel were usually separated from the laity in the nave by a screen on top of which was a loft, frequently with an altar for reservation of the Blessed Sacrament and figures of Christ on the cross supported by the Blessed Virgin Mary and St John the Evangelist. The epistle and gospel were frequently read from the top of the screen but otherwise the action of the Mass would not have been visible and key points, such as the elevation of the host, would have been announced by the ringing of bells. As in the Eastern Orthodox Churches today, there were two services taking place: the liturgy of the clergy on one side of the screen and the private devotions of the laity on the other. The links between the two were infrequent and highly formalised.

Figure 1.3   Ground plan of St Alphege's, Solihull, in the early sixteenth century

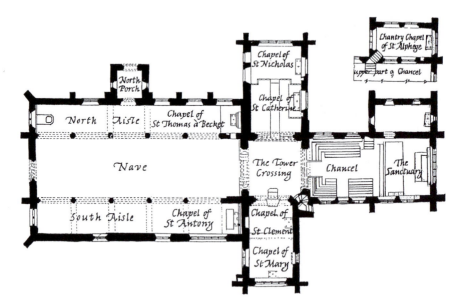

The development of the sermon, popularised by the new orders of friars from the thirteenth century, necessitated the furnishing of the nave as well as the chancel. Pulpits for preaching were installed, either at the chancel end, or in the middle, of the nave, and benches for people to sit on were gradually introduced. The proliferation of side altars and shrines led to many churches becoming extremely cramped, and the spaciousness that early Christian, and even Eastern Orthodox, churches had tried to achieve was lost. They suited the development of private devotions associated with the cults of saints and relics, the offering of prayers for the departed and the veneration of the Blessed Sacrament, but they did not work for any form of corporate worship. Consequently, although individual furnishings have survived, there is probably not a single church in Western Europe that fully reflects the liturgical climate of the Middle Ages. One exception to this will be the church of St Teilo, Llandeilo Talybont, in the process of re-erection at the Museum of Welsh Life at St Fagan's near Cardiff. This church was replaced by a new church in the largest village in the parish, Pontarddulais, in the late nineteenth century and it gradually became redundant and a target for vandals. Eventually the complete set of furnishings of 1810 were destroyed. During the process of dismantling an important series of medieval wall-paintings was discovered and this led to the extremely imaginative decision by the museum authorities to re-erect the church so as to replicate a building of c.1520, complete with facsimile paintings and furnishings. When the church opens, scheduled for some time in 2007-8, it will give as good an example as can be achieved of what the typical medieval western village church looked like on the eve of the Reformation.

Pre-Reformation Worship and the Reformers

It is not possible to understand the attitude of the Reformers to public worship and its architectural setting without also understanding their objections to the theology, liturgical practice and private devotions of the late medieval western church. Whereas the theology of the medieval schoolmen was extremely sophisticated and argued on sound philosophical principles, that of the average man and woman in the parish, or for that matter of the parish priest, rarely rose above the level of popular superstition. People on the whole were less enthusiastic about enjoying the presence of God, His angels and saints in heaven, than they were to avoid the terrible punishments waiting for them in hell, or to reduce the amount of lesser punishment that they were likely to experience in purgatory. They were reminded of the terrors of hell on at least a weekly basis by representations of the Last Judgement, frequently painted over the chancel arch, an excellent example of which has survived in St Thomas's, Salisbury. Just as the pre-Reformation church had two, largely unrelated theologies, so it also had two liturgies: the formal one conducted by the clergy, at which the laity were merely remote spectators, and the private one of the laity which focused on the repetition of popular prayers, the lighting of candles, the veneration of relics and statues and penitential devotions. The church undoubtedly used, although by no means always from disreputable motives, the credulity and superstition of the laity to provide the funding that churches needed to maintain the clergy and the regular round of church services. The early Reformers were extremely critical of such practices and it was the alleged corruption of the pre-Reformation church which was to provide the catalyst for the development of Protestant theology and Protestant forms of Christian worship.

Heresy had been a problem in the medieval western church since the twelfth century, with the emergence of Catharism in Germany and France and the Waldensians in France and Italy. In 1233-4 the Inquisition was established by Pope Gregory IX to deal with these and other heresies. However, new proto-Protestant groups were to emerge in the late fourteenth and early fifteenth centuries such as the Lollards in England and the Hussites in Bohemia. Many of their beliefs anticipated those of the sixteenth-century Reformers. The first of these was Martin Luther who, on 31 October 1517, fastened a copy of his 95 theses condemning the sale of indulgences and, by implication, the doctrine of purgatory, on which such sales depended, to the castle church at Wittenburg. Luther was a fairly conservative reformer. He was initially concerned merely to purify the church from what he considered to be its corruptions. His doctrine of justification by faith, which became the core of Lutheran belief, was not fully expressed until 1520. Luther's theological conservatism was replicated in his attitude to the reform of the liturgy. He wanted to get rid of private masses and, therefore, side altars; to permit the laity to receive not just the bread, but the wine as well, at Holy Communion; to increase the reading of the Bible and the preaching of sermons; to have at least part, and if possible the whole, of the mass in the vernacular and to remove any reference to the mass being a sacrifice. The Lutheran Sunday service was always in the form of a mass, but with a much simplified eucharistic prayer, which was not said if there was no communion. The traditional vestments and altar ornaments were retained and there was little destruction of traditional imagery in Lutheran churches. Lutherans believed that Christ was truly present in the eucharist, but they rejected the doctrine of transubstantiation, in which the bread and wine was believed to become instead the Body and Blood of Christ. They replaced this with a doctrine of consubstantiation in which it was believed that, although the bread and wine remained such after consecration, they also took on the additional reality of being Christ's Body and Blood.

Compared with Luther the other leading reformers were much more radical in their theology and they all rejected any idea of the Real Presence of Christ in the eucharistic bread and wine. For reformers like Zwingli the eucharist was really no more than a commemorative meal; for others, like Calvin, there was a Real Presence in the sacrament but it was associated, not with the bread and wine, but with the individual belief of the communicant, the doctrine usually termed receptionism. The emphasis in the services was to be even more on the reading of the Bible and preaching. The structure of the pre-Reformation mass was destroyed and replaced by a service in two parts: the first part comprised readings, prayers and preaching; the second the actual celebration of communion. However, since communion was, in effect, restricted to those worthy to receive it, it became more and more infrequent, with the result that the normal Sunday service consisted of the first part only, with the second taking place only a few times each year. The development of this new and much more radical form of Sunday service is shown in the analysis of the rites of the leading radical reformers of the early sixteenth century: Ulrich Zwingli, Martin Bucer and John Calvin (Figure 1.4). As the preaching service got longer so the communion service got shorter and even more infrequent. Along with the production of a service free from colour and ritual went the stripping from the churches of anything remotely 'popish': vestments, candles, pictures, statues, even organs were condemned to be

Figure 1.4   Outline of Sunday services adopted by Ulrich Zwingli, Martin Bucer and John Calvin

Zwingli Zürich (1525)	Bucer Strasbourg (1539)	Calvin Geneva (1542)
Preaching Service		
Opening Prayer	General Confession	Scripture Sentence (Pslam 124:8)
Lord's Prayer	Word of Grace (1 Timothy 1:15)	Confession
Ave Maria	Absolution	Psalm
Sermon	Kyrie Eleison	Collect
Commemoration of departed	Gloria in Excelsis	Lesson
General Confession	Psalm	Sermon
	Gospel	Intercessions
	Sermon	Paraphrase of Lord's Prayer

Zwingli Zürich (1525)	Bucer Strasbourg (1539)	Calvin Geneva (1542)
Communion Service		
Epistle	Apostle's Creed	Confession of Faith
Gloria in Excelsis	Lord's Prayer	Preparation of elements
Gospel	Exhortation	Words of Institution
Apostle's Creed	Words of Institution	Exhortation and Excommunication
Exhortation and Admonition	Fraction and Delivery	Communion
Lord's Prayer	Communion	Prayer of Thanksgiving
Words of Institution	Psalm or Hymn	Canticle of Simeon
Distribution and Communion	Thanksgiving	Benediction
Psalm 113: 1-9	Benediction	
Thanksgiving	Dismissal	
Dismissal		

discarded in the interests of scriptural purity. A Zwinglian or Calvinist Reformation was a very different affair from a Lutheran one.

The way in which the Reformation impacted on Europe varied greatly, not only from country to country, but even from region to region within a country. A great deal depended on whether the Reformation was a 'top down' or a 'bottom up' phenomenon. In the former case it could be a relatively speedy affair; in the latter it was usually a long-drawn-out process and could lead to more than a century of religious warfare or broken settlements. However, by the end of the sixteenth century, Lutheranism was the official form of Christianity throughout Scandinavia and large parts of Germany; either Zwinglianism or Calvinism in Scotland, Switzerland and the northern Netherlands; and a more moderate 'reformed' church in England and Ireland. Roman Catholicism remained the official religion of southern Europe, France, the southern Netherlands and parts of Germany and there were significant Roman Catholic minorities (sometimes more numerous than the established Protestant churches) in Ireland, Switzerland and the northern Netherlands. There were also strong Calvinist minorities in France and some parts of Germany. Lutheranism, because of its conservatism and the power it allowed to the ruler to determine the details of religious observance, was popular with the Scandinavian kings and German princes. In Denmark the Reformation was accomplished within a decade, the monarch simply imposing a new set of bishops and services on the Danish church. The more radical reformers were less favoured by secular rulers since their doctrines gave secular rulers little power in their churches. In France there was a long struggle between the government, which wanted to maintain the Roman Catholic church, and those who wanted to establish reformed churches wherever there was a demand for them. An attempt at a compromise, in which freedom of worship was offered to the Protestants, was offered by the Edict of Nantes in 1598, but the privileges of Protestants were further and further curtailed until they were revoked in 1685 and it became virtually impossible to worship as a Protestant in France.

In some countries the process of Reformation moved in fits and starts. A good example of this was England where King Henry VIII declared the national church independent of the papacy in 1534 but enacted no reforms other than the dissolution of the monasteries and some minor liturgical changes such as the placing of an English translation of the Bible in every church and the introduction of a new English litany which contained the phrase 'from the tyranny of the Bishop of Rome and all his detestable enormities... good Lord deliver us'. The Six Articles of 1539, the denial of which could lead to prosecution for heresy, upheld the doctrine of transubstantiation, the practice of private masses and confession and the maintenance of clerical celibacy. When Henry died in 1547 there were six years of fairly rapid reformation in which the conservative Prayer Book of 1549 was replaced by the much more radical one of 1552 (Figure 1.5). The former was basically an English translation of the pre-Reformation mass, retaining much of the traditional ceremonial, and much more like the sort of services used in Lutheran churches. The latter was strongly influenced by the reformed liturgies of Zwingli, Bucer, Calvin and others, in which ceremonial was reduced to an absolute minimum. For example the use of the traditional eucharistic vestments, which had been retained in 1549, was abolished in 1552. Although communion was still to be received kneeling this was explained in the attached rubric:

Figure 1.5   Comparison between the English eucharistic rites in the prayer books
of 1549 and 1552

1549	1552
Lord's Prayer	Lord's Prayer
Collect for Purity	Collect for Purity
Introit	
Kyrie Eleison	Ten Commandments
Gloria in Excelsis	
Collect for the Day	Collect for the Day
Collect(s) for the King	Collect(s) for the King
Epistle	Epistle
Gospel	Gospel
Creed	Creed
Sermon or Homily	Sermon or Homily
Exhortation	
Offertory Sentences	Offertory Sentences
Preface	
Sanctus and Benedictus	
Prayer for the Church	Prayer for the Church
	Exhortation
	Invitation, Confession, Absolution
	Comfortable Words
	Preface
	Sanctus
Prayer of Consecration	Prayer of Consecration
Prayer of Oblation	
Lord's Prayer	
Peace	
Invitation, Confession, Absolution	
Comfortable Words	
Prayer of Humble Access	
Communion	
Agnus Dei	
Post-Communion Sentences	
	Lord's Prayer
Prayer of Thanksgiving	Prayer of Oblation or Thanksgiving
	Gloria in Excelsis
Blessing	Blessing

> Whereas it is ordayned... that the Communicants Knelying shoulde receyve the holye Communion... Leste yet the same Kneelyng myght be thought or taken otherwyse, we dooe declare that it is not ment thereby, that any adoracion is doone, or ought to be doone, eyther unto the Sacramentall bread and wyne there bodily receyved, or unto any reall and essencial presence there beeyng of Christ's naturall fleshe and bloude... for that were Idolatrye to be abhored of all faythfull Christians.

Then for five years, following the reign of Edward VI and during that of Mary I, the Reformation was not just put on hold, but the Church of England was restored to union with the papacy and the pre-Reformation mass re-introduced. When Mary died, her sister, Elizabeth I, endeavoured to seek a compromise with her Protestant subjects. The prayer book of 1552 was re-introduced, with some minor amendments, but strenuous attempts were made during the rest of her 45 year reign to frustrate the desires of those reformers who wanted the English church to be the sort of fully fledged radical Protestant church of the sort eventually established in Scotland, Switzerland and the northern Netherlands.

The Impact on Church Buildings

Protestant reformers inherited the buildings of their Catholic predecessors and the extent that they had to be adapted for Protestant worship depended on the conservatism or radicalism of their respective theologies and their liturgical requirements. As might be expected, therefore, churches in predominantly Lutheran countries preserved medieval liturgical furnishings largely intact with the result that there are now more medieval church furnishings surviving in Scandinavia and Germany than anywhere else in Europe. In particular, medieval retables were generally retained on the main altar and only began to be replaced in the eighteenth and nineteenth centuries under the influence of pietism. Side altars, which were not needed, were generally dismantled but not always. Orders for the destruction of side altars were made in East Frisia in 1542, Mecklenburg in 1552 and Weimar in 1570, but usually the decision whether or not to remove them was left to the parishes to decide. At the former pilgrimage church of Creglingen in Baden-Württemburg there are three surviving side altars, complete with their retables, and at Sankt Olof in Skåne four of the original nine altars have survived. A similar line was taken with respect to images. The Church Orders of Hamburg (1529) and Lübeck (1531) did not require the removal of images; in Denmark it was only statues and paintings which had become the object of popular veneration that had to be removed according to the Church Order of 1539. Those that merely decorated the building, and had not become the focus of a cult, could remain. A similar line was taken by Laurentius Petri when he drew up the Swedish Church Order in 1571. There are thus many surviving examples of pre-Reformation rood figures throughout Scandinavia and North Germany. The influence of pietism did result in the eventual destruction of images that were then considered unsuitable for a Lutheran church, such as the representation of the Dormition of the Blessed Virgin Mary in the Danish church of Holstebro. The figure of the virgin was turned into one of Jacob, simply by adding a beard to her face, with the result that the figures of the twelve apostles around her became, by this ingenious change, the twelve sons of Jacob. This modest piece of iconoclasm was reversed, by the removal of the beard, in 1907.

In countries where a more radical Reformation took hold, or was attempted, the impact on church buildings was much more considerable. Not only were all the statues and pictures removed, but so was a great deal of the medieval liturgical furniture. Neither Zwingli nor Calvin saw any need for an altar. The Lord's Supper was more properly celebrated at a simple table. This might be a fixed piece of furniture or it might be a temporary one, brought in as required. Calvinist field-preaching in the Netherlands often resulted in major outbreaks of iconoclasm. A sermon at Steenvoorde on 10 August 1566 led to an outbreak of iconoclasm, especially the smashing of images, at Poperinge on 14 August, Ypres on 15 August, Oudenaarde on 18 August, Antwerp on 20 August, Ghent, Middelburg and Den Bosch on 23 August, Tournai on 23 August, Delft and Utrecht on 24 August and the Hague and Leiden on 25 August. Bands of iconoclasts roamed the countryside, frequently supported by the inhabitants of the towns and villages whose churches were being sacked. The destruction was not just restricted to images. Complete retables were destroyed, altars broken up, tabernacles dismantled, books burned and ornaments removed for secular use. In the Netherlands the only medieval furnishings that have survived are a few pulpits and fonts. Similar destruction took place in Calvinist Scotland after 1560. Here the larger town churches or former cathedrals were divided into two or more churches to serve the needs of different congregations. In Switzerland, too, most medieval furnishings have been destroyed. Although Calvinism never became the official religion of France it has been estimated that about a third of the population of France were Calvinists in the 1560s. In areas where Calvinists were strong there were similar iconoclastic outbreaks to those in the Netherlands. Many areas of France were affected by these attacks on Catholic churches. The one part of the country in which there was virtually no iconoclasm, and in which a wide range of medieval furnishings still survive, especially rood screens complete with their lofts, was Brittany.

In England some destruction of images was carried out in the late 1530s but it was very sporadic. A more resolute attempt to dismantle churches of their medieval furnishings came under Edward VI when a series of injunctions were issued ordering the destruction of images and of lights placed anywhere apart from the altar. Chantry chapels were formally abolished in December 1547. Thereafter the more Protestant bishops insisted on the dismantling, not only of side altars, but of the high altar as well, and its replacement by a wooden table standing at either the west end of the chancel or the east end of the nave, near the seating for the laity. Under Mary I (1553-8) the furnishings that had been dismantled were ordered to be reinstated. With the restoration of a modified Calvinism under Elizabeth I few churches were to remain substantially unaltered. Remaining images and altar-pieces were destroyed. However, churches were allowed to retain their screens providing the lofts and rood figures were removed. Some lofts were converted into galleries at the west end of the church. Many churches also kept their medieval benches, fonts and pulpits, frequently retaining their pre-Reformation carvings or paintings, as these were not considered to be 'images' in the full sense. They could be adapted for worship in the way that altars could not. Stained glass was also not destroyed in England to the extent that it was in Scotland, Switzerland or the Netherlands.

The Catholic Counter-Reformation

The response of the papacy to the impact of the Reformation on the national churches of Europe did not involve just passive retrenchment. There was widespread recognition that the pre-Reformation church had, to some extent at least, brought the catastrophe on itself and had been seriously in need of reform. The political difficulties of the papacy in the 1520s and 1530s, combined one suspects with a lack of realisation initially that the new Protestantism was essentially different in character from the heresies of the thirteenth, fourteenth and fifteenth centuries, prevented immediate action. However, in 1541, under the leadership of Pope Paul III, who appointed Catholic reformers to positions of authority in the Roman Curia, a meeting was held at Ratisbon between Cardinal Conterini and a number of German Catholic divines and some of the more moderate reformers led by Bucer and Melanchthon. Although a reasonable degree of understanding was reached at this meeting it had little chance of success. Extremists within both the Catholic and Protestant churches were very suspicious. Conservative forces at Rome demanded that a new Inquisition be set up to deal with heretics. Nevertheless when the Council of Trent eventually met for the first time in 1545 some attempt at conciliation between Catholics and Protestants was still on the agenda. By the end of the Council's first session in 1548 it was no longer; the bishops had decided that the doctrine of justification by faith alone was not sufficient, that the Bible and tradition were of equal importance, that private masses were acceptable and that the mass should continue to be said, for the most part, in Latin rather than the vernacular. Although Lutheran representatives attended the second session of the Council in 1551-2, their demand that the doctrinal decisions taken in the first session should be reconsidered was rejected. By the Council's final session in 1562-3 any idea that the Roman Catholic Church should adopt the core of the Protestant reformers' agenda was a dead letter. What replaced it was a distinctive Counter-Reformation which, whilst endeavouring to reform some of the abuses that had been the initial causes of Luther's protests, reaffirmed traditional doctrine. The office of indulgence-seller was abolished, as were many of the exemptions from episcopal control. Each diocese without a university had to establish a seminary for the training of the clergy. New religious orders, such as the Jesuits, were used to run these institutions. Pope Pius V (1565-72) carried out a thorough-going reform of the papal bureaucracy as well as authorising the publication of a new catechism (1566), breviary (1568) and missal (1570). These new texts eliminated the enormous regional differences that had existed in the services of the pre-Reformation church. The outcome of the Council of Trent was a centralised and highly disciplined Roman Catholic Church which was to exist until the liberalising reforms of the Second Vatican Council four hundred years later.

One of the outcomes of these reforms was a new concept of the way in which the public liturgy of the Roman Catholic Church should be celebrated and the changes that this required in the design of church buildings. Whereas pre-Reformation churches had been compartmentalised, those of the Counter-Reformation were much more open, focusing on the high altar at the east end, and with the side chapels placed in the transepts or in the outer aisles of the nave. An early example of such a church was that of Il Gesù in Rome, designed by Vignola and built between 1568 and 1575 (Figure 1.6). Churches of this type were built all over Europe between the late sixteenth and early nineteenth centuries.

Figure 1.6   Ground plan of Il Gesù, Rome, built in 1568-75

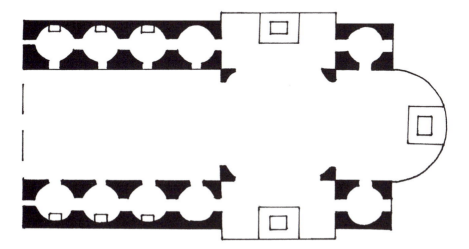

It is from them that we derived our idea of what... we expected a Roman Catholic church to be like... It has a nave and transepts, though the central aisle is very much wider in proportion to the length than it would have been in any earlier style. The transepts do not project beyond the line of the side walls of the nave, and they house the principal side altars at their ends. The side aisles of the nave have ceased to be part of a processional path; each bay has been made into a separate chapel, opening from the nave, normally with a metal screen and gates at the opening. The space where the wide nave and transepts intersect forms a large central space and is covered by a dome. But the main altar... is not under the dome but against the east wall of the shallow apse that closes the east end of the church, and which is the same width as the nave.[1]

Although private masses continued in the side chapels, the principal masses at the high altar were not just the business of the clergy behind a screen that separated them from the laity. The high altar was visible from the whole of the nave and the laity were expected to participate in what was happening at the altar, even if this participation was limited to certain well-known prayers or responses.

---

1   Basil Minchin, *Outward and Visible*, London 1961, pp 150-1.

Protestant Worship in Catholic Buildings

Opening up pre-Reformation buildings for Counter-Reformation Roman Catholic worship meant a fairly limited reorganisation, primarily the removal of screens that blocked the view of the high altar and the placing of more emphasis on this as the focus of the building through the construction of exceptionally elaborate retables and reredoses. Opening up pre-Reformation buildings for Protestant worship generally required greater adaptation. This was least the case as far as the Lutherans were concerned. Their principal service was still a somewhat truncated form of the mass and they were not adverse to imagery that did not promote ideas that they regarded as theologically unsound. Indeed, unlike Counter-Reformation Roman Catholics, they were likely to retain the pre-Reformation rood screen. The extent to which medieval furnishings were retained in Lutheran churches after the Reformation depended to a large extent on whether the country or region in which they were situated was deeply influenced by either Calvinism or Lutheran pietism at a later period. Thus in the very conservative areas of Schleswig-Holstein many medieval furnishings were still remaining in the churches until the nineteenth century or later. A.W.N. Pugin was amazed to discover on his visit to Lübeck that the city churches had

> preserved all their internal fittings... although the Catholic rites have ceased within them for nearly three centuries. The minutest ornaments remain intact, and but very trifling additions or alterations have been made in the original arrangement... although the Lutheran religion has prevailed in this city for several centuries, many of the branches set up to burn tapers in front of images of this and other churches bear the date of 1664, and even later.[2]

A comparable survival of many medieval furnishings can still be found in several churches in North Germany and Scandinavia.

The Lutheran High Mass retained much of the ceremonial associated with pre-Reformation church services. An illustration of the eucharist being celebrated at a Danish country church in 1561 (Illustration 1.1) shows the priest wearing the traditional eucharistic vestments of alb and chasuble administering the sacrament in the form of wafer bread to kneeling communicants. The altar is vested with a frontal, crucifix and two lighted candles. The liturgical conservatism of the Lutheran liturgies meant that their churches needed two focal points, the altar, at which the Eucharistic action took place, and the pulpit, for reading the scriptures and preaching. The altar stood at the east end of the church, or at least the part still used for worship. The pulpit tended to be placed in the middle of the congregation, where the people could hear better. The priest would conduct some parts of the service from the pulpit and other parts from the altar, an arrangement that the young Anglican clergyman and future Methodist leader, John Wesley, found rather disconcerting when he visited Germany in 1738. At Meissen 'the Minister's habit was adorned with gold and scarlet, and a vast cross both behind and before', a clear description of a chasuble still being worn. At Bertholdsdorf, where the priest did not wear the traditional Eucharistic vestments, 'two large candles stood lighted upon the altar'. The priest sang *Gloria in Excelsis*

---

2   A.W.N. Pugin, *A Treatise on Chancel Screens and Rood Lofts*, London 1851, pp 31-3.

Illustration 1.1   Altar frontal from Thorslunde Church, 1561, showing the retention of Catholic symbolism in Danish Lutheran worship (National Museum, Copenhagen)

and read the epistle and gospel at the altar; he used the pulpit for 'a long extempore prayer', a sermon of 75 minutes, 'a long intercession and general thanksgiving'.[3] The traditional pre-Reformation ceremonial of the early Lutheran churches, notably the wearing of vestments and the celebration of Holy Communion on most Sundays, tended to be given up for services built around the sermon during the eighteenth century, though some of the Scandinavian Lutheran churches, especially those of Sweden and Finland, never moved fully in this direction. In order to provide a better relationship between the priest in the pulpit and the laity, some Lutheran churches had their seating arranged so that it was placed facing either north or south across the nave to focus on the pulpit in the middle of the nave. The congregation were not, therefore, placed in the awkward position that occurred in some Anglican churches where, in order to face the pulpit, part of the congregation had to sit with their backs to the altar, or many Roman Catholic ones in which, in order to face the altar, part of the congregation had to sit with their backs to the preacher in the pulpit.

The adaptation of Zwinglian or Calvinist churches was much more radical, largely as a result of both Zwingli and Calvin rejecting the basic structure of the pre-Reformation mass as the core of their eucharistic liturgy. Their churches did not require a traditional altar, but they did need pulpits and seating. The arrangements for communion in what are generally termed the Reformed churches varied. In some the practice was to stand around a simple communion table. In others they sat near such a table with the ministers delivering the bread and wine to the communicants in their seats. What eventually became the normal arrangement in both Scotland and the Netherlands was for the communicants to sit at one or more tables in relays, for the celebrating minister to sit at the head of the table and for the elements to be passed from one communicant to another. Another practice, which appears to have been that favoured by the early Reformed churches in the Netherlands, was for the communicants to queue to take the elements from the minister or ministers at the communion tables, a practice known as ambulatory or walking communion. The most recent research into Reformed communion practice has shown that at Zürich the laity received communion in their seats and that at Geneva ambulatory or walking communion was the established practice under Calvin. The earliest evidence of communicants sitting around a table to receive the sacrament comes from East Friesland in 1539. The practice was adopted by John à Lasco at Emden and introduced into England by him at the church set apart for Dutch exiles at Austin Friars in London. À Lasco was unusual among Reformed clergy in not making the celebration of communion an extension of the preaching service. Every Sunday he had a service of prayer and preaching at 9am. Six times a year he had a separate communion service at 8am, preceded by a Saturday service at 2pm at which the names of those not permitted to receive communion on the following day, and the reasons for their excommunication, were published (Figure 1.7). At Calvinist churches in the Rhine Palatinate the practice was for the communion to be administered by two *Kirchendiener*, one of whom stood at one end of the table to distribute the bread, and the other at the other end to offer the wine to the communicants. The people queued to receive the bread at one end of the table and then walked alongside the table to receive the wine. In different parts of the Netherlands

---

3   F.W. MacDonald (ed), *The Journal of John Wesley*, London 1906, pp 112-15.

some congregations adopted the East Friesland practice of sitting communion whereas others adopted the walking communion practice of the Rhine Palatinate. In 1574 the Synod of Dordrecht expressed a preference for communicants to receive standing and such was also incorporated into the church regulations for the provinces of Holland and Zeeland in 1576. Even at Groningen, which from its proximity to Emden might have been expected to have adopted sitting for communion, the practice was for the laity to receive communion in the chancel of the Martinikerk standing, from two ministers positioned at each end of the table. This practice lasted from the official adoption of the Reformed faith by Groningen in 1594 until 1771 when the practice of sitting communion was introduced. Walking communion survived even longer in some other places and was officially banned, in favour of sitting communion, by the Hervormd synod in 1817. The arguments of those who favoured sitting communion were that it gave the service more of the character of a meal, that communion was simpler to administer and that it reduced the length of the service.[4]

Figure 1.7   Outline of communion and preaching services at Austin Friars, London, in 1550

Communion Service (8am)	Preaching Service (9am)
Discourse and Prayer	Exhortation
Fencing of Table	Lord's Prayer
Words of Institution	Psalm
Admonition	Scripture Reading
Sursum Corda	Sermon
Invitation	Prayer
Fraction	Decalogue
Distribution and Reception	Confession and Absolution
Admonition and Exhortation	Apostles' Creed
Thanksgiving	Lord's Prayer
Admonition	Psalm
Psalm	Commendation of the Poor
Dismissal	Benediction

The variation in communion practice across the European Reformed churches means that real caution must be exercised in trying to reconstruct the re-arrangement of medieval buildings in the post-Reformation period. Where this has been done, for example in a recent doctoral thesis by Malcolm Lovibond, conjectural arrangements have sometimes been rather heavily influenced by the later plans which almost

---

4   See J.R. Luth, 'Communion in the Churches of the Dutch Reformation to the Present Day', in Charles Caspars, Gerard Lukken and Gerard Rouwhorst (eds) *Bread of Heaven: Customs and Practices Surrounding Holy Communion: Essays in the History of Liturgy and Culture*, Kampen 1995, pp 99-117.

certainly show contemporary rather than historic arrangements. Thus Lovibond's conjectural plan of the Minster Church at Basel shows an interior with the pulpit in the middle of the south side of the nave and the communion table in front of the *lettner* or chancel screen, the chancel itself being unfurnished. This seems to conflict with a painting of the interior of the same church in 1650, reproduced by Lovibond, which shows the pulpit in the middle of the north side of the nave, no screen and stalls in the chancel.[5] Lovibond is probably on safer ground in his conjectural plan of the Grossmünster at Zurich, where the chancel was not used and the pulpit placed on top of the *lettner*. Men and women sat on opposite sides of the nave and the communion table and font were placed in front of the *lettner* and below the pulpit, an arrangement similar to that adopted in some Lutheran churches from the seventeenth century. At Berne Minster Lovibond suggests a similar arrangement, with the communion table placed in front of the *lettner*, and the font in front of the communion table, but with, in this case, the pulpit placed in the middle of the north side of the nave with the seating arranged to face it. Lovibond also produces conjectural plans of the early post-Reformation arrangement of the church at Neuchâtel, the former cathedral at Lausanne, St Thomas's Church in Strasbourg and St Peter's Church in Geneva. At Neuchâtel the pulpit was placed in the middle of the north side of the nave with seating facing it from three directions; two parallel communion tables, one for men and one for women, were placed in the otherwise empty chancel. These were designed for walking communion, a practice attested to by the Swedish traveller, Jacob Björnståhl, in 1773. At Lausanne the suggestion is that, although the chancel was left empty and retained its *jubé* or screen, the twin tables were placed in front of the pulpit which was, as at Neuchâtel, placed in the middle of the north side of the nave. Lovibond's conjectural plan of St Thomas's, Strasbourg, shows the pulpit placed in the middle of the south side of the nave. Seating faces the pulpit in the middle and western parts of the nave, but the eastern part was left empty for the font and communion table. There was seating facing the pulpit and table in the western part of the chancel and the eastern part was left empty. Unusually for a reformed church, communion was received kneeling at Strasbourg, a practice instituted by the moderately conservative Martin Bucer.[6] Lovibond and Lucien Carrive both agree on the immediate post-Reformation arrangement of St Peter's, Geneva. Here it was the nave that was left largely empty and the screen was removed. The pulpit was placed on the north-west side of the crossing with two tables, one for men and one for women, placed in front of the pulpit. The seating faced the pulpit from four sides: the eastern part of the nave, the chancel and both transepts. There were also galleries in parts of both transepts and across the eastern bay of the south aisle.[7]

---

5   Malcolm Lovibond, 'The Use of Spaces for Public Worship in the Early Reformed Tradition', unpublished PhD thesis, University of Manchester 2005, p 98.

6   *Ibid.*, pp 84, 91, 109, 117-18, 122, 137-8.

7   *Ibid.*, p 115; Lucien Carrive, 'Le Temple des Anglicans, la Conception des Lieux de Culte dans la Réforme Anglaise' in Christiane d'Hausay (ed), *Liturgie et Espace Liturgique*, Paris 1987, p 65. See also Malcolm Lovibond, 'Les Premiers Dispositifs Réformés à Saint-Pierre de Genève', *Bulletin de la Société de l'Histoire du Protestantisme Français*, clii (2006), pp 407-18.

Figure 1.8   Seating plan of the Grote Kerk at Emden in the late sixteenth century

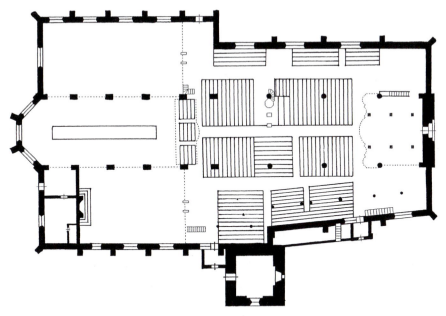

This fairly radical rearrangement of a medieval interior was to be found in other reformed churches. Where sitting communion was practised, the arrangement found at Emden (Figure 1.8), with the chancel treated as the space for communion and the nave as the space for the preaching service, tended to be replicated. In Scotland the unwanted parts of churches were allowed to fall into ruin or large churches were divided to serve as two or more parish churches. This happened at St Nicholas's in Aberdeen, in 1596, and also at St Giles's in Edinburgh, St Mary's in Dundee, St John's in Perth, the Church of the Holy Rude in Stirling and the former cathedral of St Mungo in Glasgow. At Dornoch, the nave of the former cathedral was burned down in 1570, after which the chancel and transepts were adapted to serve as the parish church. At St Andrews the former cathedral was allowed to fall into ruin as the parish church of St Nicholas was considered sufficient to house all the parishioners. In smaller parish churches the chancel tended to be turned into a private pew for the landowner, whilst the rest of the parishioners sat in the nave where the pulpit was located. In both Scotland and the Netherlands churches tended not to have fixed communion tables, except where they stood in otherwise empty chancels. If communion took place in the body of the church, as it always did in Scotland, temporary tables were brought into the church on Sacrament Sundays. Whereas in Scotland redundant medieval furnishings were, almost without exception, removed from the churches, in the Netherlands they frequently survived, so that examples of stalls and even stained glass will occasionally be found. In particular the chancel screen tended to be retained, and was sometimes replaced by a new screen, so that the chancel could be used, either as a separate place for communion, as a chapel for occasional weekday services, or as a public meeting space. A similarly conservative approach was taken to medieval buildings in Switzerland and, in particular, a significant number of medieval pulpits were retained. The Swiss, unlike the Dutch and the Scots, retained a fixed communion table, which tended to be placed either in front of the pulpit or at the entrance to the chancel.

The arrangement of churches in England and Wales before the end of the sixteenth century was more strongly influenced by Calvinism than Lutheranism. Although the Ornaments Rubric in the Prayer Book of 1559 theoretically permitted the retention of eucharistic vestments, it was effectively overturned by Archbishop Parker's Advertisements of 1566 which ordered the use of surplices and copes in cathedral and collegiate churches, but the surplice only in parish churches. Redundant chasubles were turned into carpets for the new communion tables and albs into the 'fair linen cloth' to cover the sacramental bread and wine at communion services. Even these modest ceremonial provisions were too much for the Puritan party in the Church of England. They wanted to do away completely with all vestments, music, the use of wafer bread as opposed to ordinary loaves, kneeling at communion and even parts of the authorised liturgy, such as the Nicene Creed and Gloria in Excelsis. They wanted the churches of England and Wales to resemble those of Switzerland or the Netherlands, whereas the more conservative reformers would have preferred to have church interiors that were not that different from the Lutheran ones of Germany or Scandinavia. What was eventually achieved was a slightly uneasy compromise. Archbishop Parker's Advertisements ordered the retention of the rood screen but everything above the beam, the loft and the figures of Christ on the cross with Our Lady and St John, was to be removed and replaced by the Royal Arms. The communion table was to be placed against the east wall of the chancel, except when the communion service was to be celebrated, when it was to be moved further into the chancel or even into the nave, so that the communicants could gather around it.

Anglican worship was significantly different from either the Lutheran High Mass or the services of the Reformed churches. It resembled the former in that the liturgy was fixed according to a prescribed order as set down in the *Book of Common Prayer*, but it also contained some elements of the less formal Reformed preaching service. Unlike any other church of the Reformation, the Church of England made a revised version of the pre-Reformation offices, rather than the mass, the core of its worship. The *Book of Common Prayer* made provision for the saying or singing of Morning and Evening Prayer daily, and the celebration of Holy Communion on all Sundays and holy days. This may have happened in cathedrals and collegiate churches but in most parish churches there would have been far fewer services. On Sundays the principal service comprised Morning Prayer, Litany and Ante-Communion. Almost the whole of this service was conducted from a piece of furniture unique to Anglican churches, the reading desk, usually placed near the pulpit, from which only the sermon was preached. Morning Prayer consisted of one or more sentences of scripture, a general confession and absolution, the Lord's Prayer, versicles and responses, psalm 95 and the psalms of the day, an Old Testament reading, the canticle *Te Deum Laudamus*, a New Testament reading, the canticle *Benedictus* (Luke 1, 68) or Psalm 100, the Apostle's Creed, Lord's Prayer, versicles and responses, three collects, an optional anthem, the Prayer of St John Chrysostom and the Grace (2 Corinthians 13, 13). This was followed immediately by the Litany, a series of petitions and responses, concluding with the Lord's Prayer, the Prayer of St John Chrysostom and the Grace. The Ante-Communion consisted of the first part of the Communion Service, concluding with the Sermon, Prayer for the Church, collects and blessing. On communion Sundays the priest would lead those who were going to communicate into the chancel or the eastern part of the nave after the Prayer for the Church and celebrate the communion service. He was directed to stand at the north side of the table and, in most cases, this would have stood lengthwise east-west, rather than north-south (as the pre-Reformation altar had done), so that the priest was standing on one of the long sides of the table. The surviving evidence from both two Dorset parishes and two in the Channel Islands suggests that many of these were long tables similar to those used in the Calvinist and Zwinglian churches. They would have been heavy to move and it is likely that many churches kept them permanently well away from the east wall of the chancel, even when the communion was not being celebrated. These long tables survive, though no longer used for communion services, in the Dorset parishes of Maiden Newton and Over Compton,[8] at St Lawrence and St Mary in Jersey together with a shorter one at Hailes in Gloucestershire, where it is still placed lengthwise in the middle of the chancel.

The evidence from both contemporary records and surviving buildings is that the requirements of the Elizabethan religious settlement of 1559 were carried out throughout England and Wales over the next twenty years. There were cases, especially in Wales, where rood lofts as well as the supporting screen survived. There were even cases, as at Ranworth (Norfolk) and Patricio (Powys), where side altars remained *in situ*. At Ludham in Norfolk the painting of the crucifixion on a tympanum above the rood screen was turned around to face the chancel and the blank side painted with the Royal Arms. Also in Norfolk the tympanum in the chancel arch at Tivetshall is painted with the Royal Arms and the Ten Commandments. Medieval paintings elsewhere in the church were whitewashed over but the walls were then, more often than not, painted with the Ten Commandments, Creed, Lord's Prayer and scriptural texts. Often the Ten Commandments were supported by large painted figures of Moses and Aaron. Nevertheless, although Anglican, and even Reformed, churches were not totally without colour or decoration, they were very different in ethos from what the same churches had been like before the Reformation, or from churches still under Roman Catholic or Lutheran control. What was perhaps slightly ironic was that, for all the complaints by the early reformers, about the lack of opportunity for the laity to participate fully in Christian worship before the Reformation, and the clear separation between the roles of the clergy and laity, the services of the various post-Reformation churches made few concessions towards including the laity in the new forms of worship. Anglican, Calvinist, Lutheran or Zwinglian worship all gave the dominant role to the priest or minister and, whereas before the Reformation the laity could use the services as an opportunity for private devotion, those in the Protestant churches of the late sixteenth century were obliged to sit through even longer services in which their participation was often reduced to

---

8   Nigel Yates, 'Ecclesiology in Context: Post-Reformation Church Building and Restoration in Dorset 1560-1860', *Proceedings of the Dorset Natural History and Archaeological Society*, cxxii (2000), p 28.

singing a few hymns or psalms. The Anglican Sunday morning service, for example, with a sermon, probably lasted for at least 105 minutes, and could have been even longer on days when the Holy Communion was celebrated. Sermons of 45 minutes or an hour were common in other Protestant churches. No wonder most of them had arrangements whereby the churchwardens or vergers would wander through the church with a long pole to wake up those who had accidentally fallen asleep!

In the pages that follow we will look in more detail at the ways in which church services, and the adaptation of church buildings to meet liturgical needs, changed between the late sixteenth and early nineteenth centuries in the Lutheran, Reformed, Anglican and Roman Catholic churches. Thereafter we will look at the liturgical revolutions of the nineteenth and twentieth centuries, and the way in which these impacted on church buildings. As a result of the liturgical developments of the last fifty years the mainstream Catholic and Protestant churches have developed eucharistic services which now have a lot more in common than they did four hundred years ago, and which have deliberately aimed to recapture the liturgical outlook of the Christian Church in the first few centuries of its existence.

Chapter 2

The Lutheran Churches of Germany and Scandinavia

Liturgically, as we have already noted, the Lutheran tradition within Western European Protestantism, was the most conservative, even in Germany, where competition from the Reformed churches and their eventual merger in several German states, resulted in the abandonment of some traditional ceremonial (Illustration 2.1). The most conservative of the Lutheran churches was that of Sweden, which did not finally adopt the Augsburg confession, the core theological document of the Lutheran tradition, until 1593. Similarly in the nineteenth century it was the Lutheran churches that kept their traditional architectural arrangements longest and were the last to feel the impact of ecclesiology and neo-medievalism.

Illustration 2.1   Lutheran communion service at Augsburg in the early eighteenth century (Picart, *Ceremonies*, v, between pp 428 and 429)

Lutheran Worship

Although there was some development in the structure and style of Lutheran worship between the sixteenth and nineteenth centuries, the core liturgical action remained a Sunday morning service, with or without communion, based on a modified version of the pre-Reformation Latin Mass. The only exception was in southern and western parts of Germany where Lutheranism was strongly influenced by both Calvinism and Zwinglianism. Here the normal Sunday service (*Predigtgottesdienst*) comprised hymns and sermon with the communion service held much more irregularly, its order tending to be a mix of Lutheran, Calvinist and Zwinglian influences. Even so these Lutherans did not adopt the iconoclasm of their reformed brethren and churches continued to retain many of their pre-Reformation furnishings including paintings and statues. From the late seventeenth century onwards the Lutheran churches of Germany and Scandinavia were influenced by two movements which pulled them in somewhat different directions: one was rationalism, which led to theological liberalism; the other was pietism, which put a much greater emphasis on deep personal devotion and spiritual conversion. The liturgical impact of both movements was, however, very similar. They sought to move the Lutheran churches away from traditional patterns of worship and therefore resulted in modifications being made to liturgical texts. New hymn-books were authorised for use in Lübeck in 1703, Berlin in 1704 and Hamburg in 1710. In Denmark the liturgy was revised in 1685 and the hymn book in 1699; in Sweden comparable revisions took place in 1693 and 1695. Hymns had always been an important aspect of Lutheran worship and liturgical revision was to make them more important as they replaced the more formal chanting of the ordinary of the mass inherited from the pre-Reformation church. In cases where Latin had been retained for parts of the Eucharistic rite, as in Denmark, it was now replaced by a liturgy wholly in the vernacular. The *Kyrie*, *Gloria*, Creed and *Agnus Dei* were replaced by hymns in Danish, and hymns were introduced before and after the sermon. This resulted in greatly increased congregational participation in worship. A number of Lutheran churches, influenced by pietism to acknowledge liturgically the act of conversion, reintroduced the Confirmation Service; Württemberg did so in 1722, making the service compulsory in 1785, and Denmark followed suit in 1736.

The last quarter of the eighteenth century, and the early years of the nineteenth, was a period of reform in all the Lutheran churches. In those countries which had embraced Lutheranism, especially the Nordic countries, the relationship between church and state was so close, and the former so subservient to the latter, that the due observance of the authorised liturgical rite was a matter of law. Clergy were prohibited by stiff penalties from making any changes to the authorised prayers, though many, especially those influenced by pietism, were anxious to do so. There was also pressure for change from pietist laity. As part of these ecclesiastical reforms of the late eighteenth century, consideration began to be given to further liturgical reform. New liturgies were authorised in the Rhine Palatinate in 1783 and Courland in 1785. In Berlin-Brandenburg the catalyst for liturgical reform was the desire of successive kings of Prussia to bring about a union of the Lutheran and Reformed congregations in their dominions. Liturgical reform was first proposed in 1782 and, with the authority of Frederick William III, Ludwig Borowski (1740-1832) published his *Preussische Kirchenagende* in 1789. A new draft communion rite, designed for use by both Lutheran and Reformed congregations, was produced in 1798 and used for the first time in Berlin Cathedral in 1800. Borowski's ideas on liturgy influenced the senior chaplain to the Danish royal family, Christian Bastholm (1740-1819). Bastholm saw the authorised liturgy as something mechanical, unsuited to the pastoral needs of the laity. He proposed a new order of Sunday Service comprising an opening collect, a hymn, the Ten Commandments, another hymn, scripture reading, a half-hour sermon, a shortened communion rite when this was required and a blessing. It would have been a major departure from a liturgy still based firmly on the structure of the pre-Reformation Mass with vernacular hymns replacing the former Latin chants. Bastholm and his supporters also wanted to alter the traditional ceremonial of worship and dispense with much of it, including the use of eucharistic vestments. Their proposals, however, received little public support and were not implemented.

Sweden: A Liturgical Case Study

The Swedish Reformation was the most prolonged and conservative of all those in the Lutheran churches of Northern Europe. Two kings, John III (1569-92) and Charles IX (1600-11), endeavoured to move the Swedish church in, respectively, more Catholic and more Protestant directions, without long-term success. Although Sweden was influenced by both rationalism and pietism in the eighteenth century, it retained not just the structure of the pre-Reformation Mass, but also much of its ceremonial, in normal Sunday worship. The use of eucharistic vestments was never abandoned. Many parishes retain eighteenth-century chasubles, normally in black or red damask or velvet, frequently embroidered on the back with the date when they were made. The cathedral museum in Uppsala displays a magnificent collection of chasubles, copes and mitres, from the late middle ages to the present day, a visual reminder of the continuity of traditional Catholic ceremonial in the Swedish Lutheran Church since the Reformation.

The development of the Swedish communion service is shown in Figure 2.1.[1]

The first liturgy in Swedish had been produced by Olavus Petri and was officially published in 1531. It was based on Luther's *Formula Missae* of 1523 and Andreas Osiander's *Nürnberger Messe* of 1525. It was largely a translation of the pre-Reformation Latin Mass, but with the total omission of an offertory and with the Canon reduced to the recitation of the Words of Institution immediately following the Preface, copying the precedent that Luther himself had established. Revisions of this liturgy were made in 1535, 1537, 1541, 1548 and 1557. Most were conservative modifications of an already conservative office, that of 1537 including the restoration of Latin to parts of the liturgy. In 1571 Olavus Petri's brother, Laurentius Petri,

---

1   The section that follows is base on E.E. Yelverton (ed), *The Mass in Sweden: its Development from the Latin Rite from 1531 to 1917*, Henry Bradshaw Society Vol. LVII, London 1920.

Liturgical Space

Figure 2.1   Comparison of the Swedish eucharistic rites of 1531, 1576, 1602 and
              1917

1531	1576	1602	1917
		Kyrie Eleison	
		Gloria	
		Collect	
		Absolution	
Invitation	Preparation/ Exhoration	Invitation	Preparation/ Invitation
Confession	Confession	Confession	Confession
		Exhortation	
		Examination	
Absolution	Absolution	Absolution	Absolution
Introit	Introit		
Kyrie Eleison	Kyrie Eleison		Kyrie Eleison
Gloria	Gloria		Gloria
Collect	Collect		Collect
Epistle	Epistle		Epistle
Gradual	Gradual		Hymn
	Sequence		
Gospel	Gospel		Gospel
Creed	Creed		Creed
			Sermon
			Prayer after Sermon
			Notices
			Hymn
			Intercession
	Offertory		Offertory
	Intercession		
Preface	Preface	Preface	Preface
Words of Institution	Prayer of Consecration	Words of Institution	Words of Institution
			Lord's Prayer
Sanctus	Sanctus	Sanctus	Sanctus
Benedictus	Benedictus	Benedictus	Benedictus
	Prayer of Oblation		
Lord's Prayer	Lord's Prayer	Lord's Prayer	
		Agnus Dei	

Peace	Peace	Peace	Peace
	Exhortation		
	Prayers before Communication		
Agnus Dei	Agnus Dei		Agnus Dei
Exhortation			
Communion	Communion	Communion	Communion
Hymn			
Postcommunion	Postcommunion		
	Prayers after Communion	Prayers after Communion	Collect
Blessing	Blessing	Blessing	Blessing

archbishop of Uppsala from 1531 to 1573, concerned about the growing influence of Calvinism on some sections of the Swedish Church, produced a new Church Order, designed to steer a middle path between Roman Catholics and Reformed Protestants. This provided for the confession to be said in both Latin and Swedish, for the Latin introits and graduals to be replaced by Swedish hymns, for the pre-Reformation sequences for festivals to be reintroduced, for the creed to be sung in Latin rather than Swedish on certain feast days and for a degree of liberty to be permitted in ceremonial matters, such as the elevation and the use of eucharistic vestments, altar cloths and lighted candles. Petri's church order was in turn replaced by the Red Book of 1576, a liturgy which reflected the Catholic tendencies of John III. It restored both the priest's private devotions and vesting prayers before the beginning of the public liturgy; it also restored the offertory and made provision for a simplified version of the pre-Reformation Canon. Although this liturgy was met with grudging acceptance by the bishops and clergy, it was rejected at the Uppsala Mote of 1593, which ratified the Church Order of 1571 as the official liturgy of the Swedish Church. This liturgy was, however, far too conservative for the Calvinistically-inclined Charles IX. His communion office of 1602 was the most radical reshaping of the liturgy in the history of the Swedish Church. The structure of the pre-Reformation Latin Mass was completely discarded in favour of a rite which included not just lengthy exhortations to the communicants, but a wholly memorialist approach to the sacrament. Yelverton described it as 'a glaring example of liturgical impropriety', and this was an opinion shared by the overwhelming majority of the Swedish bishops and clergy. Faced with this response to his liturgical ideas, Charles IX, 'with a grace and a humility unusual in those in authority, of his own accord... withdrew it',[2] and the Church Order of 1571 remained in use.

Although the Church Order of 1571 remained the core of the Swedish Church's eucharistic liturgy until the late twentieth century, it did not, as the Anglican prayer book of 1662 did, remain static. Significant revisions were adopted in 1614 when the use of Latin and the elevation of the elements after consecration were finally

---

2   *Ibid.*, pp 124, 126.

abandoned. Provision was also made for adapting the service on those days on which there was to be no communion, which increasingly became the practice before the high church revival of the late nineteenth and early twentieth centuries. Minor revisions were also made in 1693, 1811, 1894 and 1917. The 1811 revision pruned the number of holy days and added a new preparatory section before the confession and absolution. That of 1894 strictly regulated the way in which the notices were to be given out after the sermon and include, uniquely in a traditional Lutheran rite, commemoration of the faithful departed:

> We are reminded again today of our mortality by the announcement that [name] hath departed this life at the age of [age at death]. The Lord teach us so to consider our own coming departure, that, when we are to be taken from this transitory life, we may be prepared for a blessed end.[3]

Only two changes were made in the revision of 1917. The Church Order of 1571 had permitted either the Apostles' or the Nicene Creed to be used at the eucharist. In 1614 Luther's metrical version of the Apostles' Creed was also permitted as a third alternative. In 1811 the option to use the Nicene Creed was abolished. From 1917 the Nicene Creed was to be used in full on the greater festivals, but a metrical version of the Creed could be used on other days. The second change in 1917 was the reintroduction of the optional use of introit antiphons, as part of the preparatory introduction section of the eucharist, on certain festivals.

Lutheran Church Buildings

The conservative nature of Lutheran revisions of the pre-Reformation Latin Mass, and the general Lutheran attitude towards ceremonial as a matter of liturgical preference for individual churches, meant that it was possible, and in many respects desirable, to use pre-Reformation buildings with only the most modest modifications. This was especially true in Scandinavia where the majority of village, and even many town, churches preserve, not just the pre-Reformation liturgical arrangement of the buildings, but significant amounts of pre-Reformation church furniture and decoration. When churches were rebuilt in the eighteenth or nineteenth centuries they frequently re-used furnishings from the predecessor buildings. This was the case, for example, in Iceland, at Holar Cathedral, rebuilt in 1757-63, but retaining the sixteenth-century crucifix and Dutch triptych from the earlier cathedral; at Saurbaur, rebuilt in 1856, but retaining an eighteenth-century reredos from the former church; and at Thingeyrar, rebuilt in 1864-77, which has a fifteenth-century altarpiece and a seventeenth-century pulpit and painted font from earlier buildings. What is even more significant is that traditional furnishings did not just survive, but were replicated, in the post-Reformation Lutheran churches. In Finland the church at Tornio has a choir screen installed in 1706. Such screens continued to be retained or replaced in Finnish churches until the end of the eighteenth century and were only removed in the nineteenth century because they blocked the congregation's

---

3   *Ibid.*, pp 166-7.

view of the priest when he was standing at the altar.[4] The Swedish church of Habo is an excellent example of an eighteenth-century wooden building planned on pre-Reformation principles of church arrangement. The canopied pulpit and elaborate altarpiece are placed at the east end of the building in the normal pre-Reformation positions. Though the church is galleried, every section of the walls, ceilings and individual furnishings is covered with paintings; the only difference between Habo and a medieval church interior is that, whereas medieval paintings tended to include illustrations from the lives of the saints, the paintings at Habo are an illustrated commentary on the main themes of the Bible.

The iconoclasm that took place in other Protestant churches in the post-Reformation period, or the subdivision of buildings that took place in some of the Reformed churches, was almost entirely absent from Lutheran Germany and Scandinavia. Occasionally it did happen. When the new university of Lund was founded in 1667 the cathedral was divided so that the nave was fitted up for parochial worship (Illustration 2.2) and the chancel, complete with its medieval choir stalls, adapted to serve as a lecture hall for the university (Illustration 2.3). Such examples were, however, exceptional. Much more typical was the interior at Valleberga (Illustration 2.4) where the only major change was the replacement of open benches by box pews. In Finland seating in churches was originally provided by individual families at their own expense but these were soon replaced by sets of uniform box pews built at the expense of the whole congregation, and this became the norm throughout Scandinavia. In Iceland each parishioner had a reserved seat in church, with men sitting on the south side and women on the north. The male members of the gentry and the singers sat in the chancel, genteel women and the pastor's wife in the front pews on the north side of the nave. Traditional arrangements of furnishing, seating and liturgical order survived well into the late nineteenth, and even early twentieth, centuries. Reykjavik Cathedral was built in 1789-96, repaired in 1817, enlarged in 1847-8 and repaired again in 1879. It is fitted with box pews, a tall, canopied pulpit at the east end of the nave on the south side and a painted altarpiece illustrating the resurrection of Christ. The font of 1839 is, however, placed in front of the altar, and this was the normal practice in Lutheran churches. It marked a departure from the pre-Reformation practice of placing the font at the west end of the nave or one of the nave aisles. Sometimes fonts were made of wood, rather that stone or marble, as was the case at Oddi (Iceland), where the wooden font and cover date from 1804.

Despite, however, the conservatism of Lutheran liturgy and church furnishing, changes did take place. In order to make the preacher more easily heard by the whole congregation, pulpits were sometimes moved from the east end to about half-way down the nave, but this created difficulties when part of the service was conducted from the pulpit and part from the altar. In order to counteract this some churches were provided with seating that was reversible, facing either the altar or pulpit as required. A good example of such seating survives in the church at Stege on the Danish island of Møn. We have already noted the almost universal removal of the font from the west end to the east end of the church so that baptism could

---

4   A. Sinisalo and H. Lilius, *Kauneimmet Kirkkomme*, Jyväskylä 1962, p 59.

Illustration 2.2   The nave of Lund Cathedral, Sweden, in 1833 (Rydbeck, *Lunds Domkyrka*, opposite p 264)

Illustration 2.3   The chancel of Lund Cathedral, Sweden, in 1833 (Rydbeck, *Lunds Domkyrka*, opposite p 288)

Illustration 2.4   The interior of Valleberga Church, before restoration in 1908

take place in the full view of the whole congregation. However, the really novel
Lutheran contributions to Protestant church design were the cruciform plan with
central pulpit and altar, popular in parts of Scandinavia, and the pulpit-altar
arrangement, popular throughout Germany but only occasionally adopted in
Scandinavia.

The Cruciform Plan Church

Churches in the shape of a cross, often a Greek cross in which all four arms were of equal length, became increasingly popular in Scandinavia from the late seventeenth century. In Sweden the surviving examples include the late-seventeenth-century cathedral at Kalmar, which preserves most of its original furnishings, and they were the norm in Finland, then part of Sweden, from the 1660s.[5] Originally some of the churches were designed to retain the traditional liturgical arrangement, with one arm of the cross treated as the chancel, the altar against the ritual east wall, as at Piteå (Figure 2.2), in Sweden, a wooden church built in 1686. Such also was the case with the Finnish churches at Tampere and Puumela, though in these cases the western part of the chancel also had seats in it. In terms of seating, the interior was a T-plan, with seats facing a pulpit in one of the angles of the crossing from the nave and both transepts. Although this permitted everybody in the church a clear view of the pulpit, that of the altar was completely obscured for most of those sitting in the transepts. At Oslo Cathedral the placing of the royal pew in a gallery in the angle of the crossing diametrically opposite that in which the pulpit was located permitted its occupants a clear view of both pulpit and altar. The view of both pulpit and altar from all parts of the church could be secured where the altar was not placed in one of the arms but also in the crossing. This was achieved in Finland at Alatornio, rebuilt in 1794-7, and in the large wooden church at Ilmajoki, built in 1764-5. Here the pulpit is in the north-east angle of the crossing and the altar in the south-east.[6] An identical arrangement was shown in the contemporary plan of the district church at Skellefteå (Figure 2.3), in Sweden, where the, now much altered, church was rebuilt in 1796-9. The nearby church at Öjebyn, has, however, preserved this arrangement intact, though in this case in a pre-Reformation building to which transepts were added in the eighteenth century.

The Pulpit-Altar Arrangement

The cruciform plan church, with centrally located pulpit and altar, was only a partial solution to the problem of making both visible to the whole congregation. Very much more satisfactory was the pulpit-altar arrangement, first pioneered in Germany, which achieved, three centuries before the modern liturgical movement, a single liturgical focus, even in a larger building. The first move towards this arrangement took place at Nidda, in Upper Hesse, where a new church was built in 1618. It was a rectangular room with galleries; the altar was placed in a shallow recess, with the pulpit on one side of the recess and the font on the other. In 1649 Joseph Fürttenbach (1591-1667), whose father had built the first German theatre, at Ulm, in 1640-41, published *Kirchen-Gebaw*, in which he advocated the placing together, as closely as possible, of the font, altar, pulpit and organ, with the suggestion that the pulpit might

---

5   *Ibid.*, p 58.

6   D. Buxton, *The Wooden Churches of Eastern Europe: An Introductory Survey*, Cambridge 1981, p 345.

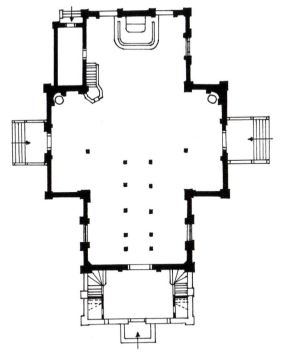

Figure 2.2   Ground plan of Piteå Church, built in 1686

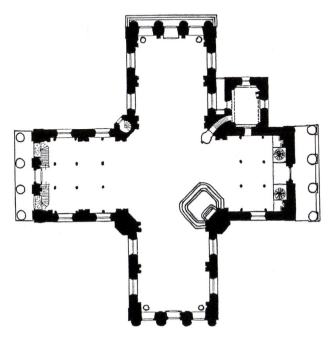

Figure 2.3   Ground plan of Skellefteå District Church, rebuilt in 1796-9

be placed over the altar, and the organ over the pulpit, with the font in front of the altar. Another advocate of this arrangement was the mathematician Leonhard Cristoph Sturm (1669-1719). Sturm argued that Protestant, as opposed to Roman Catholic, churches should resemble theatres, with the pulpit-altar replacing the stage. By the early eighteenth century, the pulpit-altar arrangement, which had been pioneered in the mid-seventeenth-century court chapels at Callenberg, Eisenberg, Gotha, Saalfeld, Weimar and Weissenfels, had begun to spread to parish churches as well: Loschwitz (1705-8), Hainewelde (1705-11), Spritzkunersdorf (1712-16), Schimedeberg (1713), Forchheim (1719-21), Niederoderwitz (1719-25), Hohnstein (1724) and Grossenhain (1735). As well as pulpit-altars, all these churches had galleries in order to increase their seating accommodation. The Pauluskirche in Frankfurt was a circular building with curved pews and the pulpit placed over the altar. There was also a handsome pulpit-altar in St John's Church at Hanover (Illustration 2.5).

Occasionally the pulpit-altar arrangement was abandoned for technical reasons. In the Frauenkirche at Dresden the pulpit was originally designed to be placed beneath a raised altar, with the organ case placed over the altar. When this arrangement was found to be impractical, the pulpit was turned into a lectern and a new, much taller and canopied, pulpit placed against one of the pillars supporting the central dome. The Frauenkirche was built between 1726 and 1734 and cost more than twice the original estimate. There were four tiers of galleries as well as a large number of fixed seats in the body of the church. Because of the height of the building and the number of galleries, the preacher was simply not audible in the original pulpit, which is why the original design had had to be modified. Dr Charles Burney, who attended Lutheran High Mass at the Frauenkirche in 1772, was extremely impressed by both the building and the worship, and noted that the congregation was close on three thousand.

The survival of the pulpit-altar arrangement in German Protestant churches, frequently an amalgamation of once separate Lutheran and Reformed congregations after official unions in several German states (Nassau and Prussia 1817, Hanau and Bavarian Palatinate 1818, Baden 1821, Hessen 1822), lasted well into the nineteenth century. An analysis of the buildings by the Hanover-based architect Friedrich August Ludwig Hellner (1791-1862) shows that, in the vast majority of his designs, the pulpit was placed over the altar, either as part of a pulpit-altar composition, or as part of a gallery behind the altar. Hellner, however, did not incorporate the organ as part of his composition, preferring instead to place it in a gallery over the entrance, on the wall opposite to that on which the pulpit and altar were situated. Towards the end of his career Hellner moved away from this arrangement, clearly influenced by the Gothic revival in other parts of Europe. At Suderbruch the altar was placed in an apse with the pulpit, entered through the wall from the vestry behind, placed on the south side of the entrance to the chancel. A similar design was employed at Molzen and Gross Lobke.[7]

Outside Germany the pulpit-altar arrangement was far less common and was more quickly abandoned. There are exceptionally fine examples in Denmark in Christian's Church at Copenhagen and in Norway at Kongsberg. In both of these churches the

---

7   U. Muller (ed), *Friedrich August Ludwig Hellner*, Hannover 1991, pp 75-149.

Illustration 2.5   The pulpit-altar at St John's, Hanover, in 1913

pulpit is placed over the altar and the organ over the pulpit and there are three tiers of galleries, those for the more distinguished pew-holders resembling boxes in a theatre. In Sweden the church at Nor was given a pulpit-altar in 1804 but it was dismantled in 1859.[8] There were also interesting examples of the arrangement in proposed plans for new churches at Nedertorneå-Haparanda by E. Hollström in 1820 and C.G. Blom-Carlsson in 1821, at Överluleå by Hollström in 1821 and at Överkalix by R. Brouhn

8   H. Kjellin, *Sveriges Kyrkor, Värmland: Grums Härad*, Stockholm 1924, p 130.

in 1841. In all four cases what was designed was an internally rectangular building with a projecting tower on one side and a projecting vestry exactly opposite. The pulpit-altar, placed in front of the vestry, was thus in the middle of one of the long sides. At Överluleå the ends of the rectangle were designed to be semi-circular. All of these plans, and the correspondence attached to them, survive in the archives of the Board of Public Works and Building (*Overintendentsämbetet*), which had a statutory duty to control the building of new churches, and the repair of existing ones, in Sweden from the late eighteenth century. There is an Icelandic example of the pulpit-altar arrangement at Reynistadur.

The Lutheran Church Interior

The cruciform plan church and the pulpit-altar arrangement were not the only examples of a particularly Lutheran approach to the re-ordering of church interiors, though they were the most radical. In Sweden during the eighteenth century the most common alteration in small village churches was for the chancel screen, if it survived, to be dismantled and for the chancel itself to be shortened and provided with a three-sided apse in which the altar was placed. This was generally provided with a painted reredos and lit by a window on each side. The elaborate Baroque reredoses of the late seventeenth century were replaced by more severe altar paintings or, in some cases, by a draped cross. However, many churches, as has been noted, frequently re-used existing furnishings wherever they could. Very occasionally acts of Puritan iconoclasm occurred but it was as likely to be in the late nineteenth century, at a time when other European churches were trying to reverse the iconoclasm of the past, than in the immediate post-Reformation period. Thus at Borgvik, in Sweden, all the internal paintings, together with the altar-piece, pulpit and wooden font, dating from 1718, and the painted organ-loft of 1745, were whitewashed over in 1880. Thirty-two years later, in 1912, the whitewash was removed and the paintings restored to their former glory.[9]

In Scandinavia in particular, and to a lesser extent in Germany, the practice of seating the congregation in box pews of uniform size was very common. The square pews with seats on three sides, frequently found in Anglican and Reformed churches, were virtually unknown. Whereas box pews tended to be replaced by open benches in other parts of Europe during the nineteenth century, those in Scandinavian churches were usually allowed to remain and their survival, especially in village churches, is still very common. In Denmark the town churches of Køge and Ringsted have complete sets of elaborately carved seventeenth-century box pews. In Sweden box pews are seen as such a feature of traditional church furnishing that they have even been included in some modern interiors, such as the late-twentieth-century refurbishment of the cathedral at Växjö. Lutheran churches normally included special seats for important people, either in the form of galleries or lofts, or as canopied seats in the body of the church. Genarp church in Skåne preserves some handsome sixteenth-century family pews at the east end of the nave, with later box pews behind

---

9   *Ibid.*, p 62.

them, and a series of elaborate family lofts in the north aisle, facing the pulpit. At the former abbey church of Varnhem, restored by the Chancellor of Sweden, Magnus Gabriel de la Gardie, between 1654 and 1672, canopied pews were placed on either side of the chancel for the King and Queen.[10] There are similar royal pews with elaborate canopies in the cathedral at Stockholm.

The major difference between Lutherans and other Protestants was that they were happy to retain medieval altars intact, and also for them to retain the traditional ornaments. In the seventeenth and eighteenth centuries many earlier reredoses were replaced, not for doctrinal but for purely aesthetic reasons, by new retables of classical, Baroque or Rococo design. There was virtually no difference stylistically between the altar-pieces of Lutheran and Roman Catholic churches in Germany, except that those of the former largely restricted the paintings or statuary in them to biblical themes. Altars were also provided with new Baroque crucifixes and candlesticks. In those churches where the eucharistic vestments were retained new chasubles followed the fiddle-back design favoured by Counter-Reformation Roman Catholics. In the late eighteenth and early nineteenth centuries Baroque altar-pieces in some Lutheran churches were replaced by more severe classical ones; an interesting comparison can, in this respect, be made between the late-seventeenth-century altarpiece in Kalmar Cathedral and the late-eighteenth-century one, a draped cross with supporting angels, in the cathedral at Karlstad. However, even in Germany, where Lutheran worship and furnishings tended to be modified by the desire of secular rulers to unite the Calvinist and Lutheran churches in their realms, travellers in the late nineteenth century were surprised by the Catholic atmosphere of Protestant churches. T.F. Bumpus noted that

> the communion table is invariably provided with a crucifix, and one or more pairs of candlesticks, and vested in frontals varying in colour with the Christian seasons, while the walls, roof and windows glow with frescoes and stained glass.[11]

At St Peter's, Soest, he noted that

> in the cathedral apse or *Haupt Chor* stands the Communion table, apparelled in a richly embroidered frontal of purple velvet. A cross encircled with a scroll bearing the inscription *Kommt, es ist alles bereit* (Come for all things are now ready) fills the central space formed by the orphreys and a graceful arrangement of wheat and grapes (the latter issuing from the chalice) the one on either hand. Upon the table stands the crucifix framed by lights, of which there is a pair in simple candlesticks of Early Renaissance design, whilst others are in branches. The general effect of these arrangements is very rich, and it is materially enhanced by a tall handsome altar-piece in the Italian variety of Corinthian, its five divisions enclosing as many paintings.[12]

The medieval screens and choir fittings had been preserved in the former cathedrals at Havelberg, Lübeck, Magdeburg, Halberstadt and Naumberg; this was made possible

---

10   R. Edenheim and I. Rossell, *Varnhems Klosterkyrka*, Stockholm 1982, p 83.

11   T.F. Bumpus, *Holiday Rambles among the Cathedrals and Churches of North Germany*, London 1903, p 125.

12   *Ibid.*, p 210.

by the Lutheran retention of the Holy Cross or people's altar which traditionally stood to the west of the screen of cathedral and monastic churches in Germany. At Halberstadt the altar before the screen was used when there was no communion, and the altar in the choir on the days when the sacrament was celebrated. At Naumberg there were no fewer than three surviving altars. In the western choir, which formed the Lady Chapel, there stood

> an altar vested … back, front and ends in an ancient frontal of crimson damask with figures of saints embroidered on the orphreys and supporting a crucifix and candlesticks. A second altar, apparelled in green, stands under the central arch of the rood screen at the opposite end of the nave, and a third is in the apse of the eastern choir, which with its episcopal throne placed at the west end and therefore facing the altar, its stalls with their elaborately carved poppyheads, its sedilia, *Sakraments-haüslein* [tabernacle], piscina, and other furniture, retains almost all its old arrangements undisturbed. Here the Holy Table backed by an early Renaissance altar-piece, had on a richly worked green antependium, while its superfrontal bore the legend *Ecce panis angelorum*.[13]

It is not surprising that some English Protestants should have been amazed, and some even shocked, by the retention of such furnishings and ornaments in a church which had abandoned a fully episcopal structure and had, in many cases, altered its liturgy to accommodate Calvinists and Zwinglians.

The long disintegration of the traditional Lutheran liturgy in parts of Germany had begun in the early eighteenth century as a result of the influence of pietism. In many places the first section of the liturgy had shrunk to the introit hymn, salutation, collect, one scripture reading and a hymn before the sermon; the eucharistic prayer had generally lost the Preface but otherwise remained intact; however, there were few churches in which there was communion every Sunday. It was not until the nineteenth century that high church reformers in Germany began to revive the full eucharistic liturgy and weekly communion. In the intervening period proposals were made to move the liturgies of the German Lutheran churches in a more Calvinist or Zwinglian direction. There were proposals for sitting communion and the use of individual communion cups. It was also suggested that the eucharistic rite, shorn of communion, should cease to be the principal service on Sundays, and rather that it should be replaced by a separate preaching service every Sunday, with an additional communion service on occasional Sundays during the year, every few weeks, on the model of John a Làsco's practice at Emden and the Austin Friars Church in London in the 1540s and 1550s. No such movement took place in the Scandinavian Lutheran churches to abolish the normal Sunday liturgy, but there was an increase in the number of churches in which there was not a weekly communion service. German visitors to Sweden in the early nineteenth century still commented on the solemnity of the Swedish rite, the entrance procession of the priest with chalice and paten, the churchwarden with wafer-box and flagon of wine, and the threefold bow of the communicants. Although communion continued to be celebrated weekly in some town and large village churches, the norm throughout much of Sweden varied from fortnightly communion to communion every sixth week and at the major

---

13 *Ibid.*, pp 271-2, 328-30.

festivals. Most communicants received at least twice to four times a year and some as many as eight times. Reports to Diocesan Synods noted a significant decline in the number of communicants in the second half of the nineteenth century. In Norway a second wave of pietism in the nineteenth century resulted in the virtual abandonment of communion services in favour of missionary ones. Communion became 'a service for the few who had their accounts with God in order'.[14]

Despite these trends there was little change in the externals of worship or church furnishings in the Lutheran churches of Scandinavia. In Denmark the altars of most churches had richly embroidered altar frontals, usually in crimson velvet, and with 'a deep superfrontal of lace', and were furnished with a crucifix 'flanked by two or more candlesticks... besides one or more branches of small candles'. Danish clergy mostly wore chasubles at the altar though the black gown was used for preaching. The eastward position was taken, the priest standing with his back to the congregation, and it was common practice for both clergy and laity to cross themselves and to bow to the altar.[15] In Sweden the clergy always wore chasubles, even when the full communion service was not celebrated. These were usually red except in Lent 'when it is invariably black with silver embroidery or lace'. Bishops carried crosiers and they also wore copes, mitres and pectoral crosses; the archbishop of Uppsala wore a diamond pectoral cross at the coronation of King Oscar I in 1844. The Swedish liturgy directed the celebrant to take the eastward position in front of the altar for most parts of the service. Communicants knelt to receive the sacrament on a railed and cushioned altar step; 'the use of wafer-bread is universal... it is stamped with the crucifix... and it is always placed in the mouth by the priest'.[16]

In the 1840s and 1850s a number of high church Anglicans, including the Secretary of the British Legation in Stockholm, G.J.R. Gordon, were fascinated by the Catholic outlook of the Swedish Church and saw in it a possible model for the reintroduction of traditional ceremonial into the services of the Church of England. Gordon wrote an account of the services in the Swedish church, noting that the normal pattern on Sundays was Matins at 8am, High Mass at 10am and Evensong at 4pm. In many parts of Sweden communicants received fasting, and all intending communicants had to attend a preparation service, *Skriftemål*, held beforehand and, in effect, replacing the compulsory private confession of the pre-Reformation church.[17] Both in their services and in their architecture and furnishings, the Lutheran churches of Germany and Scandinavia had, with relatively few exceptions, preserved and developed the ethos of the pre-Reformation church, whilst at the same time adopting a theological position which was uncompromisingly Protestant. It was a position which, before the nineteenth century, was not replicated by Protestant churches in either the Reformed or the Anglican traditions.

---

14   E. Molland, *Church Life in Norway 1800-1950*, Westport 1978, pp 45-6.

15   T.F. Bumpus, *The Cathedrals and Churches of Norway, Sweden and Denmark*, London 1908, pp 31, 80.

16   *Ibid.*, pp 92-3.

17   *The Ecclesiologist*, lxxxviii (1852), pp 30-46.

Lutheran Worship and Buildings in Perspective

Whilst from the perspective of the Anglican and Reformed traditions, and that of the nineteenth-century ecclesiologists, Lutheran worship and buildings must have been seen as incredibly old-fashioned, there is a sense in which both anticipated, in a rather uncanny manner, and with certainly no intention to do so, much of the liturgical agenda of the modern church and the ecumenical approach to both worship and church buildings since the 1960s. Lutheran worship aimed at purging the liturgy of the pre-Reformation church from its perceived corruptions, without seeking to destroy, in the way that most other Protestants did, the overall order and structure of the Mass. Since the 1960s a broad sweep of churches, from the Roman Catholics to some of the Reformed churches, have sought to create a liturgy which maintains exactly that order and structure but which sweeps away the unnecessary accretions that came to form part of the pre-Reformation Mass, many of which the Roman Catholic church had retained as part of its own Counter-Reformation remodelling of the eucharistic rite. The sort of eucharistic rites now in use throughout much of western Europe, Catholic and Protestant, reflect very much the Lutheran ethos, even though the Lutheran churches themselves were rather slower at adopting them than most Anglican, and even some Reformed, churches.

Similarly, in adapting their buildings to meet their liturgical requirements, some Lutherans anticipated the sort of changes that are commonplace today. The pulpit-altar arrangement that created one liturgical centre and focus, bringing together not just the pulpit and altar, but the organ and font as well, has not been directly imitated in the arrangement of many modern church buildings, but the principle of creating one liturgical centre – for baptism, reading the scriptures, preaching and celebrating Holy Communion – to a large extent has. The compartmentalisation of the church building, inherited from the pre-Reformation church, was, with important modifications, retained by both Anglicans and Counter-Reformation Roman Catholics, as well as many, more traditional, Lutherans. Those Lutherans who experimented with the pulpit-altar arrangement abandoned compartmentalisation of the church building as much as most European churches, Catholic and Protestant, have attempted to do, wherever they could, over the last forty years. The ideal at which virtually everyone now aims, though not all are able to achieve it in important historic buildings, is a flexible sanctuary, visible from all parts of the building, in which the essential furniture for the different parts of the service – the altar, the font, the pulpit, the lectern or reading or prayer desk – can be brought together, in close proximity to one another. It was an arrangement which some Lutherans, alone among the churches of western Europe, achieved more than three hundred years before the Second Vatican Council.

Chapter 3

The Calvinist and Reformed Churches

Churches in the Calvinist and Reformed tradition covered a much wider swathe of Europe than those of the Lutherans by the late sixteenth century. They existed in France, the Netherlands, Switzerland, Hungary, parts of Germany and Scotland. By the early seventeenth century they were beginning to make an impact in other parts of Britain and Ireland. As with Lutheranism these churches did not follow the same pattern of organisational structure or liturgical practice and their buildings also could be very different. In this chapter we will start by considering the general approach of these churches to the conduct of public worship and then look at how this developed in detail in the different groups of these churches across Europe.

The Reformed Approach to Public Worship

It would be fair to say that the Reformed churches had a great suspicion of the sort of rigid liturgical structure that the Lutheran churches were happy to preserve from the pre-Reformation church, or any liturgical practices that could not be justified from scripture. However, there was a wide variation of liturgical attitudes among the Reformed churches and significant differences in their approaches, both to the treatment of pre-Reformation church buildings, and to the building of new churches. Although Zwingli and Calvin had certainly wished to create a more radical liturgy than the simplified mass of the Lutheran churches, they were not opposed to some form of set liturgy, and indeed made provision for this. It was only in the late sixteenth and early seventeenth centuries that some of the Reformed churches took the view that there should be no set liturgy and that individual ministers should be free to order the service as they and their congregation preferred. One of the main groups that pushed this agenda was the Puritans in England, a group that looked back as much to the radical reform tradition of the Münster Anabaptists, and other groups of this type, as to the more mainstream theology of the principal non-Lutheran reformers. The development of this tradition can be seen in a comparison of Knox's *Book of Common Order*, produced for the Reformed Church of Scotland in 1564, the liturgy produced for the Puritan congregation at Middelburg (Netherlands) in 1586, the Westminster Directory of 1644 and the Savoy Liturgy produced by Richard Baxter in the discussions over the revision of the English *Book of Common Prayer* in 1661 (Figure 3.1). Knox's liturgy had included a number of set prayers, such as the Apostles' Creed and the Lord's Prayer. A move towards a much freer liturgy in which, apart from scriptural texts and psalms, the minister could pray *extempore*, is seen in the Puritan Liturgy of 1586 and a further move in this direction in the Directory of 1644, where both the ordinary Sunday service and the eucharistic rite

Figure 3.1 Comparison of Knox's *Book of Common Order* (1564), a Puritan Liturgy of 1586, the Directory (1644) and the Savoy Liturgy (1661)

1564	1586	1644	1661
		Opening Prayer	Opening Prayer
			Nicene or Apostles' Creed
			Ten Commandments
	Scripture Readings	Scripture Reading	
	Psalms	Psalm	
Confession	Confession		Confession
Prayer for Pardon			
Psalm	Psalm		Psalms
Prayer for Illumination	Prayer before Sermon	Prayer before Sermon	
Lesson	Text		OT Reading
			Psalm or Te Deum
			NT Reading
			Psalm, Benedictus or Magnificat
			Prayer before Sermon
Sermon	Sermon	Sermon	Sermon
Intercession	Prayer for Church		
Lord's Prayer			
Apostle's Creed			
	Psalm	Prayer after Sermon	Prayer after Sermon
	Blessing or Grace		Blessing

Communion Service			
Preparation of Elements			
Words of Institution			
Exhortation	Exhortation	Exhortation	Exhortation
Prayer of Thanksgiving	Prayer of Thanksgiving		
Fraction	Words of Institution	Words of Institution	Prayer over Elements
		Prayer of Thanksgiving	
Distribution	Distribution	Distribution	Distribution
	Prayer of Thanksgiving	Prayer of Thanksgiving	Prayer of Thanksgiving
Psalm	Psalm	Psalm	Psalm
Blessing			Blessing

were reduced to their bare minimum. Baxter's Savoy Liturgy, however, showed a willingness to return to set forms as the price for achieving a religious settlement acceptable to Puritans, even though his suggestions were not found to be acceptable to the bishops of the Church of England. The three elements common to all four liturgies were the sermon, always the core of Reformed worship, the communion exhortation and the words of institution or prayer over the elements. Apart from these there was much variation in both the form and the content of the four liturgies and, because all included provision for extempore prayer, there would clearly have been significant differences in the way each was celebrated by individual ministers.

The major debate within the Reformed churches was over provision for the sacraments. There was a universal rejection of kneeling for communion, but a wide variety of other practices. In the churches influenced primarily by the liturgical standards of Calvin's Geneva the preference, at least by the late seventeenth century, was to receive Holy Communion sitting at long tables. Sometimes these were permanent, sometimes they were temporary, brought in as required. However, in the more eastern parts of Europe the preference was for fixed communion tables and for communicants to receive standing, or walking, or to have the elements brought around to them in their seats. Where Reformed churches retained fonts they were normally placed near the pulpit, itself always the main liturgical focus of the building. However, many Reformed churches abandoned use of the font and baptised from 'a ewer or basin set on a table or bracketed from the pulpit'.[1] In the Netherlands small fonts on wrought-iron stands were frequently placed in the enclosure that separated the pulpit from the seating. The level of destruction of pre-Reformation furnishings varied greatly from one Reformed tradition to another. It was least in Hungary and greatest in Scotland which, consequently, has hardly any surviving medieval stained glass or woodwork. There was also much debate over the permissibility of music in worship. In Hungary, southern Germany, Switzerland and even the Netherlands the decision eventually went in favour of music, so organs were either retained or reinstated. In the British Isles the decision went the other way and it was not until the nineteenth century that Reformed churches began to consider the introduction of organs. Such decisions frequently led to schisms, the anti-organ party setting up a new place of worship, and even today there are parts of Scotland, especially the western highlands and islands, where metrical psalms are still sung unaccompanied, line by line after the precentor, as they were in many Reformed, and even many Anglican, churches four hundred years ago.

Reformed Churches in France and the Netherlands

These were the churches which were most strongly influenced by the theology of John Calvin. Eventually the church in the Netherlands was divided by the Remonstrant Schism following the condemnation of the teachings of Jacobus Arminius (1560-1609) at the Synod of Dort (Dordrecht) in 1618-19. The church in France was eventually forced underground by persecution after the Revocation of the Edict of Nantes in 1685. Whereas both Luther and Zwingli had been priests who

---

1   Lovibond, 'Use of Spaces for Public Worship', p 70.

retained, to a greater or lesser extent, a respect for the liturgy of the pre-Reformation church, Calvin did not have this background and was less restrained by tradition in restructuring the Sunday liturgy. Although he arguably supported the idea of weekly communion, Calvin always saw the Lord's Supper as essentially an extension of a preaching service. It is therefore not surprising that, when weekly communion was found to be impossible, it was a simple service of prayer, bible-reading, psalms and sermon that became the normal liturgical form of the Reformed churches west of the Rhine, with the Lord's Supper tacked on between one and four times a year. This type of service was generally maintained in the Reformed churches of France and parts of French-speaking Switzerland, though during the eighteenth and nineteenth centuries occasional attempts were made to enrich the liturgy with borrowings from Anglican or Lutheran sources. Although the eucharistic rites of the Dutch Reformed Churches were based on that introduced by John à Lasco at Emden, they followed a similar pattern to the Calvinist rites in France and French-speaking Switzerland. The communion service was an addition to the Sunday preaching service (Illustration 3.1). The minister read an excommunication of those unworthy to receive communion from the pulpit, followed by a prayer for worthy communion and an account of the institution of the sacrament. He then took his place at the table where he broke the bread and poured the wine. Originally there was some variety of communion practice in the Dutch churches, some standing around or walking past the table, others physically sitting around it, until sitting became the invariable practice in the Netherlands (Illustration 3.2). After all had received there would be a prayer of thanksgiving and a brief discourse on a topic connected with the sacrament.

In arranging their churches Calvinists in France and French-speaking Switzerland also took their lead from Calvin's Geneva and churches were arranged so that seeing and hearing the preacher was paramount. French Calvinist churches before the Revocation of the Edict of Nantes tended to be either simple galleried rectangles with a tall pulpit against one of the short walls, as at Charenton (1623), or with apsidal short sides, as at La Rochelle (1577), or else round or octagonal buildings with all the seating focused on the pulpit, as at Lyons (1564) and Rouen (1601).[2] There were no fixed communion tables and temporary ones were set up when required. Arrangements in the Calvinist churches of those parts of Switzerland adjacent to France were similar. Nineteenth-century illustrations of the churches of St Gervase and St Mary Magdalene in Geneva show galleried naves and aisles with their respective pulpits placed in the middle of one of the long sides.[3] There were identical arrangements in the churches at La Neuveville and Le Locle. The church at St Sulpice, built in 1820, had an elliptical interior with the pulpit on one of the long sides and seats curved to focus on it.

Whereas all the Calvinist churches in France were new buildings, all the earliest Reformed interiors in the Netherlands were adaptations of pre-Reformation buildings. In small village churches the necessary adaptations could be very radical and normally involved treating the nave and chancel as a single liturgical space. The pulpit was normally placed in the middle of one of the long sides of the

2   Plans in Carrive, 'Temples des Anglicans', p 65.
3   Lovibond , 'Use of Spaces for Public Worship', p 120.

Illustration 3.1   Service in a Dutch village church in 1624 (Rijksmuseum Het
Catharijneconvent, Utrecht)

church, so that the seating in the western part of the nave would face east; that in
the eastern part, and frequently the chancel, would face west. Where chancels were
apsidal the space formerly occupied by the main altar tended to be occupied by a
canopied pew for the leading landowner in the parish or other important people.
Examples will be found all over the Netherlands: Achlum, Buitenpost, Dalen,
Huizinge, Niebert, Tinallinge, Tzum and Vrouwenparochie. Despite this radical
reordering, and the destruction of most pre-Reformation imagery, Dutch churches
were not totally devoid of colour. The canopied pews and pulpits were frequently
very elaborate, and in the church at Borne the early sixteenth-century stone pulpit
was preserved and re-used. The seventeenth-century wooden pulpit at Augsbuur
incorporated carvings of Moses and Aaron displaying the Ten Commandments. The
early sixteenth-century organ case was preserved at Naarden until replaced by a
new one in 1863. One of the traditional features of Dutch Reformed churches were
elaborate painted boards for the Ten Commandments and the suspension of model
ships from the ceilings. The latter, and its inconsistency with Reformed theology,

Illustration 3.2   A Calvinist communion service in the early eighteenth century
                     (Picart, *Ceremonies*, v, opposite p 469)

has been commented on by Willem Frijhoff.[4] A fine example of a commandments
board, painted in 1687 and in the form of a triptych, with the commandments on the
central panel and the Creed and Lord's Prayer on the insides of the doors, survives at
Poortugaal. At St Peter's, Leiden, the commandments board was placed on top of the
chancel screen. Even more remarkable, when one compares Dutch church interiors
with those in Calvinist Scotland, was the survival of stained glass and the installation
of new painted glass in churches in the seventeenth and eighteenth centuries. In the
Grote Kerk of St John at Gouda there are some 57 stained glass windows. Some
of these date from before 1571, when the church became a Reformed one, but
many were installed later. The pre-Reformation glass probably survived because
it illustrated biblical stories rather than the lives of saints. The post-Reformation
windows include both religious and secular subjects: the Pharisee and the Publican
(1597), the Woman Taken in Adultery (1601) and the Relief of Leiden (1603).[5] An
illustration of the Oude Kerk of Amsterdam in 1786 shows visitors being invited to
inspect the painted glass in one of the windows. These windows date, respectively,

4   The practice of placing replicas of ships in churches in the Netherlands began
before the Reformation but was continued well into the nineteenth century. See Willem
Frijhoff, 'Votive Boats or Secular Models? An Approach to the Question of the Figurative
Ships in the Dutch Protestant Churches', *Embodied Belief: Ten Essays on Religious Culture
in Dutch History*, Hilversum 2002, pp 215-34.
5   For a detailed description of these windows see Rachel Esner, *The Netherlands*,
London 1998, p 238.

from 1655 and 1761. There are also examples of post-Reformation painted glass in windows at Egmond aan den Hoef (1633-4), Schermerhoorn (1642), Broek in Waterland (1729), Akkrum (1762) and Appingedam (1777).

Town churches in the Netherlands tended to be treated rather differently from village ones. In most cases the chancels were left empty, or used only for communion services, with the result that chancel screens were frequently left *in situ*. This was the case at St Peter's, Leiden, where temporary tables were placed in the chancel for communion services. The pulpit and baptism enclosure were placed in the middle of the north nave arcade and, by the eighteenth century, seating was arranged to face this enclosure in the nave and both aisles. There were also canopied pews for magistrates and other officials at both the east and west ends of the nave.[6] However, in some Dutch town churches, the practice was to leave the central part of the nave empty so that it, rather than the chancel, could be used for sitting communion. The seating in the nave consisted largely of canopied pews for important people against the nave arcades and other seating, mostly in the form of simple benches, was placed between these pews or in the nave aisles, as shown in a late-seventeenth-century illustration of the Grote Kerk at Hoorn (Illustration 3.3). A feature of most town churches was the organ. At St Bavo's, Haarlem, this was placed on top of the chancel screen (Illustration 3.4). There was much debate about the use of organs in the Dutch Reformed Church in the late sixteenth and seventeenth centuries. Organs were normally owned by the municipalities, who wanted them played for secular purposes. The Calvinist clergy, however, felt that it was inappropriate to use them in public worship and preferred unaccompanied singing led by a precentor (*voorsanger*). The somewhat ridiculous situation in which organs were played before and after, but not during, the service, together with the practical experience of the relatively unharmonious congregational singing of metrical psalms, led to many churches agreeing that the organ could be used to accompany singing.[7] By the late eighteenth century virtually all Dutch churches, not just in towns, but in villages as well, had been provided with organs.

New churches built in the Netherlands during the seventeenth century tended to replicate the internal design of reordered pre-Reformation ones. Thus the Westerkerk in Amsterdam is an aisled rectangle with the pulpit placed in the middle of one of the nave arcades. It originally had no galleries though one across one of the short walls was added in 1685. The Zuiderkerk of 1603 in Amsterdam was also an aisled rectangle with the pulpit in the middle of one of the nave arcades and a canopied magistrates' pew in the middle of the opposite arcade. However, other types of churches were built in this period. The Nieuwe Kerk of 1647 at Emden was designed as a T-plan with seating in the three arms of the church facing a central pulpit.[8] Some medieval churches were extended by adding a transept opposite the pulpit, thus making the interior a T-plan, examples of which include the churches at Breukelen and Ouderkerk aan de IJssel. Some T-plan interiors were formed within what was outwardly a Greek cross, the fourth arm serving as a vestry. This

---

6   Lovibond, 'Use of Spaces for Public Worship', p 230.

7   I owe this information to a current PhD student, the Rev'd Randall Engle, who is currently completing a thesis on the use of organs in the Netherlands before 1700.

8   Lovibond, 'Use of Spaces for Public Worship', p 144.

Illustration 3.3   The interior of the Grote Kerk, Hoorn, in 1695 (Westfries Museum, Hoorn)

was the case in the church of 1771 at Harlingen. Other examples of Greek cross churches in the Netherlands were the Nieuwe Kerk at Haarlem and the Nieuwe Kerk at Groningen. At the latter the pulpit was placed against one of the central pillars with a magistrates' pew directly opposite, and seating angled to face the pulpit in three blocks in the central part of the church. Another common design in the post-Reformation Netherlands was the octagonal church: the Marekerk of 1638-40 in Leiden,[9] the Oostkerk of 1647 at Middelburg and the village churches of 1653 at Sappemeer and 1682 at St Annaparochie.

---

9   *Ibid.*, p 231.

Illustration 3.4   The interior of the Grote Kerk (St Bavo's), Haarlem, in 1789 (Geemente Archief, Haarlem)

Although the long wall arrangement remained popular in the Netherlands, a late example being the church of 1865 at Farnsum with seating arranged to face the pulpit in a semi-circular pattern, a number of Dutch Reformed churches also adopted an arrangement whereby the pulpit was placed on one of the short walls. One of the earliest examples of this arrangement was shown in an eighteenth-century illustration of the Remonstrant church in Amsterdam. The pulpit was placed against the short wall opposite the entrance, with an organ above and canopied pews on each side. The pews and galleries were placed against the long walls, with an empty space, presumably for the temporary communion tables, in the middle. Such arrangements were also to be found in the pre-Reformation churches of Ter Apel and Westerwijtwerd as well as several new churches built between the late seventeenth and early nineteenth centuries: at Lellens and Oudeschans (both 1667), Urmond (1685), Nieuweschans (1751), Hoofdplaat and Zweins (both 1783), Osterwijk (1811), Eersel (1812), IJhorst and Veghel (both 1823) and Heteren (1837). At Ter Apel the pulpit was placed at the west end of the nave with the chancel, retaining its pre-Reformation stalls, left largely empty. At Westerwijtwerd the pulpit was placed against the east wall of the chancel with benches along the chancel walls and the rest of the seating, facing east, in the nave. In the pre-Reformation church at Abbenbroek the pulpit was placed at the east end of the nave and the chancel left empty. During the nineteenth century several Dutch Reformed churches were 'turned' so that what had been long wall arrangements became short wall ones, as was the case at Vlaardingen when it was refurbished in 1865 (Figure 3.2).

Figure 3.2   Seating plans of the Reformed Church at Vlaardingen before and after
               reordering in 1865

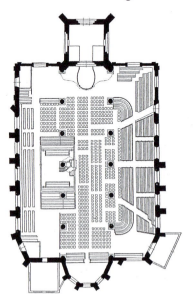
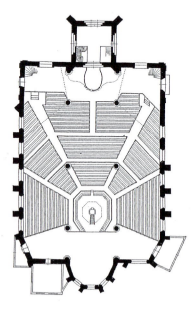

Reformed Churches in Switzerland and Hungary

Although Zwingli had favoured sitting communion, the practice in Reformed churches in most parts of Switzerland and throughout Hungary was for fixed communion tables, and therefore for communicants not to receive sitting at tables. The liturgical arrangement of buildings was, however, similar to that in the Netherlands, with a mixture of the long or short wall positions for the pulpit, but with the communion table placed in front of the pulpit, and the font also in a central position. Good examples of Swiss churches with the pulpit on the long wall are those at Wilchingen (1678), Yverdon (1753-7), Wadenswil (1764) and Horgen (1779-82). At Wilchingen stalls for the elders are placed on either side of the pulpit. The church at Horgen is elliptical with the font placed in the middle of the seating. Short wall arrangements were created at Holy Ghost, Berne (Figure 3.3), with the organ placed behind the pulpit, the French Reformed Church at Königsberg (1733-6) and at Morgues (1769-76), which had a raised apse at one end of the building, containing the pulpit and communion table, and the organ at the opposite end, in a gallery over the entrance. As was eventually the case in the Netherlands, organs were the norm in Swiss churches, though the most striking features are the fixed communion tables, often of considerable elaboration, and the much more traditional types of font, a far cry from the bowls on brackets or stands found in the Netherlands or Scotland. Indeed Swiss churches were not afraid of elaborate decoration in other respects. Although the majority of Baroque churches in Switzerland, as in southern Germany and Austria, are Roman Catholic, there were Protestant examples as well. Both Holy Ghost, Berne, and the church at Horgen, respectively short and long wall arrangements, were built in the Baroque style.[10] An interesting example of a Roman Catholic church in Switzerland imitating the arrangements in neighbouring Reformed churches is at Wattwil. Here the Roman Catholic church has a galleried interior with a shallow recess for the high altar in the middle of one of the long walls. Side altars are placed on each side of this recess, with the pulpit high up on one side of the sanctuary arch. Seating along the short walls faces inwards across the church as it would in a Reformed church.

As one moves east Calvinism becomes even more conservative in its attitude to worship and the arrangements of church buildings. Hungary had a majority Roman Catholic population but substantial minorities of Calvinist, Lutheran and Orthodox Christians, all of whom were granted a degree of toleration within a strict regulatory framework. Hungarian Calvinism was a strange phenomenon compared with the models for Reformed churches in Western Europe. It did not have a fully Presbyterian structure but a largely hierarchical one with superintendents (bishops) and archdeacons. Influences from English Puritans in the seventeenth century led to pressure for the introduction of a more presbyterian structure, but it was firmly resisted. Most churches had daily, as well as Sunday, services and Holy Communion was normally celebrated six times a year (Advent, Christmas, Ash Wednesday, Easter, Ascension Day and Pentecost). The traditional calendar and some holy days were retained. Imagery, in the form of paintings or statues, was permitted to remain in

---

10   John Bourke, *Baroque Churches of Central Europe*, London 1978, p 199. Plates 26-43 in this book show excellent examples of Roman Catholic Baroque churches.

Figure 3.3   Seating plan of the Holy Ghost Church, Berne, in 1725

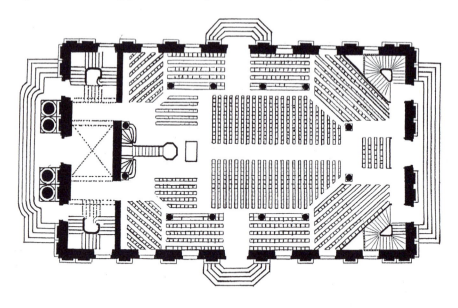

Figure 3.4   Ground plan of the Great Church at Debrecen, completed in 1819

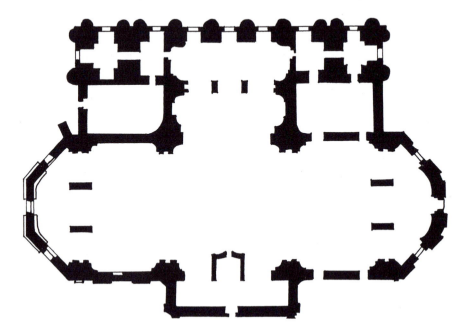

churches provided the subject was scriptural. There was controversy in the seventeenth century over whether the bread and wine should be elevated at communion, but some churches retained the practice. The theological and liturgical conservatism of the Hungarian Reformed Church was reflected in its attitude to church buildings which, alone among the Calvinist churches of Europe, retained elements of colour and symbolism more normally associated with Lutheran or Roman Catholic places of worship. Nevertheless, despite this, the liturgical arrangement of these buildings had a good deal in common with other Reformed churches elsewhere in Europe. The norm in Hungary was the long wall arrangement with the communion table placed in front of the pulpit and the seating organised to face this central liturgical focus from three directions. In the Great Church at Debrecen (Figure 3.4) the pulpit and the communion table are in this position with the organ placed over the entrance on the opposite wall. Medieval churches could be treated in quite a cavalier manner. That at Vámosoroszi has a gallery across the apsidal chancel providing seating at two levels. The typical arrangement in post-Reformation churches, such as that at Tiszacsécse (1820-25), is for the pulpit, communion table and a canopied seat for the minister to be placed on the long wall and for there to be galleries across the two short walls. Woodwork and plasterwork in Hungarian churches tended to be painted in very lively colours, with the walls of many medieval churches painted with scriptural texts in the seventeenth century, making the buildings much more attractive than the much plainer Reformed churches elsewhere in Europe. Alternatives to the long wall arrangement can, however, be found. At Szilvásvárad there is a circular church of 1820. The church of 1835-70 at Cegléd is in the form of a Greek cross with seating in each arm and a pulpit with a suspended canopy attached to one of the crossing pillars.

A particularly distinctive feature in Hungarian churches is the treatment of the communion table. They were frequently round or oblong, rather than square or rectangular, normally covered with an elaborate fringed carpet but with no ornaments on them. They were also frequently railed on four sides, as was the case at Cegléd and Egerlövö (1828). At Sárospatek (1776-81) the enclosure was octagonal. Fonts tended to be of the pedestal variety, stone with a wooden lid at Kéttornyúlak and of wood throughout at Litér. Organs were mostly nineteenth-century additions. Many churches had canopied seats for the minister and other important people. The rest of the congregation sat in pews without doors and there was never a fashion for box pews. The earliest complete surviving set of pews in Hungary is at Nádasdaróc, where they date from 1687.

> These seats were distributed on the basis of social position, gender and age and the front seats were secured for the most eminent families of the congregation, often on an hereditary basis. Two galleries... was the norm, one being used by young men and the other by young women.[11]

Békés Church, built in 1820 and enlarged in 1850, has special seats for the county recorder, judge, village magistrate, mayor's counsellors, school teachers, churchwardens, sextons and presbyters.

---

11   Balázs Dercsényi et al, *Calvinist Churches in Hungary*, Budapest 1992, p xxxiii.

Presbyterianism in Scotland and Ireland

The Reformation in Scotland was initially a rather patchy affair. There was a sense in which the country was 'partitioned' for two generations after 1560 between reforming and orthodox clergy. Three of the Scottish bishops, Robert Stewart of Caithness, Alexander Gordon of Galloway and Adam Bothwell of Orkney, were early supporters of the Reformation but there were Catholic bishops at Aberdeen until 1577, Argyll until 1580, Dunkeld until 1585 and Ross until 1592. These surviving Catholic bishops effectively prevented reforming clergy or laity from gaining ground in their dioceses. There were Reformed ministries soon after 1560 in most parts of Fife, Angus and Mearns, but not until the 1570s in Ayrshire, Perthshire, Berwickshire and East Lothian, or until the 1580s in Aberdeenshire. In much of the western highlands and islands Catholicism remained entrenched even longer. There were no appointments of Reformed clergy to the Hebridean parishes before 1609 and Islay was still predominantly Roman Catholic in 1615.[12] The study of the Reformed Church of Scotland, and its later plantations in Ireland, cannot be understood properly without some parallel discussion of events in England and Wales. In 1603 King James VI of Scotland became James I of the rest of the British Isles. His policy, and that of his successors until 1688, was an attempt to create a single national Protestant church for all their kingdoms. Early Presbyterianism in Scotland had encouraged Puritans in late sixteenth-century England, dissatisfied with the incompleteness of Elizabeth I's Reformation. In turn English Puritans proved a powerful influence on the Scottish church, encouraging it to reject episcopacy and adopt less structured forms of worship. Although liturgical and architectural developments in Presbyterian Scotland and Ireland are treated separately in the pages that follow from similar developments in the non-episcopal Protestant churches of England and Wales, it will be necessary, at various points, to make the necessary cross-references between them.

The earliest reformers in Scotland used the only fully Protestant liturgy available to them, the Second English Prayer Book of 1552. In 1562 the General Assembly of the Reformed Church of Scotland formally adopted Knox's *Book of Common Order*, which was itself based on Calvin's *La Forme des Prières*, used in the churches of Geneva, and this was first published with a complete psalm book in 1564. The main features of Knox's book was the rendering of the psalms in metrical versions, which could be easily learned, sitting for communion and the abolition of traditional vestments and ceremonial much more radically than had been done in Lutheran, or was to be done in Anglican, churches. Knox recommended that the normal preaching service should be extended to a full communion service once a month but in practice this rarely happened. Part of the reason for this was the solemnity with which the sacrament was approached in the Church of Scotland and, as Margo Todd makes clear, the form that remained common in Scotland for the best part of three centuries, and has still not been abandoned in some parts of the western highlands and islands, had been adopted long before the end of the seventeenth century.

---

12   I.B. Cowan, *The Scottish Reformation*, London 1982, pp 159-81.

Every communion… was celebrated over a period of at least two weeks, so that communion effectively comprised a season in itself. The sacrament was offered twice on each of two successive Sundays, even in quite small parishes, in order to allow time for all the designated segments of the congregation to take it in turn to sit at the communion table.[13]

Most parishes had only one communion season a year, a few had two or three, and Aberdeen after 1606 had as many as four. Although the Church of Scotland had, in principle, abolished the liturgical calendar, in practice the annual celebration tended to be in the spring, at or about the time of Easter (Pasch). The season was announced well beforehand to allow everyone time to prepare. This comprised at least one preparatory sermon, fasting and examination. Only those considered worthy were issued with a 'token' admitting them to the communion table. The services on the Sundays on which the sacrament was administered were very long affairs, frequently beginning as early as 4am and lasting through to the evening. Temporary tables were erected in the churches and sometimes, where the churches were too small, in the churchyards. The minister stood at one end of the table but the congregation administered themselves, passing the bread and wine to each other, and not being served by the clergy as they were in Anglican, Lutheran, Roman Catholic and even some Reformed churches. After the communion services had taken place the season ended with one or more services of thanksgiving. The numbers of communicants, despite the rigid examination process and the denial of the sacrament to those under sixteen, was very considerable: 2200 communion tokens were issued at Perth in 1621, 4000 at Glasgow in 1604 and even 950 in the small town of Burntisland in 1609. In the last case, where fifty communicants could be seated at one time, this meant seven sittings in the morning and twelve in the afternoon. Despite the overwhelmingly Protestant ethos of communion in the Church of Scotland a few pre-Reformation practices appear to have survived. Many churches used a type of shortbread rather than ordinary bread, and therefore more analogous to wafers, and some continued to mix water with wine in the chalice.

The treatment of pre-Reformation church buildings in Scotland was ruthless in the extreme. Spaces no longer required for worship were allowed to fall into ruin or else larger churches were divided so that they could serve more than one congregation. Nowhere is the resulting iconoclasm more clearly seen than in the treatment of cathedrals. At Aberdeen the chancel, transepts and Lady Chapel fell into ruins after being sacked by Protestant insurgents in 1560. At Brechin the chancel was abandoned after 1580. At Dornoch the cathedral was in ruins between 1570 and 1614, but all but the nave was re-roofed in 1614-17 to serve as a T-plan church. At Dunblane the nave was abandoned before 1600 and allowed to remain roofless for three hundred years. At Dunkeld the same happened in 1560 and the building remains in that condition. Four cathedrals, those at Elgin, Fortrose, Iona and St Andrews, were abandoned altogether, Elgin from c.1640, Fortrose in 1720, Iona from the late seventeenth century (though later rebuilt) and St Andrews after 1570. The cathedral at Lismore was roofless by 1679 but later restored for use as the parish

---

13   M. Todd, *The Culture of Protestantism in Early Modern Scotland*, New Haven and London 2002, p 85.

church. That at Whithorn, of which only the nave had remained in use after 1600, was finally abandoned in 1822 when a new parish church was built. The cathedral at Glasgow had been divided into three separate churches by the 1630s. Only one Scottish cathedral, that at Kirkwall, remained completely intact, though even there only the chancel was used for services.

Between 1560 and 1610 there was a battle for religious supremacy in Scotland between the crown and the church's leading reformers. An unsatisfactory compromise was reached, whereby bishops continued to exist but had no power and were not consecrated, but the church had, *de facto* if not *de jure*, a Presbyterian structure with a General Assembly, presbyteries and kirk sessions. It was the kirk sessions which effectively regulated both the local minister and his congregation and which imposed a moral discipline on the inhabitants unparalleled in the rest of western Europe. In 1610 James VI and I made his first significant move to integrate the established churches in his realms when he insisted on the consecration of three of the Scottish bishops by those in England. Those consecrated then consecrated the remaining members of the Scottish episcopate. In 1616 the General Assembly agreed, under royal pressure, to set up a committee to consider a revision of the *Book of Common Order*, but work on the revision proceeded very slowly. In 1618 the General Assembly, meeting at Perth, approved the Five Articles designed to bring the Church of Scotland more into line with that of England: the liturgical calendar, in a modified form omitting saints' days, was to be reintroduced; private baptism and communion were to be permitted; bishops were to administer confirmation before first communion; and, most controversially, communicants were to receive kneeling and not sitting. In 1619 a revision of the *Book of Common Order*, essentially a compromise between that and the English *Book of Common Prayer*, drafted by Bishop Cowper of Galloway, was approved but never published. It is now generally accepted that the direction to kneel at communion, issued in 1618, was widely disregarded, and in 1626 King Charles I instructed the Scottish bishops not to enforce it on ministers ordained before 1618 if they had scruples about kneeling. However, by no means all the Scottish clergy objected to kneeling. Those who supported kneeling included Dr David Lindsay, minister of Dundee and later bishop of Brechin, and John Michaelson, minister of Burntisland, who 'pointed out that in the Gospel accounts, the apostles did not sit "at an high Table, as wee doe at Dinner or Supper", but reclined'.[14]

The real catalyst for liturgical confrontation in Scotland was the new communion rite, eventually published in 1637. The evidence of growing popularity in Scotland for some Anglican customs, such as the replacement of temporary long tables by a fixed square communion table of the type being promoted by the English bishops, and the decoration of churches with flowers and hangings in velvet, damask or brocade, encouraged some of the more high church Scottish bishops to press for further liturgical change. In 1633 Charles I prescribed the use of the surplice in Scotland. Concerned that this suggested that the king wanted to introduce the English *Book of Common Prayer* in Scotland, the Scottish bishops argued for a liturgy that would be designed to meet the needs, and respect the traditions of, the Scottish church. In a

---

14   B.D. Spinks, *Sacraments, Ceremonies and the Stuart Divines: Sacramental Theology and Liturgy in England and Scotland 1603-1662*, Aldershot 2002, pp 60-61.

sense the liturgy of 1637 did exactly this. The word 'priest' was replaced by 'presbyter' throughout. The rite provided an epiclesis, contained in Knox's *Book of Common Order*, but not in the *Book of Common Prayer*, and readings from the Apocrypha were largely excised. These concessions to Scottish tradition were, however, more than counterbalanced by features many Scottish clergy and laity found objectionable: the reintroduction of a full liturgical calendar, including saint's days; references to prescribed ornaments, presumably to be ordered by subsequent canon; and the rubric about the position of the minister at the consecration, which implied that he should face eastwards and elevate the bread and wine. These were all considered signs of popery. The bishops who compiled the new liturgy, Wedderburn of Dunblane and Maxwell of Ross, had modelled it on the English Prayer Book of 1549 rather than that of 1552, and that was enough to condemn it in the eyes of all good Protestants. The final proof that the book was 'popish' was the confession of Archbishop Laud, who had originally wanted to impose the English *Book of Common Prayer*, that 'if a comparison must be made, I do think the order of the prayers, as they now stand in the Scottish Liturgy, to be the better, and more agreeable to use in the primitive Church'.[15]

The attempt to impose a new liturgy on the Church of Scotland was a disaster. It was to lead to its formal condemnation and abolition of episcopacy by the General Assembly, and was a major factor in launching the civil wars that resulted in the execution of both Archbishop Laud and King Charles I. When bishops were re-introduced into Scotland after 1660 no attempt was made to re-introduce any type of fixed liturgy. By that date influence from English Puritans had made Scottish Presbyterians dubious about any sort of fixed liturgy and to find even Knox's *Book of Common Order* too restrictive. A few Scottish clergy, such as Bishop Leighton of Dunblane and Gilbert Burnet, minister of Saltoun and later bishop of Salisbury, favoured, or even used, the new English Prayer Book of 1662, but most of Scotland used the form of worship prescribed by the Westminster Directory of 1644. This simply provided a framework for both the preaching service and communion. In practice each minister and kirk session had the freedom to adopt the standard of worship with which they were most comfortable. Communion services became more and more infrequent. There were only two celebrations at Glasgow between 1660 and 1688. The minister at Rattray was admonished by the presbytery of Meigle after an enquiry by the bishop of Dunkeld found that he had only celebrated communion four times in nine years. This situation continued after the final abolition of episcopacy in the Church of Scotland after 1690. Shapinsay, in Orkney, had not had a communion service for fifty years in 1795 and had no tables, cloths or cups. Archibald Rennie never once celebrated as minister of Muckhart between 1734 and 1786. It was during this period that it became common practice for parishes to unite for these infrequent communion services. At Culross (Fife) in 1708 communicants came from as many as twenty neighbouring parishes.

In terms of its worship, the Church of Scotland has, until recently, been one of the most conservative of the Reformed churches in Europe. Even so changes have taken place since 1800. One of the most influential of these occurred in 1824 at St John's, Glasgow, when, instead of administering communion sitting at long

---

15   *Ibid.*, p 97.

tables, the elders administered to the congregation in their seats. Although initially condemned by the General Assembly, the innovation quickly gathered pace and has been responsible for the virtual disappearance of the long tables in most Scottish Presbyterian churches. A further innovation was made at Anderston Parish Church in Glasgow (following an abortive attempt at St Andrew's, Glasgow, in 1807) in 1860 when the first organ was introduced to accompany the psalms and replace the traditional practice of 'lining out' by a precentor. In the 1860s many churches began to abandon the earlier practice of 'fencing the tables' before, and exhorting the congregation after, communion. A decade later even the communion seasons, and the services of preparation and thanksgiving, were also being abandoned. Churches replaced the use of shortbread or oatcakes at communion with ordinary bread, that of communion wine with unfermented grape juice, that of the common cup with individual glasses and that of communion tokens with communion cards. Although communion services became more frequent in the late nineteenth and early twentieth centuries, the statistics for 1956 showed that only one Scottish church (St Giles, Edinburgh) had a weekly communion service and only 53 had communion services more than four times a year. 648 churches had four communion services a year, 457 had three, 1104 had two and 27 had only one. The observation of the liturgical calendar, reintroduced by high churchmen in the Church of Scotland in the 1870s, was still negligible. Only 191 congregations had a communion service on Easter Sunday, 79 on Christmas Day and 24 on Whit Sunday. Traditional communion seasons, with fasting, preparation and thanksgiving, were still being observed, and indeed still are today, in the Western Isles, Skye and Wester Ross.

From the late sixteenth century, Scottish churches were arranged primarily for preaching. Mostly pre-Reformation churches were adapted for Reformed worship and filled with pews and galleries. A few new churches were built in the late sixteenth and early seventeenth centuries: Kembach (1582), Burntisland (1592), Prestonpans (1595), Greyfriars at Edinburgh (1612-20), Dirleton (begun 1612), Dairsie (1621), Anwoth (1627), Portpatrick (1629), Auchterhouse and Kingsbarns (both 1630), South Queensferry (1633), Anstruther Easter (1634) and Elie (1639). The standard plan for a Scottish church was either a simple rectangle with the pulpit placed on one of the long walls, or else the T-plan arrangement in which seating faced the pulpit from three directions, the two ends of the cross aisle and a separate aisle opposite the pulpit. The first of these T-plan churches, which became increasingly common between the mid- seventeenth and mid-nineteenth centuries, was probably that at Weem in 1609. The church at Burntisland was highly innovative, since it was built as a square with a central space for the pulpit and communion tables, but this arrangement was not copied elsewhere. Only one Scottish church seems to have adopted the high church arrangement favoured by some of the Scottish bishops. This was the church at Dairsie in Fife. It was described in the 1640s as having a raised chancel and 'a glorious partition dividing the body of the church from the choir, on which were displayed the royal arms of England and Scotland with divers crosses above and about them'.[16]

---

16   G. Yule, 'James VI and I: Furnishing the Churches in his Two Kingdoms', *Religion, Culture and Society in Early Modern Britain: Essays in Honour of Patrick Collinson*, ed. A. Fletcher and P. Roberts, Cambridge 1994, p 207.

Figure 3.5   Seating plan of Thurso Parish Church before 1833

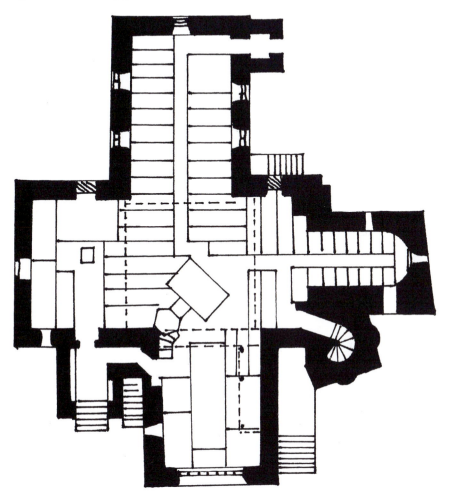

The liturgical changes of the nineteenth century – the abandonment of sitting communion and precentors, the introduction of organs – have meant that very few Scottish Presbyterian churches retain pre-1850 liturgical arrangements intact. As has been noted above, the earlier preference was for rectangular or T-plan arrangements. Interesting variants of the T-plan arrangements were the cruciform arrangements that existed at Thurso before 1833 (Figure 3.5) and still exist at Lauder (Figure 3.6). During the eighteenth century other types of churches were built, such as the octagonal one at Dreghorn (1780) and the elliptical St Andrew's at Edinburgh (1785). In all these cases the pulpit was central with the seating arranged to focus on it. During the first part of the nineteenth century this type of church began to be replaced by the hall church, aisled or unaisled, in which the pulpit was placed against one of the short walls. An early example was Ceres (Fife) of 1806 (Figure 3.7). Here the seats for communion were square pews with tables in them, which

Figure 3.6   Seating plan of Lauder Parish Church, refitted in 1820

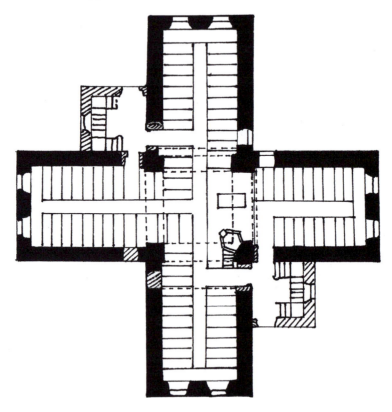

Figure 3.7   Seating plan of Ceres Parish Church, built in 1806

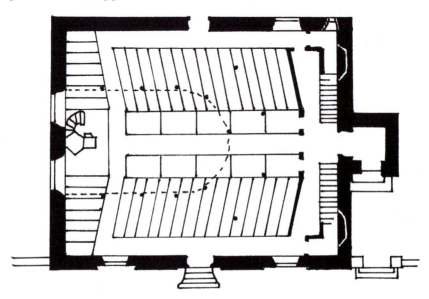

Figure 3.8   Seating plan of Lochbroom Parish Church, built in 1844-5

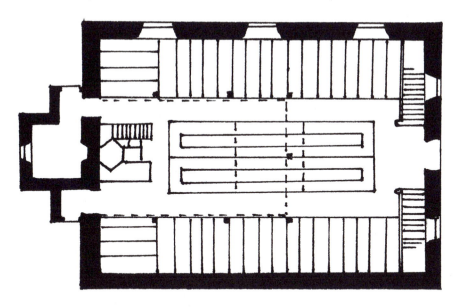

Illustration 3.5   The interior of St Callan's Church, Rogart (Highland), refitted in
1817

could be joined up on sacrament days. In other churches of the hall type, such as Lochbroom (Figure 3.8) the communion tables were placed down the middle of the church with benches on each side and were not used on ordinary Sundays. Whereas in earlier churches the galleries were in the form of individual lofts, against the short walls of rectangular buildings, or in each projection of T-plan or cruciform buildings, galleries in hall-type churches were placed along the long walls and across the short entrance, frequently, as at Ceres, in a U shape. Although table pews were normally placed in the central part of the church they could be placed on one side as they were at Rogart (Illustration 3.5). Pulpits were normally canopied and had in front a box pew for the precentor who led the psalm-singing. Except for the communion proper the minister conducted the whole service from the pulpit, which was usually provided with a seat that he could use during the singing of the psalms. Baptismal bowls were attached to the pulpit on a bracket and baptisms took place during the Sunday service. Most churches also had a penitent's stool on which those found guilty of misdemeanours would be obliged to sit during the service. These were normally, as survive at Bourtie (Aberdeenshire) and Duirinish (Highland), placed to the side of the pulpit, convenient for the full onslaught of the minister's rant and making the penitent visible to the whole congregation. The chief feature of most Scottish Presbyterian churches before the middle of the nineteenth century was their unrelenting plainness and lack of colour in their internal arrangements.

The Scottish experience was largely replicated in Ireland. Irish Presbyterianism was essentially an import from Scotland, through the plantation policies of the early seventeenth century. Thereafter Irish Presbyterian ministers continued to be trained at the Scottish universities until the opening of the Belfast Academical Institution in 1810. During the 1820s there were enormous theological divisions within the main Presbyterian body in Ireland, the Synod of Ulster, over the appointment of an alleged Arian, William Bruce, to the chair of Hebrew and Greek at the Belfast Academical Institution. By 1827 a majority within the Synod insisted that all its members must reaffirm their Trinitarian orthodoxy and a small minority, who had issued a *remonstrance* against the proceedings, withdrew from the Synod in 1830. The Remonstrants later united with the Presbytery of Antrim and the Synod of Munster to form the Non-Subscribing Presbyterian Association. Several of the Association's meeting houses, notably those at Banbridge (1844-6), Crumlin (1835-7), Downpatrick (1711-29, extended 1787), Dunmurry (1719) and Rademon (1787-9), retain late-eighteenth- or early-nineteenth-century interiors intact. Presbyterian churches in Ireland tended to be either rectangular, with the pulpit on one of the long walls, or T-plan, though there were occasional exceptions, such as the elliptical interior of the Rosemary Street Meeting House in Belfast, built in 1793, and the earliest Presbyterian church in Ireland to introduce an organ (Figure 3.9). Elsewhere in Ireland the introduction of organs was as controversial as it was in Scotland. When an organ was introduced at Enniskillen in 1861 the innovation was formally condemned by the General Assembly of the Presbyterian Church of Ireland, the body formed in 1840 by the union of the Synod of Ulster with the Secession Synod.

Figure 3.9   Plan of ground floor and galleries of Rosemary Street Presbyterian Church, Belfast, built in 1793

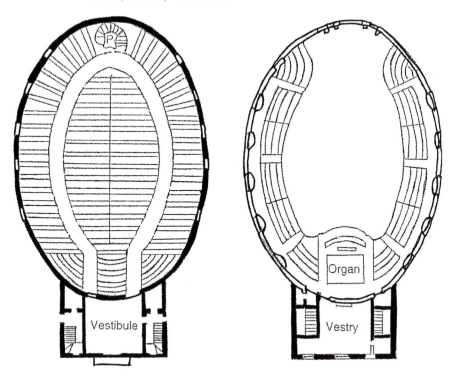

The Free Churches in England and Wales

The Free Church tradition in England and Wales stemmed from those who were dissatisfied with the religious settlement of 1559 and the way in which this was subsequently interpreted by Elizabeth I and her bishops. The majority of those dissatisfied with the settlement remained in the Church of England until the Civil Wars and Interregnum of the 1640s and 1650s, and only after the failure to make the revised *Book of Common Prayer*, finally imposed in 1662, a more Reformed liturgy, did they leave the established church. However, well before that date, a number of separate gathered congregations had been established in England and Wales. It was these congregations of Baptists, Independents and Presbyterians, much strengthened by the secessions of 1662, that formed the nucleus of what eventually became known as the Free Churches. Their numbers were further strengthened in the late eighteenth and early nineteenth centuries by the secessions from the Church of England resulting from the Evangelical Revival. Dissenting or nonconformist chapels, some dating from the seventeenth century, are found all over England and Wales, but with particular strengths in the areas remotest from London, in the north and west of the country.

The worship of the Free Churches generally followed what might be termed the Geneva tradition and was particularly influenced, as that of the Church of Scotland had been, by the Westminster Directory of 1644. The early Separatists rejected what they termed the 'idolatry' of the *Book of Common Prayer*: its fixed liturgy, its retention of a liturgical calendar, its failure to exclude all but the 'elect' from Holy Communion. By contrast, those Puritans who remained in the Church of England despite their criticism of its structure and practices, accepted some sort of fixed liturgy, such as that published at Middelburg in 1586, and it was only later that divisions began to occur in their ranks over whether or not a fixed liturgy was desirable. The Westminster Directory of 1644 was a victory by the Independents over the Presbyterians, in both England and Scotland, in which, for the first time, a published liturgy no longer comprised, to a greater or lesser extent, a series of fixed prayers and ceremonies, but permitted the minister to conduct the service as he wished within a very flexible framework. After the secessions of 1662 all the new separatist churches adopted liturgies that followed the model of the Westminster Directory and it was not until the late nineteenth century that any serious attempt was made to introduce more formal services into any of the Free Churches in England and Wales.

Independent and Presbyterian worship in the eighteenth century was basically very similar, and this pattern of worship was continued by those congregations that later became Unitarian in doctrine.

> In the morning we begin with singing a psalm, then a short prayer follows to desire the Divine Presence in all the following parts of worship; after that, about half an hour in the exposition of some portion of Scripture, which is succeeded by singing a psalm or an hymn. After this the minister prays more at large, for all the variety of blessings, spiritual and temporal, for the whole congregation, with confession of sins, and thanksgiving for mercies; petitions also are offered up for the whole world, for the Churches of Christ, for the nation in which we dwell, for all our rulers and governors, together with any particular cases which are represented. Then a sermon is preached, and the morning worship concluded with a short prayer and the benediction.[17]

Holy Communion was celebrated either, as in Scotland, at long tables with the communicants seated, or else the elements were distributed to people in their seats by elders or deacons. The history of the institution was read out, either from Matthew's Gospel or the first epistle to the Corinthians, followed by a blessing and breaking of the bread and pouring out of the wine prior to the distribution. Whilst the distribution was taking place the minister would frequently read out appropriate scriptural passages and, after all had communicated, there would be a psalm or hymn during which a collection was made for the poor. The service would end with prayers of thanksgiving and a blessing.

Meeting Houses tended to be organised so that all the seating was focused on the pulpit, the communion tables being placed in a pew or pews either in front of,

---

17   Description of service at the Bury Street Independent Meeting House in London recorded in Horton Davies, *Worship and Theology in England 1690-1850*, Princeton 1961, p 101.

or to the side of, the pulpit. The singing of psalms and hymns was initially led by a precentor, who occupied a desk in front of the pulpit, but later organs were introduced in a gallery, either behind or opposite to the pulpit. The earliest Independent or Presbyterian meeting houses tended to have the pulpit on one of the long walls, and this arrangement can still be seen in the Old Meeting of 1699-1700 at Ipswich and in the chapels of 1703 at Rivington (Lancs), 1721-2 at Chowbent (Lancs), 1723 at Halebarns (Ches) and 1727-9 at Middle Lambrook (Som). There are later examples at Walpole (Illustration 3.6), of 1769 at Nanhoron (Gwynedd), of 1773 at Glanaman (Carms), of 1774 at Toxteth (Lancs) and exceptionally late ones of 1826-7 at Heol Awst, Carmarthen, and 1845 at Ainsworth (Lancs). By the late eighteenth century chapels were being 'turned' so that their pulpits were placed on one of the short walls. The earliest surviving example of this arrangement appears to be at the Caebach Chapel of 1715 at Llandrindod Wells (Powys), but there are later surviving examples of 1794 in the Old Meeting at Bridport (Dorset) and of 1808 at Roxton (Beds).

Illustration 3.6   Early-nineteenth-century seating arrangements at Walpole Independent Meeting House, Suffolk

Independents and Presbyterians, even when the majority of the latter became Unitarians, were the more conservative of the Free Churches. The Radical elements were represented by the Baptists and the Society of Friends, more commonly known as Quakers. The Baptists were themselves divided into General or Arminian and Particular or Calvinist Baptists. The Particular Baptists generally followed a similar approach to liturgy as that already outlined for the Independents and Presbyterians. The General Baptists added a number of unusual features in their approach to worship. They opposed the singing of psalms or hymns so that the whole service was entirely without any form of music. They also approved of the washing of the feet of their members, though this custom began to be given up in the late eighteenth century. Both groups of Baptists also rejected infant baptism and insisted that baptism could only occur after an adult confession of faith and that the rite must be performed by total immersion. The earliest Baptist congregations built their meeting houses near streams, which could be used for baptism; by the nineteenth century most chapels used specially-constructed baptismal pools. These could be placed either outside the chapel or within the chapel itself, usually under the platform on which the pulpit and communion table were located. Before the nineteenth century communion was usually administered to communicants sitting at tables (Illustration 3.7). Baptists appear to have adopted the short wall, as opposed to the long wall, position for the pulpit somewhat earlier than the Independents and Presbyterans: early examples are at Derry Hill (Wilts, 1814), Winslow (Bucks, 1821) and Atch Lench (Worcs, 1829). Exceptions are the completely square meeting houses of c.1800 at Goodshaw (Lancs) and 1829 at Hengoed (Glam).

Illustration 3.7   A Baptist communion service in the early eighteenth century (Picart, *Ceremonies*, vi, opposite p 184)

Whereas the Baptists preserved a formal liturgy, at least in terms of its framework, the Quakers dispensed with any type of structured worship, sacraments or ordained ministry. Congregations would assemble at stated times on Sundays and wait for the spirit to move them. Voltaire described his experience of attending a meeting house of the Society of Friends in London in 1726.

The Brethren were already assembled at my entering... All were seated and the silence was universal... The silence lasted a quarter of an hour, then at last one of them rose up, took off his hat, and, after making a variety of wry faces and groaning in a most lamentable manner, he... threw out a strange fashion of words... which neither himself nor any of his hearers understood.[18]

All that Quaker meeting houses required was a series of benches on which the congregation could sit, though there was normally a platform for the seats on which the more senior members of the congregation would sit. There are excellent surviving examples of eighteenth-century Quaker meeting houses at Come-to-Good (Cornwall) and the Pales at Llandegley (Powys).

The secessions from the Church of England, which took place in the late eighteenth century and comprised such groups as the Wesleyan Methodists, the Countess of Huntingdon's Connexion, the Huntingtonians (the followers of William Huntington), and the Presbyterian Church of Wales (Calvinistic Methodists), also resulted in the building of new places of worship. The Huntingtonians and the Calvinistic Methodists tended to adopt the service patterns and the liturgical arrangements of 'old dissent'. The Huntingtonian or Calvinist Jireh Chapel of 1805 at Lewes, and the Providence Chapel of 1809 at Chichester, have handsome galleried interiors with their box pews focused on the pulpits placed on the short wall opposite the entrance. The Calvinist Methodist chapel at Pentrebach in the parish of Llandeilo'r Fan (Powys), refitted in 1858, still has its pulpit on one of the long walls, placed within a *sêt-fawr* with seats for the elders and a communion table. Later Calvinist Methodist chapels generally adopted the short wall arrangement by then preferred by Baptists, Independents, Presbyterians and Unitarians. Box pews rather than open benches were the preferred form of seating in nonconformist chapels and many, especially in Wales, have retained their box pews even if the other furnishings have been altered.

The Wesleyan Methodists were the longest to retain services and liturgical arrangements based on the Anglican *Book of Common Prayer* and it was only in the second half of the nineteenth century that the interiors of their chapels began to resemble those of the older branches of Protestant dissent. The earliest, and best preserved, Methodist chapel, the New Room of 1739-48 at Bristol, has a two-decker pulpit placed behind the communion table and against the short wall opposite the entrance. However, the City Road Chapel in London (1778) and the St Peter's Street Chapel at Canterbury (1812) adopted the contemporary Anglican practice of placing the communion table behind the pulpit; and the communicants knelt at the communion rail to receive the sacrament. This arrangement still survives, though the other furnishings have been altered, in the Methodist chapel at Newbury (1837). The organ is placed in a gallery over the communion table and the pulpit stands well forward of this gallery. Behind the table, as in most Anglican churches of this date, are framed panels inscribed with the Ten Commandments, Creed and Lord's Prayer.

---

18   Quoted in *ibid.*, p 120.

Quasi-Anglican services and liturgical arrangements were also adopted by the Countess of Huntingdon's Connexion. The sect's chapel at Worcester, built in 1804, extended in 1815 and partly refurbished in 1845, having ceased to be used for worship, was adapted to serve as a concert hall between 1977 and 1987. This involved the removal of a few of the box pews and the building of a stage over the former communion enclosure, but otherwise the original furnishings remain *in situ*. A gallery surrounds the whole interior with the organ being placed in that part of the gallery behind the pulpit. There are two eagle lecterns flanking the pulpit and against the back wall of the communion enclosure, under the gallery, are panels inscribed with the Ten Commandments, Creed and Lord's Prayer.

The family of Reformed churches in Western Europe provided for their congregations wide variation in liturgical practice and the ordering of their buildings, but there was clear agreement between them about the centrality of preaching and the need to focus the interior on the pulpit. After that the provision of fixed or temporary tables for communion, the arrangements for baptism – from a traditional font to a bowl attached to a bracket on the pulpit to a total immersion baptistery – and whether or not an organ was part of the furnishings, depended on differing attitudes to worship and different interpretations of Holy Scripture in that respect. The extent to which these arrangements have been preserved has likewise depended on the extent to which Calvinist and Reformed churches were influenced by more Catholic attitudes to worship in the nineteenth and twentieth centuries.

Chapter 4

The Worship and Buildings of the Anglican *Via Media*

The picture postcard image of the Anglican village church is largely an invention of the nineteenth century. Between 1840 and 1900 Anglican churches were transformed, liturgically and architecturally, by, respectively, 'movements' established at Oxford and Cambridge in the 1830s. As the future Dean Close remarked at the time

> Romanism is taught *Analytically* at Oxford, it is taught *Artistically* at Cambridge... it is inculcated theoretically in tracts at the one University and it is *sculptured, painted* and *graven* at the other.[1]

Before 1840 Anglican churches were designed, not to meet certain architectural or theological principles, but primarily to meet the liturgical needs of the worshipping community. In this chapter we will explore the development of Anglican liturgy and architecture between the late sixteenth and early nineteenth centuries.

The Elizabethan Settlement

The religious settlement of 1559, which reintroduced the Prayer Book of 1552 with minor modifications, was essentially a compromise between the different religious groups in post-Reformation England and Wales. The settlement was also extended to Ireland, though with very much less success, and the established Church of Ireland never managed, before its eventual disestablishment in 1869, to capture the support of more than a fifth of that nation. It is by no means clear how permanent Elizabeth I intended her religious settlement to be. There are indications, in the revisions to the liturgy, especially the ornaments rubric, and in the furnishings of her own chapel, that the queen would have preferred a less Protestant settlement. However, with the refusal of all Mary's Catholic bishops, apart from Kitchin of Llandaff, to accept her authority, Elizabeth was obliged to rely on the returning Protestant exiles to provide the leadership of a church no longer in communion with the Holy See. These exiles wanted a church modelled as far as possible on the reformed churches of Geneva and Strasbourg. They obtained this in the Thirty-Nine Articles of 1563 and in Archbishop Parker's Advertisements of 1566. The articles were broadly Calvinist in tone and the Advertisements dashed any hopes that Catholic ornaments and vestments might be retained in use, as the ornaments rubric had implied. Copes were to be used in

---

1   Quoted in Peter Toon, *Evangelical Theology 1833-1856: A Response to Tractarianism*, London 1979, pp 66-7.

cathedral and collegiate churches, but in parish churches only a surplice was to be worn. Old vestments were cut up to be turned into carpets for the altar or hangings for the pulpit.

In the immediate aftermath of the Elizabethan settlement there were two groups who found it profoundly unsatisfactory: those who wanted to maintain pre-Reformation doctrine and liturgical practices and those who felt that the settlement had not created a church sufficiently purged of popish error to be considered truly reformed. The first group gradually disappeared. As clergy died congregations conformed to legal practice and only a small number joined those known as recusants who were determined to maintain their allegiance to the Roman Catholic Church. The second group was a much more long-term problem. They were usually termed Puritans, from their determination to achieve a more 'pure' church, free from the retention of what they considered 'popish' practices. They either objected to episcopacy entirely or they wanted a modification of episcopacy, which would lead to a presbyterian church on the Genevan model. They disliked many of the set forms and ceremonies enjoined by the *Book of Common Prayer*, especially kneeling at communion and the use of the surplice. They wanted more control over clerical appointments and, where they could, used their wealth to establish lectureships attached to parish churches to which they would appoint clergy who shared their views. A significant number of puritans were to be found among the beneficed clergy, and even among the early Elizabethan bishops, though those with Puritan sympathies were less likely to become bishops by the latter part of Elizabeth's reign. The puritan lobby exercised constant pressure in Parliament and elsewhere to achieve their aims but with little success. When Elizabeth died in 1603 they hoped that her successor, James VI of Scotland, would be more sympathetic to their cause but they were to be bitterly disappointed.[2]

Puritans, however, remained a minority within the fledgling Church of England, albeit a vociferous one. By the end of Elizabeth's reign the evidence is that the majority of both clergy and laity had come to appreciate the services provided in the *Book of Common Prayer*. Among churches in the Reformed tradition, the Church of England was unusual in two respects. The first was its retention of cathedrals in which the daily offices of Morning and Evening Prayer were still sung by the members of the cathedral establishment. The second was its use of a reformed version of the pre-Reformation divine office as the core of its liturgical practice. Morning Prayer was a continuation of the pre-Reformation services of Mattins and Lauds, Evening Prayer that of Vespers and Compline. When the Holy Communion was celebrated, usually weekly in cathedrals, monthly in town churches and less frequently in village ones, it formed the last part of the Sunday morning service, which otherwise consisted of Morning Prayer, Litany and Ante-Communion with a sermon. Despite many attempts to change it over a period of four hundred years, the *Book of Common Prayer*, as published in 1552, and very slightly altered in 1559 and 1662, remained the only legal service book for Anglicans in England and Wales until the 1960s.

---

2   For a detailed discussion of late-sixteenth- and early-seventeenth-century Puritanism see Patrick Collinson, *The Elizabethan Puritan Movement*, London 1967, and *The Religion of Protestants: The Church in English Society 1559-1625*, Oxford 1982.

We know remarkably little about the way English and Welsh parish churches were adapted for Prayer Book worship in the late sixteenth and early seventeenth centuries. Archbishop Parker's Advertisements of 1566 ordered rood-screens to remain *in situ* but everything above the beam, the loft and the figures of Christ on the cross with Our Lady and St John, was to be removed and replaced with the Royal Arms. The communion table was to be placed against the east wall of the chancel, except at the time of celebration when it could be moved further into the chancel or even into the nave, and the Ten Commandments were to be set up over the table. A seat for the minister to read the service, when there was no communion, could be placed either just outside the chancel or in the body of the nave. Organs were permitted in Anglican churches but in practice were only found in cathedrals and the larger parish churches. The arrangements that had been proposed by Parker for a movable communion table were found in practice to be rather tiresome. Canon 82 of 1604 ordered the table to be placed 'in so good sort, within the church or chancel, as thereby the minister may be more conveniently heard by the communicants in his prayer and ministration, and the communicants also more conveniently, and in more number, may communicate with the said minister'. The purpose of this canon was to regularise what had become widespread, the placing of the table in the east-west position in the middle of the chancel, surrounded by seats for the communicants. In the church at Hailes (Glos) the seventeenth-century communion table has been replaced in this position, though the effect is somewhat compromised by the retention of a later altar at the east end of the chancel.

The result of this arrangement was to create a two-room church, the nave for the normal services of Morning and Evening Prayer and for preaching, and the chancel for communion, as in some Calvinist churches. The major Anglican contribution to post-Reformation church furnishing was the so-called three-decker pulpit. This incorporated desks from which the minister read the service and for the parish clerk, who led the congregational responses and sometimes the singing as well. Three-decker pulpits were not *de rigeur*. Sometimes they were only two-deckers, pulpit and reading desk, with separate accommodation for the parish clerk in one of the pews. Sometimes pulpit, reading and clerk's desks were separate pieces of furniture. In Anglican churches pulpits were only ever used for preaching and not, as was the case in most other Protestant churches, for reading parts of the service. Canon 81 of 1604 ordered the provision of a stone font for baptism and this was normally placed either at the west end of the nave or near one of the entrances to the church. Seating had been introduced into many English and Welsh churches before the Reformation, but it now became essential as the services were much longer. The normal Sunday morning service would rarely last much less than two hours, if there was a sermon, and could last as long as three hours on sacrament Sundays. Early post-Reformation seating seems to have been in the form of open benches, of the type found before the Reformation, but these were soon replaced by box pews, which kept out the drafts. At Laxfield (Suffolk), Old Dilton (Wilts) and Torbryan (Devon) later box pews have been built over, and incorporate, medieval benches. Pews in churches were generally assigned to particular families or properties, people of higher social rank occupying the more prominent and better located seats. When Richard Gough wrote his history of the Shropshire parish of Myddle in 1701 he described the families according to the order in which they sat in church.[3] It was normally the responsibility of churchwardens, elected by the parish ratepayers, to assign the pews in church and such assignments are frequently to be found in surviving parish registers. At Botley (Hants) they survive for 1605, 1680 and 1715.[4] In addition, from time to time, faculties were granted by the diocesan authorities to individual families to erect their own pews in parish churches.

There are only two surviving churches in England which preserve furnishings of about 1600 and they reflect the wide variation that must have existed between one church and another as they sought to interpret the relevant canons. At Brooke (Rutland) the nave is fitted with a canopied pulpit, reading desk and box pews and the chancel is stalled for the use of communicants. At Langley Chapel (Salop) the communion table stands well away from the east wall with rails or seats on the east, north and south sides of the chancel. Pulpit and reading desk stand on opposite sides of the church, unlike Brooke, where they are placed together, and the seating is provided by open benches rather than box pews.

The Laudian Transformation

By the second decade of the seventeenth century the high church party in the Church of England had begun to become prominent among the senior clergy and by the 1630s they had seized virtually complete control of the Anglican agenda. Their aims were both theological and liturgical, and, more to the point, they had the support of both James VI and I (1603-25) and his son Charles I (1625-49). Theologically many, though not all, of them were Arminians, determined to move the Church of England away from orthodox Calvinism and to develop a distinctive Anglican theology which sought, in practice if not in actual motivation, to place Anglicanism in a sort of *via media* between Calvinism and Lutheranism.[5] Part of their programme was to enrich the church's services and ceremonial, and to resist any Puritan demands for the alteration of the *Book of Common Prayer*. The placing of the communion table in the middle of the chancel, with seats around it, although not specifically designed for the purpose, was seen to encourage the desire to receive communion sitting rather than kneeling. Anglican high churchmen noted that where the table was placed permanently against the east wall of the chancel such practice was impossible, and that if the table was not railed in there was a danger that it might be used for non-sacramental purposes, and therefore not treated with appropriate reverence. The future Archbishop Laud, as Dean of Gloucester, persuaded his cathedral chapter in 1616-17 to place the altar at the east end of the choir. During the 1620s and 1630s the Laudian bishops used their powers of visitation to enforce the placing of altars against the east wall of the chancel in parish churches, their covering with a carpet

---

3   R. Gough, *History of Myddle*, ed. D. Hay, Harmondsworth 1981, with plans showing the allocation of pews on pp 80-83.

4   Hampshire Record Office, Winchester 40M75 PRI.

5   See especially Nicholas Tyacke, *The Anti-Calvinists*, Oxford 1987, and Julian Davies, *The Caroline Church in Captivity: Charles I and the Remoulding of Anglicanism*, Oxford 1992.

and their enclosure with rails. They also encouraged the erection of paintings or panels inscribed with the Ten Commandments, Creed and Lord's Prayer behind the altar and even the placing of candlesticks on the altar. All these innovations were highly unpopular with those of Puritan sympathies.

Opposition to the Laudian transformation of churches, and what was considered to be the revival of 'popish' ceremonial, was a major factor in the Civil Wars of the 1640s which were to lead to the execution of both Archbishop Laud and King Charles I and the abolition of bishops, the *Book of Common Prayer* and the monarchy. There was particular criticism of cathedrals. The Kentish puritan clergyman, Richard Culmer, was vehement in his denunciations of Canterbury Cathedral in 1644:

> The Pettie Cannons, and Singing men there, sing their Cathedral Service in Prick-Song after the Romish fashion, chanting the Lord's Prayer, and other Prayers in an unfit manner, in the chancel, or Quire of that Cathedral; at the East end whereof they have placed an Altar (as they call it) dressed after the Romish fashion, with candlesticks, and tapers, for which Altar they have lately provided a most Idolatrous Costly Glory-Cloth or Back-Cloth; towards which Altar they crouch, and duck three times at their going up to it, and reade there part of their service apart from the Assembly.[6]

After the Puritan triumph in the Civil Wars cathedrals were either used for secular purposes or partitioned for use by different congregations, much as large churches in Scotland had been. At Exeter the cathedral choir was used by Presbyterians and the nave by Independents. At Canterbury Richard Culmer destroyed many of the furnishings and most of the stained glass. The main part of the cathedral was not used at all but an Independent congregation worshipped in the chapter house. Although Anglican worship was officially illegal, surviving diaries and letters from the Commonwealth period (1649-60) suggest that those who wanted it had no difficulty in finding a service which approximated to that in the banned *Book of Common Prayer*. Some long-serving clergy who were not ejected from their parishes by Puritan extremists were able to recite much of the liturgy from memory.

The Restoration Church

The recall of Charles II from exile in 1660 was not meant to lead to the revival of Laudianism in the Church of England, though in practice that was what happened. The more extreme Laudians wanted to celebrate their reinstatement in their bishoprics and benefices by adopting a revised Prayer Book more along the lines of that of 1549, or the version that had been so unsatisfactorily attempted to be imposed on Scotland in 1637. These moves were skilfully resisted and the chief Anglican negotiators went out of their way to accommodate the more moderate Puritans who eventually accepted a modified variation of the 1559 Prayer Book in 1662. The more extreme Puritans could not accept this and a number of clergy were ejected from their benefices. Those clergy and laity who could not in conscience use the new Prayer Book set up their own gathered congregations of Baptists, Independents or Presbyterians, using their own

---

6   Centre for Kentish Studies, Maidstone, U235 Z1.

forms of worship. As a result the leadership of the Church of England gradually passed into the hands of those whose views were much the same as their Laudian predecessors, and gradually churches were restored to their pre-1640 appearance. In the diocese of Rochester, Archdeacon John Warner used his 1670 visitation to order several churches to place the altar at the east end of the chancel and to rail it in. Chancel screens were introduced in some churches in the late seventeenth century and even later. Those at St Paul's Walden (Herts) and Crowcombe (Som) date from 1727 and 1729 respectively; that at Thorpe Market (Norfolk) from 1796; and that at Haccombe (Devon) from 1821. Cathedral services which had been attacked by Puritans were now vigorously defended, as in William Dingley's *Cathedral Service Decent and Useful*, published in 1713. There was long a popular view that during the eighteenth century both Anglican churches, and the services that took place within them, suffered from deliberate neglect. Recent research has shown that such was not the case. Some Anglican high churchmen, amongst the non-juring clergy,[7] produced interesting revisions of the *Book of Common Prayer* and more mainstream Anglican clergy produced manuals of private devotion closely linked to the Prayer Book services. A large number of new churches were built, or older churches rebuilt, in this period. Many churches, if not wholly or partially rebuilt, were restored or refurnished. To take one county virtually at random, sixteen churches were substantially enlarged and thirteen churches entirely rebuilt or newly built in Devon; between 1737 and 1799 no fewer than 51 churches had licences granted for the erection of galleries to increase the accommodation for the parishioners and 65 had major reseating schemes. Samuel Butler, the future bishop of Coventry and Lichfield, was so successful in ordering the repair of churches as archdeacon of Derby between 1821 and 1836 that his successor found only three out of 186 churches in the archdeaconry to be 'out of repair'. Archdeacons were also diligent in ensuring that parishes were provided with the requisite number of Sunday services and celebrations of Holy Communion. Cathedrals and some parish churches had daily services. At Exeter Cathedral Morning and Evening Prayer were sung every day and there were celebrations of Holy Communion on every Sunday, on Good Friday and on 29 May (the anniversary of Charles II's restoration). The state of church music was also generally healthy with many town churches installing organs. In Norfolk, the organ at St Margaret's, King's Lynn, introduced in 1672, was replaced by the corporation as 'a symbol of civic splendour' in 1753. St Peter Mancroft in Norwich had an organ in 1709 and St George's, Great Yarmouth, was built with one in 1714. Organs were introduced into the parish churches of the smaller market towns of Aylsham in 1769, East Dereham in 1785 and Wymondham in 1793. Even village churches, with small groups of musicians and singers, attempted some quite ambitious settings of the psalms and canticles, and occasionally an anthem, as is clearly revealed in the surviving church music books from the Kentish parishes of Kemsing and Trottiscliffe.

---

7   Non-jurors were those Anglicans who, whilst loyal to the formularies of the Church of England, refused, for theological reasons, to accept the legitimacy of those English monarchs after the abdication and exile of James II in 1689 whilst he, his son and grandsons were still alive.

Illustration 4.1   Seventeenth-century furnishings at Staunton Harold Church, Leicestershire

Figure 4.1   Seating plan of Ballymakenny Church, Co. Louth, built in 1785-93

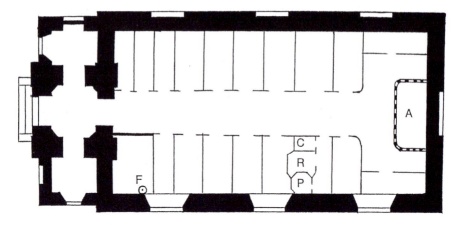

The vitality of the eighteenth-century church in England and Wales, as well as in Ireland, is shown in the variety of liturgical arrangements adopted in new or refurbished buildings. There was not a single type of Anglican arrangement and there was much more variety in the different types than there was among the churches of either Lutheran Germany and Scandinavia or Calvinist Holland, Hungary, Scotland and Switzerland. Basically, Anglican church designs fell into one of six main types. The most popular, certainly on the evidence of surviving buildings, was the traditional interior adopted by the Laudian clergy in the seventeenth century, in which the pulpit and reading desk were placed together in one of the eastern angles of the nave and with the chancel empty apart from the altar. Excellent surviving examples are the churches of 1653-65 at Staunton Harold in Leicestershire (Illustration 4.1) and 1785-93 at Ballymakenny in County Louth (Figure 4.1). The former church was built by a high church Anglican landowner as an act of defiance against the Puritanism of the interregnum. There is an organ in the west gallery, the box pews are complete with candle-holders, the pulpit and reading desk, set at an angle across the nave, retain their original hangings, the ceilings are painted, the chancel is paved in black and white marble and is empty apart from the altar still vested in its original frontal of pale purple. The celebration of Holy Communion (Illustration 4.2) was an occasion of great solemnity. After the Prayer for the Church the minister would lead the congregation into the chancel where they either sat in the stalls or gathered around the altar rails. All knelt to receive communion and the communion plate not actually being used in the service was frequently arranged along the back of the altar. The idea that communion could be celebrated at temporary or movable tables, briefly accepted in the immediate post-Reformation period, was an idea that would have horrified any devout Anglican in the eighteenth century. The altar had to be fixed and treated with great reverence. An excellent example of a church in which the altar and pulpit are so arranged that both are the objects of liturgical focus is that at Shobdon (Hereford) built in 1752-6 for the Honourable Richard Bateman (Illustration 4.3). It is an early example of the Gothic Revival style, but of the romantic rather than the correct type favoured by the later ecclesiologists. It is a cruciform building, with a shallow chancel and transepts, with an open space in front of the altar.

The pulpit, slightly separated from the reading and clerk's desks, stands on the north side of the entrance to the chancel, with the font on the south side, thus grouping together so that all are visible, as in some Lutheran churches, the principal foci of the liturgical action. The north and south transepts formed pews for the Bateman family and their servants, with the rest of the congregation sitting in the nave and with the musicians and singers in the west gallery. Many similar churches were built throughout the seventeenth, eighteenth and early nineteenth centuries.

Illustration 4.2   Anglican communion service at St Paul's Cathedral, London, in the early eighteenth century (Picart, *Ceremonies*, vi, between pp 78 and 79)

Some Anglicans, however, adopted designs for their buildings which had some elements in common with their nonconformist contemporaries, or Reformed churches throughout Europe. These were churches in which the pulpit and reading desk were placed in the middle of one of the long or short sides of a rectangular building. The long wall arrangement is shown in the surviving plan for the proposed rebuilding of Epping church in 1786 (Figure 4.2). There are excellent surviving examples of such churches throughout England, Wales and Ireland: Wilby (Norfolk) of 1637, Bramhope (Yorks) of 1649, Ballinderry (Co. Antrim) of 1664-8, Disserth (Powys) of c.1687, Llangar (Denbs) of 1716-32, Chislehampton (Oxon) of 1762-3 and Skelton-in-Cleveland (Yorks) of 1785. In all these cases the long wall arrangement was used in churches with unaisled naves but it was also used in churches with one or more aisles

Illustration 4.3   Late-eighteenth-century   furnishings   at   Shobdon   Church, Herefordshire

Figure 4.2   Seating plan of Epping Church, Essex, 1786

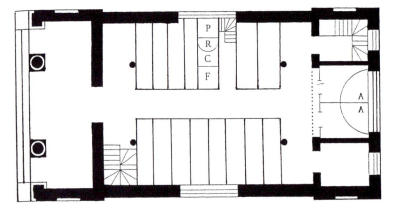

to the nave. Good surviving examples will be found in the late seventeenth century interior at Compton Wynyates (Warws) and the eighteenth century ones at Old Dilton (Wilts) and Stanstead Abbots (Herts). The great advantage of this arrangement was that, as all services apart from Holy Communion were conducted from the pulpit and reading desk, they were placed in a position where the minister was likely to be most audible and visible to the whole congregation. The disadvantage was that it effectively cut off the chancel from the rest of the church but, as such, this did not matter since the chancel was used separately from the nave and only for communion services. A greater concern, however, for some high churchmen was that part of the congregation sat with its back to the altar and they thought this was disrespectful. In the plan of Epping church there were galleries across both the east and west ends of the church. Clearly the occupants would have had an excellent view of the pulpit and reading desk, but those in the eastern gallery were actually sitting over the sanctuary. In medieval churches with long chancels it was customary to place seats, facing west, in the western part of the chancel which, for some high churchmen, seemed to imply further lack of reverence for the altar.

An alternative arrangement, which placed altar, pulpit and reading desk at the east end of the building, became extremely popular, especially in town churches, during the eighteenth century but it engendered some debate as to whether the altar should be placed in front of or behind the pulpit. From the point of view of creating a single liturgical focus the former was more effective and was comparable with the Lutheran pulpit-altar arrangement popular in Germany and used occasionally in Scandinavia. It was not, however, popular with Anglicans, for two reasons. The first was that it was found to be impractical. If the sanctuary was effectively treated as a separate room for communion the arrangement worked better if the altar was placed behind the pulpit. The second was a concern that if the pulpit was placed behind the altar, and therefore towered above it, it implied that the word was more important than the sacrament, an idea to which high church Anglicans were implacably opposed. Whilst placing the pulpit behind the altar seems to have occasioned little concern among Scottish episcopalians or Anglicans in the American Colonies, this was not the case in England, Wales or Ireland. The result is that very few Anglican churches were ordered in this manner and the arrangement will now only be found at Dale Abbey (Derbys), the disused former prison chapel in Lincoln Castle, the Gibside Chapel (Durham), a former mausoleum fitted up for Anglican worship in 1812 (Illustration 4.4), and two churches in Ireland, Clonguish (Co. Longford) and Timogue (Co. Laois). At Clonguish the pulpit does indeed dominate the altar, projecting over it in the form of a canopy. Concerns about the relationship between pulpit and altar were to result in three changes being made to the internal arrangements of All Saints, Newcastle upon Tyne, between its opening in 1789 and 1812. It was designed with the pulpit and reading desk behind the altar, but in 1790 they were moved to stand in front of the altar, thus creating a separate communion room behind them. This apparently created accoustical difficulties and in 1812 they were moved back to their original position. The fact that such an arrangement might not be considered theologically sound was recognised by the contemporary defence of the change, in which it was noted that the alteration

> effected an improvement not generally found, which was in affording the congregation an opportunity of hearing and attending to the communion service as well as to the prayers and sermon... The advantages derived... are very obvious, and the arrangement might be adopted to great advantage in similar structures where one or other of the services is rendered nearly inaudible by the distance of the places in which they are performed.[8]

---

8   T. Sopwith, *An Historical and Descriptive Account of All Saints Church*, Newcastle upon Tyne 1826, p 93.

Illustration 4.4   Central three-decker pulpit at the Gibside Chapel, County Durham,
                     fitted out in 1812

This was a case where practical need was allowed to overcome theological scruples, but such was not so everywhere.

The arrangement that was felt to be both theologically sound and generally practical, though it was to be vilified in the most aggressive terms by later ecclesiologists, was that in which pulpit and reading desk stood in front of the altar. Although criticism from ecclesiologists meant that few such arrangements still survive, they were enormously popular, especially in town churches, in the eighteenth and early nineteenth centuries. Since the recent removal of the central pulpit at St Peter's, Congleton, the only surviving examples of the arrangement will be found at King's Norton (Leics) of 1757-75, St John's in Chichester of 1812-13 and St Clement's, Toxteth, in Liverpool of 1841. There are, however, countless surviving plans and illustrations of the arrangement such as those of Holy Trinity, Sunderland (Figure 4.3), and St Peter and St Paul's, Buckingham (Illustration 4.5). The great advantage of the arrangement was that it retained the space behind the pulpit as a separate communion room on sacrament days, at a time when the number of communicants in relation to general worshippers was relatively small, whilst enabling all the seating to face either directly towards, or at least sideways on, to the pulpit and reading desk, as well as the altar, even though this was hidden behind the pulpit. It was therefore, from a theological point of view, preferable to the long wall arrangement. Advantage was frequently taken of this arrangement to make the box pews uniform in size, with seats facing only in one direction, rather than large square pews, with seats on three sides, that had been popular in the late seventeenth and early eighteenth centuries. In churches of this type it was normal for there to be galleries across the north, south and west walls. Occasionally, as at St John's Chichester, there was an east gallery across the sanctuary in which the organ was placed, but the more normal location for this was with the singers in the west gallery.

Figure 4.3   Seating plan of Holy Trinity Church, Sunderland, 1825

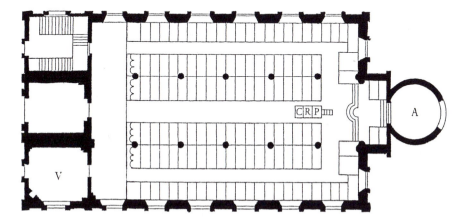

Illustration 4.5   The interior of St Peter and St Paul's Church, Buckingham, before its restoration in 1862

Figure 4.4   Seating plan of Little Hadham Church, Herts, 1692

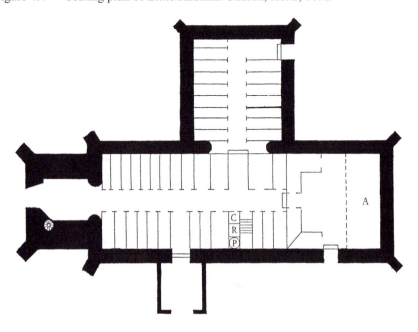

The fourth type of Anglican liturgical arrangement, and much more popular than has been realised, was the T-plan. The difference between Anglican and Reformed churches, in which the arrangement was even more popular, was that Anglicans had to make provision for a fixed altar so that one of the arms of the T had to incorporate the sanctuary. This was normally achieved, as it was at Little Hadham (Herts), shown in a plan of 1692 (Figure 4.4), by building a transept at right angles to the nave and placing the pulpit and reading desk in one corner of the nave so that seating faced them from two directions. In cruciform churches it was possible to place the pulpit and reading desk at the entrance to the chancel so that seating faced them from three directions, in the nave and both transepts. Excellent examples of Anglican T-plan churches survive, in addition to Little Hadham, at Llanfaglan (Gwynedd) of c.1780, Aldfield (Yorks) of 1783, Minstead (Hants) and Stelling (Kent) of 1792, and Weston (Yorks) of 1806-19. In all of these the T was created by the addition of either a north or a south transept, or a shortened aisle treated as a transept for seating purposes. Another way of forming the T was to add a chancel against one of the long walls of a rectangular interior. This was done at St Iberius, Wexford, in the 1770s, though the interior has been refurbished, and it survives more completely at Petersham (Surrey), refurnished in 1839-40 and only slightly altered in 1874. No pure example of the cruciform T-plan, with seating facing a central pulpit and reading desk from nave and two transepts, survive, apart from those shown in surviving seating plans, but one does survive, somewhat disguised, at St Mary's, Whitby, one of very few major urban parish churches to retain its pre-1840 fittings intact. Here the north transept dates from 1744 and the south from 1759. In 1818 the T-plan arrangement was distorted by the addition of a substantial and galleried north aisle, making a square addition to the nave and north transept. Another interesting variant of the T-plan arrangement is that at Dromard (Co. Sligo), refurnished in c.1820. Here two shallow transepts project from the western part of the nave and the pulpit and reading desk are placed against the middle of the west wall. The altar is at the east end with the result that most of the seats in the nave have their backs to the altar in order to face the pulpit and reading desk.

A few Anglican churches in the eighteenth and early nineteenth centuries were built with circular, elliptical or octagonal interiors. No church of this type survives with its interior intact but there are good, refurnished, examples of octagonal churches of 1758-9 at Stoney Middleton (Derbys), of 1794-6 at Madeley (Salop), of 1805 at Malins Lee (Salop), of 1806 at Micheldever (Hants) and of 1820 at St James, Teignmouth (Devon). The one surviving circular church, also refurnished, is at St Chad's, Shrewsbury, built in 1790-92. A plan of the interior in c.1850, before its extensive late-nineteenth-century reordering, shows the pulpit, reading and clerk's desks, standing, one in front of the other, before the altar in the eastern part of the circular building. To the west of this were open benches and in the middle of the circle stood the font. On the north side of the pulpit and desks was a seat for the town's recorder and on the south side one for the mayor, with seats for members of the corporation in front of each. There were special seats for the churchwardens and overseers of the poor at the back of the circle. A gallery surrounded the whole of the interior, apart from the area over the altar, and the organ was placed in the western part of the gallery opposite the altar.[9] There were elliptical interiors at All Saints, Newcastle upon Tyne, of 1789 and St Andrew's, Dublin, of 1807 but neither interior survives and the buildings are no longer used for worship. In both these cases the original location of the pulpit and reading desk was behind, rather than in front of, the altar. St Mary-in-the-Castle, Hastings, built in 1828, comprised a semi-circular auditorium with a gallery along the external walls, and a shallow chancel in the middle of the long wall, with entrance porches on either side. There was also a proposal, shown in a plan of 1818,[10] to add a semi-circular north aisle to the existing nave at Bedlington (Northumberland) and to place the pulpit, reading and clerk's desks in the middle of the south wall of the nave.

A few Anglican parish churches, or private chapels in large houses, were modelled on the interiors of college chapels at Oxford and Cambridge, their seating ranged in blocks facing one another across a central passageway as in a cathedral choir. There are excellent surviving examples of such buildings at Gwydir Uchaf (Gwynedd) of 1673, Belton House (Lincs) of 1685, Petworth House (Sussex) of 1690-92, Woodhey (Ches) of c.1700, Wimpole Hall (Cambs) of 1724, Halston (Salop) of c.1725, Withcote (Leics) of 1744 and Audley End (Essex) of 1786. All these were private chapels but early examples of parish churches built in the same style survive at Langton-by-Partney and Well (Lincs) of c.1725 and 1733 respectively, Ravenstonedale (Cumb) of 1738-44, Teigh (Rutland) of 1782, Stapleford (Leics) of 1783 and Glenealy (Co. Wicklow) of 1791-2. Several churches of this type were built or refurnished in the middle years of the nineteenth century, such as those at Gatton (Surrey) in 1834, Killerton (Devon) in 1838-41, St Wilfrid, Brougham (Cumb) and Rushbrooke (Suffolk) in c.1840, Roecliffe (Yorks) in 1843-4, Thornton (Bucks) in 1850 and Llandwrog (Gwynedd) in 1860. The last of these was a cruciform church in which inward facing stalls line the walls of both nave and transepts. A similar arrangement is shown in the proposed plan for the reordering of Wendlebury Church (Oxon) in 1761 (Figure 4.5).

Figure 4.5   Seating plan of Wendlebury Church, Oxon, 1761

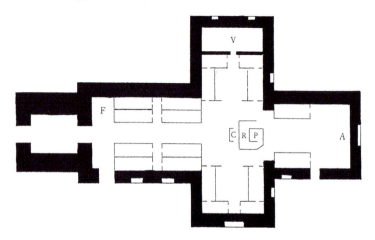

9   Shropshire Record Office, Shrewsbury, 1148/5125.
10   Northumberland Record Office, Gosforth, Faculties 23.

The Road to Ecclesiology

A popular view of ecclesiastical development in the design of Anglican churches is that what were, often rather dismissively and quite incorrectly, dismissed as Georgian preaching boxes were suddenly swept aside by the ecclesiological movement of the 1840s. Not only, as we shall see, was the ecclesiological movement a much more complicated and long-drawn-out phase in Anglican church design than has generally been realised, but recent research has shown that there was in the Anglican churches of England, Wales and Ireland a pre-ecclesiological movement which, to some extent, anticipated, in a somewhat less rigid manner, some of the ideas of the ecclesiologists. Determining dates for this is a tricky business but the indications are that this movement had its beginnings in the 1780s, perhaps even earlier, and that it was in full swing by the 1820s. It also coincided with the most extensive period of Anglican church building in the British Isles since the days when the British churches were still in full communion with Rome. In Ireland the church building initiative began with a series of substantial parliamentary grants to the Irish Board of First Fruits every year from 1777 until 1823. In the twenty years following the Act of Union with the rest of Britain in 1801 grants were made towards the building, rebuilding or enlargement of no fewer than 697 churches, which represented more than a third of the total number of Anglican churches in Ireland. Large programmes of church building and repair were promoted in the Welsh dioceses of Bangor and St Davids by their respective bishops. In the Isle of Man Bishop Mark Hildesley carried out a meticulous inspection of the island's churches as part of his primary visitation in 1757, issuing instructions for the carrying out of essential repairs. Between then and 1846, when Bishop Thomas Vowler Short was translated from the diocese of Sodor and Man to that of St Asaph, no fewer than thirteen of the island's seventeen parish churches and four chapels-of-ease had been either rebuilt or extensively refurbished and a total of nine new churches built. Braddan Church, rebuilt in 1773, retains its interior intact, but substantial remains of these refurbishments or original interiors also survive at Dalby, Malew, St Jude's and Santan. In England and Wales a major initiative for new churches and repairs to existing buildings took place as a result of the establishment of the Church Building Commission and the Incorporated Church Building Society in 1818.

These bodies, the Irish Board of First Fruits, the Church Building Commission and the Incorporated Church Building Society, as well as individual bishops, did not just promote the building and repair of churches, but advocated rather different types of liturgical arrangement than those that had been the norm in most Anglican churches. These new ideas comprised three main elements: one was the breaking up of the old three- and two-decker pulpits and the placing of the pulpit and reading desk on opposite sides of the entrance to the chancel or sanctuary; another was the desire to give greater prominence to the altar, making it more visible by raising it a few steps above the level of the congregation in the nave; a third was the final abolition of square box pews and their replacement with regular pews with doors, provided with seats at the back and kneeling boards at the front. There was also a move to reduce the number of appropriated or rented pews so that more seating was available for the poor and in better locations within the buildings. Bishop Richard

Mant of Killaloe and Kilfenora, addressing his clergy at his 1821 visitation of these two Irish dioceses, stated that he would not consecrate churches that did not comply with certain liturgical principles:

> the reading desk and the pulpit should be situated towards the eastern extremity of the building, but not within the rails of the communion table, so that the minister may in either position see, and be seen by, the whole congregation, and so that at the same time the view of the Communion table may not be obstructed, nor the place appropriated to it suffer encroachment; and that the pews, if pews there must be, should be regular in their dimensions and arrangement upon the principle of containing only single parallel benches behind, and accommodation for kneeling in front; so that in every posture, whether sitting, standing or kneeling, the people may naturally be turned towards the officiating minister, whether he be in the reading desk, or at the Communion table or in the pulpit.[11]

In his *Church Architecture Considered in its Relation to the Mind of the Church*, published in 1843, Mant produced a plan of the ideal Anglican church: uniform seating, with open benches rather than closed pews, all facing east; a chancel three steps higher than the nave and with the altar placed against the east wall; the pulpit on the south side of the entrance to the chancel and a lower reading desk on the north side; the font placed in the middle of the nave towards its western end. Altars were to be railed in and have decent coverings; reading desks should have two ledges, one facing east and the other, depending on its position in the church, north or south; pulpit and desks were not to be placed directly in front of the altar; credence tables were not essential but were to be commended as consistent with the practice of the primitive church.

Similar attitudes to those espoused by Mant were adopted by both the Church Building Commission and the Incorporated Church Building Society. The Commission disapproved of pulpits that blocked the view of the altar and strongly advocated the placing of pulpit and reading desk on opposite sides of the entrance to the chancel, with the parish clerk being relegated to a pew elsewhere in the church. The Commission preferred open seats to closed pews but insisted that, if closed pews were to be installed, there should be a wide passageway between them in which benches for the poor could be placed so that they should have a clear view of the liturgical action. Previously much seating for the poor, where it existed at all, had been relegated to the backs of galleries or benches in the side aisles where the occupants could hear or see little. In 1839 the Incorporated Church Building Society refused to make a grant to the new church at Hersham (Surrey) until the plans had been amended so that a three-decker pulpit was not shown as standing in front of the altar. The amended plans, which the Society sanctioned, showed the pulpit on the south side of the altar recess, with the reading and clerk's desks on the north side. This was exactly in line with the plans of Grayrigg Church (Cumb) in 1839 (Figure 4.6), and it became the standard type of church approved by both the Commission and the Society. Where they differed from the later views of the ecclesiologists

---

11   Richard Mant, *A Charge delivered to the Clergy of the Diocese of Killaloe*, Dublin 1821, pp 12-15.

was in their insistence that chancels should be shallow. At a time when chancels were usually empty, apart from the altar, except where stalls in them were used by communicants, there was no requirement for a long chancel, especially as it did not normally permit a clear view of the altar from the nave. The Church Building Commission recommended that the chancel should be from eight to fifteen feet deep and that panels inscribed with the Ten Commandments, Creed and Lord's Prayer should form a reredos behind the communion table. Galleries were not to be placed over the altar. Side galleries in which the seats faced north or south were permitted as they increased the available accommodation for parishioners, but in the body of the church all the seats were expected to face east, and square pews were not permitted. High pews, common before 1800, were not allowed. Pews needed to be sufficiently low to allow their occupants to see the minister. Pulpits and reading desks had to be approached from either the body of the church or the front of the chancel. Early plans for St George's, Kidderminster, were criticised because the approach to the pulpit and reading desk was from behind the altar, even though the altar was still visible between them.

Figure 4.6   Seating plan of Grayrigg Church, Cumb, 1839

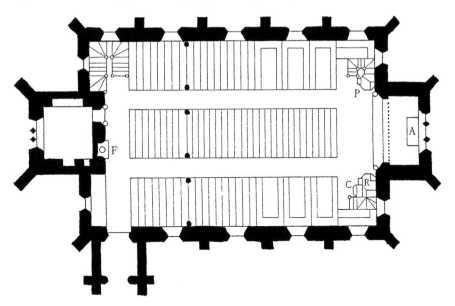

The Church Building Commission insisted that all the churches it funded had to have a reasonable mix of open and free, as well as closed and rented or appropriated, seating, and that the open and free seats must remain so in perpetuity. Regulating the design of churches, though strictly enforced by the Commission, was not entirely new. In 1712 the Committee for Building Fifty New Churches in London had resolved

> That the pewes be single and of equal height, so low that every person in them may
> be seen either kneeling or sitting, and so contrived that all persons may stand or kneel
> towards the Communion Table. That movable forms or seats be so contrived in the
> middle isles, as to run under the seats of the pewes and draw out into the said isles.
> That the chancel be raised three steps above the nave or body of the churches.[12]

Fonts were to be large enough to allow baptism in them by dipping, if desired.

Plans of churches built after 1800 show an increasing preference for buildings in which pews were uniform in size and in which the pulpit and reading desk were placed, either on opposite sides of the entrance to the chancel, or, in very small buildings, the altar itself. There are also many surviving examples of such churches: Hillsborough (Co. Down) of 1772-4, Mildenhall (Wilts) of 1815-16, Calke (Derbys) of 1826, Wreay (Cumb) of 1835, Kilfenora Cathedral (Co. Clare) of 1837, Long Lawford (Warws) of 1839, Birtles (Ches) and Fugglestone (Wilts), both of 1840. At Mildenhall the canopied pulpit and reading desk are of equal height. At Hexton (Herts), refitted in 1824, the pulpit is considerably higher than the reading desk, itself a two-decker with the clerk's seat attached (Illustration 4.6). An interesting variant of the arrangement is St George's, Portland, conservatively refitted in 1849-52. The church, built in 1744-66, is cruciform with a west tower and a central dome. A deep west gallery for an organ and singers covers much of the nave and there are also galleries across both transepts. Pulpit and reading desk, of equal height, stand, on opposite sides of the nave, at the crossing, with the result that the seating between them and the chancel faces west. The altar is placed in a shallow apse and the whole sanctuary is raised well above the level of the nave. Nevertheless this was not the sort of church which would have been approved of by Bishop Mant, the Church Building Society or the Incorporated Church Building Commission, and the reordering had to be paid for by the seat-holders according to a sliding scale laid down by the churchwardens.

Anglican Worship on the Eve of the Oxford Movement

Older historians of Anglicanism from the 1840s to the 1960s have been keen to portray the pre-Victorian church as one that was spiritually dead. Depending on their own perspective it was either the Evangelical Revival or the Oxford Movement, or a mixture of the two, that had brought the church alive. The former, of course, had its roots in European Pietism and had begun to make an impact in the middle years of the eighteenth century. Many of its initial supporters had, however, left the Anglican churches to join the Calvinistic or Wesleyan Methodists, and it was not until the 1820s that the Evangelicals became a powerful lobby in the United Church of England and of Ireland. Eventually both Evangelicals and Tractarians were to want changes made to the liturgical practices of their church but this was not the case before 1840. By and large, Anglicans, whether high churchmen, liberals or Evangelicals, had been content with the form and style of worship provided by the

---

12   P. de la R. du Prey, *Hawksmoor's London Churches: Architecture and Theology*, Chicago and London 2000, p 144.

Illustration 4.6   Early-nineteenth-century   furnishings   at   Hexton   Church,
                   Hertfordshire

Book of Common Prayer. Evangelicals had made some modest experiments. Several
Evangelical clergy introduced communion services in the early morning, separated
from the office of Morning Prayer and the Litany, and additional evening services.
They were also not averse to incorporating hymns into worship, a practice that most
high churchmen were uncomfortable with, since there was no provision for their
use in the Prayer Book. Apart from these differences it would have been difficult for
the average worshipper to determine, apart perhaps from the content of the sermon,
which wing of Anglican theological opinion the officiating minister belonged to.
Such was not the case by the end of the nineteenth century, when it was perfectly
clear, from the interiors of church buildings and the forms of service that took place
in them, which brand of Anglican churchmanship was favoured by the clergy and
their congregations.

If we imagine ourselves back into an Anglican church anywhere in England,
Wales or Ireland before the 1840s, the scene that would have greeted us would have
been much the same everywhere. The church would have been pewed, rather than
fitted with open benches, and a pew-opener would have opened the pew door for us to
take our places before the service. Pews tended either to be appropriated to particular
persons or properties by tradition or else to be rented by particular families. If the
pew-holders were not in church their seats would have been left empty. Visitors would
have been shown to seats reserved for 'strangers'. At the opening of the service the
minister would have ascended the reading desk wearing a full-length white surplice,

a black scarf and the hood of his degree, which most had. The Sunday morning service would have consisted of Morning Prayer, Litany and Ante-Communion. Apart from the sermon everything would have been done from the reading desk. Congregational responses would have been led by the parish clerk. By that date few also led the singing. The psalms, canticles and possibly an anthem would have been sung by a choir, usually in a west gallery, accompanied either by an organ or a small orchestra. In small country churches simple metrical versions of the psalms and canticles would have been used, but in those with a good group of singers the music might have been quite elaborate. After the Nicene Creed the minister would have left the reading desk to change his surplice for a black Geneva gown, in which he would have preached the sermon from the pulpit. He would have changed back into the surplice for the Prayer for the Church and the final prayers and blessing. On Sacrament Sundays, after the Prayer for the Church, the minister would have led those intending to communicate, most of the congregation having now left, into the chancel or space in front of the altar, and have taken a position on the north side of the communion table, from which he would have celebrated the Holy Communion. The choir might have sung appropriate texts, often the words of the *Sanctus*, whilst the congregation was moving forwards but, except in cathedrals, college chapels or the larger parish churches, the communion service itself was not normally sung. The afternoon service, though shorter, followed a similar pattern to Morning Prayer, with prescribed prayers, lessons, psalms and canticles, but the sermon was frequently replaced with the public catechising of children and servants.

The furnishings of the church would have been decent but simple. Pulpit and reading desk, and perhaps the clerk's desk as well, would have had damask or velvet hangings in a rich colour and brackets for candles. The communion table would have been similarly vested in a richly-coloured damask or velvet carpet, over which a white cloth would have been placed when the Holy Communion was to be celebrated. It would have had some sort of reredos, either a painting of a scriptural subject, or panels inscribed with the Ten Commandments, Creed and Lord's Prayer. The table itself might have been furnished with candlesticks and an almsdish. By the 1830s, even in cathedrals, the only vestments in use would have been surplices. Copes, although still worn in some cathedrals during the first half of the eighteenth century, had been abandoned except for use at very special occasions, such as coronations. The use of incense to perfume the church, though not unknown in the early eighteenth century, also seems to have been abandoned. Anglican services, though they certainly suffered from a degree of tediousness, caused by excessive length, and lack of variety, appear to have been, on the whole, conducted with great solemnity and were much praised by contemporaries, whether regular worshippers or foreign visitors. Later criticism of them was determined largely by changes in liturgical taste and the unscrupulous use of the few examples of churches which were not kept in good repair and in which the services were conducted in a slovenly manner.

Anglicans before the 1840s considered themselves to be part of the family of Protestant churches but to occupy a special position within it. They, except for some Evangelicals, rejected orthodox Calvinism and they regarded the much less rigidly-structured services of the Reformed churches as somewhat improper and not really decent. On the other hand they regarded Roman Catholics, and even Lutherans, as liturgically corrupt, adopting practices that fuelled superstition among a poorly-educated laity and retaining ornaments and vestments that were not consistent with worship based on the teachings of Holy Scripture. Anglican theological distinctiveness was, for Anglicans, manifested to the world in the services of the *Book of Common Prayer*, and in the arrangement of their churches, which was designed to permit the decent celebration of those services.

Chapter 5

Counter-Reformation Roman Catholicism

The Reformation did not just produce the Protestant churches of Europe, considered in the previous three chapters. The Roman Catholic Church too was substantially reformed and, by the late sixteenth century, had very little in common with its pre-Reformation predecessor. Not only was the official liturgy of the church reformed and standardised, but its buildings were transformed, both to meet the new liturgical requirements, and to reflect the taste of the age. The history of these developments in the seventeenth and eighteenth centuries is one of two, very different, manifestations. In Catholic Europe – Austria, France, Italy, Portugal, Spain, parts of Germany and much of the eastern fringes – the architecture and furnishings of this period were openly demonstrative of Catholic power and the defeat of the Reformers. However, there were in Protestant Europe, especially Ireland and the Netherlands, Roman Catholics who had to worship in a much more restrained and secretive way, and those buildings were rather different from the triumphant ones of Catholic Europe. In this chapter we will consider both aspects of Roman Catholic worship, and the buildings associated with it, between the late sixteenth and early nineteenth centuries.

The Tridentine Mass

One of the last acts of the Council of Trent (1545-63) was to request a reform of the liturgical rites of the Roman Catholic Church. The Council had been summoned by Pope Paul III, partly to respond to the allegations made against the church by the reformers. The Council had redefined that the mass was 'a true, proper and propitiatory sacrifice for the living and the dead',[1] but had acknowledged that the wide variations in which the mass had been celebrated, according to different local rites, had both caused confusion and offered an opportunity for practices and teachings which were not in line with the official doctrines of the church. The work of revision was entrusted to a papal commission and in 1570 Pope Pius V issued the new *Missale Romanum*. Whereas many copies of pre-Reformation missals had contained few rubrics for the celebration of the Mass, leading to some fairly exotic practices by some clergy, the new missal laid down what was to happen in precise detail. Although the new missal did not outlaw all local rites, it did result in their gradual disappearance. Any local rite that could show that it had been in existence for at least two hundred years could continue to be celebrated. This, for example, permitted the continued celebration of the Mozarabic rite, with its very strong Eastern Orthodox influences, in a few churches in Spain. In addition to the official copies of

---

1 George Every, *The Mass*, Dublin 1978, p 129.

the new missal, the interpretation of which was to be controlled by the Congregation of Rites (set up by Pope Sixtus V in 1588 and which led to an improved edition of the text being issued by Pope Urban VIII in 1634), a large number of manuals were published for the benefit of the clergy illustrating the prescribed ceremonial; they usually included diagrams showing what the exact position of the celebrant ought to be, or the way in which he should perform liturgical actions, during the mass.

The new missal banned many practices which had been common in the pre-Reformation church: the interpolation of additional material into the text of certain prayers; the introduction of special masses for the feasts of local saints by replacing them with common prayers to be used for all but the most important feasts in the liturgical calendar; the replacing of the mass of a particular feast by votive masses for special intentions, by reducing the days on which such masses might be celebrated. Along with the revision of the missal, energetic attempts were made by reforming clergy, especially the new order of Jesuits, to encourage more frequent communion. Those who were members of sodalities, societies of lay people who adopted a rule of life, were encouraged to communicate weekly, and others were recommended to do so monthly. Indulgences were used to promote more frequent communion. However, as Andreas Heinz has pointed out, the encouragement of more frequent communion was, to some extent, at variance with the rubric of the 1570 missal, since, for the laity to receive communion, a separate communion rite, based on that prescribed for the communion of the sick, had to be inserted into the normal eucharistic rite. The rubrics only demanded a congregation of two, so that private masses, without communion, remained the norm in many Roman Catholic churches. When communion did take place it did so after the following form. The priest placed sufficient altar breads, consecrated during the mass, on the paten and a server spread a linen cloth across the top of the communion rail. The priest then said the confession in the name of the communicants and pronounced the absolution. He then proclaimed *Ecce Agnus Dei* and repeated *Domine, non sum dignus* three times. After the communicants had received the sacrament in one kind it was common practice for them to be handed a vessel containing a mixture of unconsecrated wine and water to enable them to swallow the bread whole. In some parts of Europe it was common for the priest to give an address before communion. Provision for it was found in the *Rituales* or *Pastorales* produced by the dioceses of Trier in 1574 and Mechelen in 1607. The earliest ones tended to prescribe an address in Latin, the later ones in the vernacular. There was provision for one in German in the *Rituale* of the diocese of Passau in 1686, and one in French in that of the diocese of Metz in 1662. By the late eighteenth century some diocesan *Rituales*, such as that of Amiens in 1784, were also prescribing the use of a post-communion exhortation. In addition, during the seventeenth century, it became common for the Latin confession, said by the priest, to be replaced with a vernacular confession said by the congregation. It was normal for communicants to receive the sacrament kneeling and to place their hands under the cloth spread over the altar rails, which they then lifted slightly so as to prevent any particles of the altar bread being spilt on the floor. Although receiving the wine as well as the bread was not specifically rejected by the Council of Trent, it was not encouraged, and indeed specifically prohibited by some diocesan *Rituales*, largely to emphasise the difference between Roman Catholics and Protestants in this matter.[2]

The one change that the Council of Trent declined to make to the liturgy of the Roman Catholic church was the language in which it was celebrated. Except in the case of some of the Uniate Eastern churches, the liturgy remained in Latin until the reforms of the Second Vatican Council in the 1960s. However, as we have seen, provision was made by individual dioceses to have a few congregational parts of the mass in the vernacular. In addition, except in universities or seminaries, the sermon was also preached in the language of the country. Although local rites were effectively suppressed after the publication of the Tridentine missal, there were some attempts to preserve, or even revive them, in a few parts of the Roman Catholic world. This was especially so in France, where a long tradition of Gallicanism was encouraged by the French monarchy. However, even here, there were limits. Cardinal Mazarin obtained a brief from Pope Alexander VII in 1661 to prevent a French translation of the Tridentine missal, convinced that its author was planning to celebrate mass in the vernacular. Some Gallican clergy did, however, celebrate mass in a manner somewhat removed from the rubrics in the missal. At Asnières, near Paris, the parish priest never used the high altar except on Sundays and festivals and did not have a permanent cross or candlesticks on the altar, the processional cross and the candles being carried by the acolytes and put into position, behind the altar, at the beginning of the mass. He involved the whole congregation in the preparation, the responses and the psalm, as well as the confession at the start of the mass. He would not begin the canon of the mass until the choir had finished singing the *Sanctus* and *Benedictus*, and then said it loud enough for the words to be heard by the congregation, whereas it was meant to be said inaudibly. There were similar practices in some German churches. Priests celebrated only one 'parish' mass on Sundays, always with communion, and with prayers in German said by the congregation whilst the priest said the canon. It was also common for the *Gloria*, *Sanctus* and *Benedictus* to be sung in German rather than in Latin.

Church Services and Buildings in Catholic Europe

Despite the single liturgical standard of the Tridentine missal, there was a great deal of difference between the way in which services were conducted, or the architectural setting of the liturgy, between countries in which Roman Catholicism was the main religion and those in which Roman Catholics worshipped in much more constrained circumstances. The extravagance of the Roman Catholic high mass at the Cathedral of Notre Dame in Paris is shown in an early-eighteenth-century engraving (Illustration 5.1). Vestments, ornaments, ceremonial, music; all were extremely lavish. So, too was the architectural setting. The proto-type Counter-Reformation church, noted earlier at Il Gèsu in Rome, was replicated throughout Catholic Europe. Occasionally, as at the church of Santa Agnese, in the Piazza Navona in Rome, built in 1642, the Greek cross plan with nave, chancel and transepts of equal length, was

---

2   See, especially, Andreas Heinz, 'Liturgical Rules and Popular Religious Customs Surrounding Holy Communion between the Council of Trent and the Catholic Restoration in the Nineteenth Century', in Caspers, Lukken and Rouwhorst (eds), *Bread of Heaven*, pp 119-43.

Illustration 5.1   Solemn High Mass at Notre Dame Cathedral, Paris, in the early
                     eighteenth century (Picart, *Ceremonies*, i, between pp 334 and 335)

adopted,[3] but normally it was the much longer nave with side chapels, shallow
transepts and apsidal chancel. The internal decoration of these buildings could be
extremely ornate. With some German architects, such as Balthasar Neumann (1687-
1753), Baroque church architecture reached its zenith, but equally ornate sculpture
could be found in many parts of southern Europe. Churches, such as those at
Collioure and Prades in the Pyrénees-Orientales Départment of southern France,
are furnished with elaborate Baroque altars of the late seventeenth and eighteenth
centuries, not only in the chancel but in the side chapels as well. This type of church
will also be found throughout Portugal and Spain. The church of St Paulin at Trier,
built in 1738-43, has a long stalled apsidal choir with a Baroque high altar at the east
end and equally lavish side altars flanking each side of the entrance into the chancel
in a church without aisles or transepts. Bruchsal church, built in 1738, was cruciform
with the high altar in an apsidal chancel and altars at the apsidal ends of the north and
south transepts; the nave was also apsidal, the apse forming the entrance portico.[4]
Even cities like Paris, with many existing pre-Reformation churches, were provided
with new Baroque or classical churches, such as those of St Roch and St Sulpice,
erected in the late seventeenth and early eighteenth centuries.[5]

---

3   T.F. Bumpus, *The Cathedrals and Churches of Italy*, London 1926, p 350.

4   C.F. Otto, *Space into Light: The Churches of Balthasar Neumann*, New York 1979,
illus. 37, 60, 63.

5   E. Tyrrell-Green, *French Church Architecture*, London 1928, p 200.

Pulpits as well as altars could be lavish pieces of furniture in Roman Catholic churches. In southern Europe they tended to be placed at the eastern end of the nave as their pre-Reformation predecessors, when they had existed, had been, but in northern Europe they were more likely to be placed well down the nave as they were at St Paulin's, Trier, or at St Riquier (Ilustration 5.2). Seating was most frequently provided by benches, as it was at St Riquier, but there are certainly examples of Roman Catholic churches in which the seating was provided by box pews. Good examples of such churches survive in France at Cheverny, Richelieu, Souvigny-en-Sologne and Thionville. This use of box pews and the positioning of pulpits well down the nave, frequently, especially in Belgium, approached by double staircases, creates interesting parallels between the architecture of Protestant and Roman Catholic buildings which have tended to be overlooked. In the former cathedral at St Omer, in northern France, not only is the pulpit placed halfway down the nave but immediately opposite it is a large pew, facing the pulpit, for the mayor and members of the municipal corporation.[6] Sermons were an important part of Counter-Reformation Roman Catholic spirituality and preachers dedicated as much care to the preparation of sermons as their Protestant counterparts. As in many Protestant churches during the eighteenth century, they tended to concentrate on issues of personal morality and the virtues of charity. A more evangelical style of preaching, concentrating on the fires of hell, tended to be associated with parochial missions, frequently promoted by reforming bishops.

The fact that the services were largely in Latin meant that the Roman Catholic laity were more likely to be isolated from official religion than their Protestant counterparts, and in many Roman Catholic countries there was a deep division between 'official' and 'popular' religion. In this respect many of the problems of the late medieval church had not been resolved by the reforms of the Council of Trent. The bishop of Amiens complained that the inhabitants of neighbouring parishes were attending the very short low masses provided by a neighbouring abbey rather than the longer masses, with sermons, in their own parish churches. In 1706 the bishop of Toul endeavoured to deal with the problem of dogs in the churches of his diocese; they interrupted the services with their barking and soiled the buildings with their excrement. In other churches children sitting in the galleries would amuse themselves by spitting on the heads of the adults below them. There were major problems with the maintenance of church buildings. Tithe owners were responsible for this, and for the provision of ornaments and vestments, but they were frequently reluctant to fulfil their responsibilities and priests had to make the difficult choice of either paying for such items themselves or trying to raise an additional tax from their parishioners to meet the costs. The greatest problem faced by bishops and their clergy was that the laity preferred to make their main spiritual efforts through religious processions and other extra-liturgical devotions, rather than through mass attendance, confession and communion, as enjoined by the ecclesiastical authorities.

---

6   Nigel Yates, 'Unity in Diversity: Attitudes to the Liturgical Arrangement of Church Buildings Between the Late Seventeenth and Early Nineteenth Centuries', in W.M. Jacob and W.N. Yates (eds), *Crown and Mitre: Religion and Society in Northern Europe since the Reformation*, Woodbridge 1993, p 55.

Illustration 5.2   Late-eighteenth-century furnishings at St Riquier, France

All too often processions were occasions, not just for spiritual devotion, but for popular enjoyment. Religious processions became pageants or carnivals, frequently associated with drunkenness and riotous behaviour. Another popular religious practice was the exposure of the relics of the church's patron or other saints. The cathedral at Angers had, among its relics, the arm of its patron, St Maurice, as well as a phial of his blood and a lock of the hair of the Blessed Virgin Mary. On certain festivals these relics were brought out and exposed on the high altar to be venerated by the laity, or to be carried in procession. Many of these relics were alleged to have supernatural powers, so that veneration of them was considered to be more effective than regular attendance at mass or the other official services of the church. Several people attested to having illnesses cured, or other benefits conferred on them, by direct contact with relics. Another, though more expensive, popular devotion was the pilgrimage. Major sites, such as Santiago de Compostella, continued to attract large numbers of pilgrims throughout the seventeenth and eighteenth centuries, but there were many more local, and therefore accessible, pilgrimage sites: in France they included Mont St Michel, Notre Dame de Marienthal, Notre Dame de Liesse and the chapel of the Blessed Virgin Mary at Puy. Large numbers of chapels were built, especially in southern France, to house statues of the Virgin Mary and these in time achieved a reputation as local sanctuaries at which benefits could be conferred on the devout. Reforming bishops and clergy made strenuous attempts to suppress some of these popular religious observances, or at least to separate them from the secular activities that tended to surround them, but it was a difficult task, as so many laity found that they met their religious needs more effectively than the official religious observances which they regarded as boring. In some dioceses local observances, which had traditionally taken place during the week, were switched to the nearest Sunday, in the hope that they would become more spiritual, and less secular occasions. Major reductions in the number of festivals were decreed in the dioceses of Bordeaux in 1740, Autun in 1753, Orléans in 1763, Rouen in 1767 and Paris in 1778.

Roman Catholicism in the Netherlands

Outside Catholic Europe the practice of the faith was rather different. A Dutch archbishopric, in the historic former bishopric of Utrecht, had been established, on the eve of the Reformation, in 1559, with suffragan bishoprics at Deventer, Groningen, Haarlem, Leewuarden and Middelburg. By the time the first archbishop, Schenck van Toutenberg, had died, in 1580, the Netherlands had been mostly overrun by Calvinism. Although, eventually, a new archbishop, Philip Rovenius, was appointed to give leadership to the surviving Roman Catholic community in the Netherlands in 1620, and although he resided in Utrecht, he was legally the archbishop of Filippi *in partibus infidelium* (in the regions of the unbelievers). During the French occupation of Utrecht, in 1672-3, the city churches were refurnished for Roman Catholic worship and the then archbishop, Johan van Neercassel, both celebrated Mass in the cathedral and presided at a Corpus Christi procession through the streets of the city. The French connection was to lead to Jansenist influences in the Dutch Roman Catholic church and an eventual schism within it. When Neercassel's successor as archbishop, Petrus Codde, was himself accused of Jansenism, he was initially suspended, and in 1704 deprived, by the pope. A substantial section of the Dutch Roman Catholic church remained loyal to Codde and, through the offices of a suspended French missionary bishop, Dominique Marie Varlet, the episcopal succession was maintained. This was the origin of the Dutch Old Catholic Church, a church that maintained traditional Catholic doctrine and ceremonial but was not in communion with the Holy See. It was not until the early nineteenth century that the Roman Catholics in the Netherlands were provided with their own bishops *in partibus infidelium*, with the eventual restoration of a Dutch hierarchy under a rival archbishop of Utrecht in 1853.[7]

During the late seventeenth and early eighteenth centuries both Roman Catholics and Old Catholics had freedom of worship in the Netherlands, provided this was observed with discretion, though they did not have full political rights in a country where the Reformed Church was the religion of the majority of the population. They worshipped in what were known as 'hidden churches', of which a number of outstanding examples survive. These were either chapels in houses, or buildings, the fronts of which were designed to look like houses, but which were churches behind the secular frontage. The best surviving example of the first type is the former church of St Nicholas, also known as Our Lord in the Attic, which now forms the core of the Museum Amstelkring in Amsterdam (Illustration 5.3). Good examples of the second type of church, their severe domestic frontages hiding a wealth of elaborate Baroque furnishings, are the Old Catholic churches of St James and St Augustine in The Hague and of St Mary and St Ursula in Delft. The former was built in 1722, and furnished between then and 1734. The latter has a complete interior of 1743. Even where Old Catholic churches have been wholly or partially rebuilt they often retain furnishings from their eighteenth-century predecessors. This is the case in the church of St Michael at Oudewater, rebuilt in 1882, where the reredos, altar rails, pulpit and font date from the early eighteenth century.

Roman Catholicism in England and Wales

Before the second half of the seventeenth century, Roman Catholicism was a largely proscribed religion in England and Wales. Roman Catholics were regarded as political traitors, houses of Roman Catholics likely to be raided and priests executed. Roman Catholic worship was a 'hole in the corner' affair in rooms in the houses of recusant aristocratic or gentry families. From the second half of the seventeenth century conditions for Roman Catholic worship in England and Wales were more analogous to those in the Netherlands. Roman Catholics were politically and socially restricted but they could, with discretion, worship without interference from the authorities. During the reign of James II (1685-8) England and Wales were divided into four districts, each administered by a vicar-apostolic who was also a titular bishop *in partibus infidelium*. This structure survived until the number of districts was doubled in 1840 and then replaced by a proper hierarchy, with non-titular bishops, in 1850. It was during James II's reign that the first Roman Catholic places of worship not in private houses were opened, such as the Franciscan Chapel in Birmingham in 1687, though most continued to be in private houses. A shortage of priests meant that many chapels did not have a mass every Sunday or holy day. When a priest was not available the local congregation would improvise its own 'prayers', which were often incorporated into the mass when a priest was available. Whereas the mass itself was in Latin, the prayers were in English. They consisted of psalms, the Lord's

---

7   See D. Bouvy (ed), *From Willibrord to World Council: Some Aspects of the Spiritual Life of Utrecht through the Ages*, Utrecht 1972, pp 32-40.

Illustration 5.3   The chapel of Our Lord in the Attic, Museum Amstelkring, Amsterdam, built in 1661-3 and extended in 1735-6 (Museum Amstelkring)

Prayer, the Acts of Faith, Hope, Charity and Contrition, the Litany of the Saints, *Te Deum* and prayers for the sick, the departed and the royal family. Roman Catholics were not encouraged to participate in the formal parts of the mass, but had private devotional manuals which they used for their own private prayers whilst the mass was said or sung.

On the whole the masses celebrated in country-house chapels were modest affairs, maintaining the discretion required by law. In London, however, more elaborate buildings and services were, by the middle years of the eighteenth century, being provided by the embassies of Roman Catholic states: Bavaria, France, the Holy Roman Empire, Naples, Portugal, Sardinia, Spain and Venice. Some of these chapels maintained an elaborate ritual with a series of low masses on Sundays, a sung high mass, vespers and, once a month, Benediction of the Blessed Sacrament. In about 1740 the Portuguese embassy also had Compline on Wednesdays in Lent and the full liturgy for Holy Week and Easter. Some private chapels were also able to maintain high liturgical standards. At Thorndon in Essex the Petre family maintained the traditional ceremonies of blessing candles at Candlemas, ashes on Ash Wednesday and palms on Palm Sunday, Tenebrae on the Monday, Tuesday and Wednesday of Holy Week, an altar of repose on Maundy Thursday, creeping to the cross on Good Friday and the lighting of the paschal fire and candle on Easter Eve. The chapel also had Benediction monthly with full exposition of the Blessed Sacrament between mass and vespers on at least seven of the major feast days.

The growing confidence and more elaborate liturgical practice of Roman Catholics in the late eighteenth century, together with the provisions of the Catholic Relief Acts of 1778 and 1791, led to the erection of some ambitious places of worship, of which a few survive with their furnishings intact. The private chapel at Milton House, south of Oxford, erected in 1773, is typical of the more modest chapels in houses, which provided the main settings for Roman Catholic worship before the 1780s. Even so it is furnished with a tasteful altar, benches and painted glass (Illustration 5.4). By the second half of the eighteenth century Roman Catholic churches, such as some of the embassy chapels in London, were being built in such a way that they were no longer being hidden away behind domestic frontages but could be seen for what they were. There are free-standing chapels, with substantially complete furnishings, of 1786-7 at East Lulworth (Dorset), 1789 at Marton (East Yorks) and 1796-1800 at Stonor (Oxon). The most elaborate is, however, the chapel at Wardour Castle (Wilts), begun in 1761 and extended in 1788, though some of the furnishings are later. There are also surviving illustrations of the 1792 chapel at Winchester and the 1798 one at Newcastle upon Tyne.[8] During the 1790s two chapels were erected on the Isle of Wight, at Newport in 1792 and West Cowes in 1796. The buildings themselves survive, though the interiors have been altered.[9] Churches of this date, and the early part of the nineteenth century, tended to follow a fairly standard design. Most were rectangular buildings, frequently galleried, with the emphasis on the single altar against the short wall opposite the entrance. A few, as did the chapel at Winchester, had pulpits on one side of the entrance to

---

8   Bryan Little, *Catholic Churches Since 1623*, London 1966, Plate 4.
9   *Ibid.*, Plate 6.

Illustration 5.4   Private chapel at Milton House, Oxfordshire, opened in 1773 (Milton House)

the sanctuary, but many appear not to have done, the priest preaching from the altar steps. Some chapels had benches for the people to sit on, but others had box pews, as still survive in the North Yorkshire chapels of Crathorne (1834) and Leyburn (1835). With the growth in the elaboration of their chapels, and with total freedom of worship, the vicars-apostolic tried to bring their clergy and congregations into line with Roman Catholic worship in Europe by abolishing the vernacular prayers that had traditionally formed part of, or even substituted for, the mass. Bishop Milner was the first to do so as vicar-apostolic of the Midland District in 1803, but others endeavoured to follow his example. There was, however, some resistance to such innovations from some of the leading Roman Catholic landed families in England and Wales, which very much valued the older forms of worship and resented any attempts to impose what they regarded as 'foreign' innovations upon them. A major feature of English and Welsh Roman Catholicism in the late nineteenth and early twentieth centuries was the continuing tensions between the old recusant families and the, much larger, new Roman Catholic community comprised of converts from Anglicanism and immigrants from Ireland or mainland Europe.

Roman Catholicism in Scotland

Scottish Roman Catholics, supporters of the exiled Stuarts, remained politically tainted until the end of the eighteenth century, and, like Scottish Episcopalians, were much restricted as a worshipping community. Their main strength lay in the north-east, also a stronghold of episcopalianism, and in parts of the western highlands and islands, especially Barra and South Uist. In 1731 a vicar-apostolic, Hugh Macdonald, was consecrated for this Catholic *Gaidhealtachd*. In 1778 Scotland was divided into two vicariates, one for the Lowlands and the other for the Highlands, until the restoration of a full hierarchy in 1878. A serious shortage of priests to serve this small, but widely dispersed, Roman Catholic community meant that in many places mass could only be celebrated, usually in barns or private houses, three or four times a year. On those Sundays and festivals, usually the majority, when mass could not be celebrated, 'prayers' consisted largely of recitation of the rosary, a devotion which became central to Roman Catholic spirituality in late-eighteenth- and early-nineteenth-century Scotland. Only one substantially unaltered church, that at Tynet in Moray of 1787, a long low building converted from a house and byre, survives from this period. By this date, however, some more prestigious churches were being erected. St Gregory's at Presholme was the scene of the first High Mass to be sung in Scotland since the Reformation when it was consecrated in 1792. High Mass was also sung at the opening of a new church in Aberdeen in 1803. New churches, with imposing facades, were opened in Edinburgh in 1814 and Glasgow in 1817. By this date Roman Catholics in Scotland had moved on from a Sunday service of vernacular prayers, followed, if a priest was available, with a simple low mass, and possibly a sermon in either English or Gaelic, to masses with singing. Organs were installed in the new churches and choirs were established. In 1816 the church at Aberdeen became the first in Scotland to introduce Benediction of the Blessed Sacrament. At Traquair House, between Peebles and Selkirk, where Roman Catholic worship had been maintained by a strong recusant family throughout the seventeenth and eighteenth centuries, the upper room in which mass had been celebrated by the resident chaplain, was replaced by a, still fairly modest, chapel in the courtyard of the house, fitted up with an altar-piece, sacred pictures, a large pew for the family and benches for their servants and tenants, in c.1820.

Roman Catholicism in Ireland

Between 1560 and 1870 the religious situation of Ireland was unique in Europe. An established Protestant church could only count on the support of about an eighth of the population by the early eighteenth century. Almost as many Protestants worshipped in Presbyterian meeting houses and three-quarters of the population were Roman Catholics. Strenuous efforts had been taken by the Dublin-based government to weaken the Roman Catholic allegiance of the Irish people through the imposition of severe economic, political and social restrictions on Roman Catholics. Although some of the landed families had converted to the Church of Ireland, in order to retain their estates and their political influence, the policy was a failure, and by the 1720s was openly recognised to have been such. By the 1750s a full Roman Catholic hierarchy had been restored in Ireland, and the bishops appointed were prepared to collaborate with the British authorities to secure a stable political regime in Ireland in return for various measures of relief for the Roman Catholic population. From the 1770s the economic, political and social restrictions on Roman Catholics were gradually lifted, though full political emancipation, not just for Roman Catholics in Ireland, but in the rest of the British Isles as well, was not achieved until 1829.

As in England, Wales and Scotland, Roman Catholic worship in the post-Reformation era had developed rather differently in Ireland from the way it had in those European countries where Roman Catholicism was the official religion of the state. Ignatius Murphy has commented on the general state of worship and church building in the diocese of Killaloe before 1800:

> Most chapels had no other formal religious services apart from mass on Sundays and holy days. The Blessed Sacrament was reserved in the priest's house... Ceremonial and its accompanying trappings were reduced to a minimum... a stole worn by the priest was the only indication that a sacred rite was taking place... Altars were made of mud, boards or stone, or a combination of these materials, and at times were raised on timber or stone landings... Some chapels had a crucifix while others had only a painted image of a crucifix... Unsuitable or worn-out vestments were often ordered... to be destroyed... [and] parish priests to ensure that the altar coverings were not torn and that in particular the corporals and purificators, used on the altar during mass, were in good condition.[10]

There were parts of Ireland, even in the early nineteenth century, where there were few Roman Catholic churches and where mass was still celebrated, as it had been in the seventeenth century, in the open air at traditional mass rocks. In the rural areas, where churches existed, they tended to be simple, thatched, barn-like structures, frequently used for secular as well as religious purposes. A good example of such a church, built in 1768 at Tullyallan, and re-erected with a reconstructed interior at the Ulster-American Folk Park, has a rectangular interior with the altar on one of the long walls. The projection behind the altar was used as both a sacristy and living accommodation by the parish priest, and the fact that the church has a hearth on one of the short walls suggests that it doubled up as a schoolroom. Very similar churches were described in the visitation reports of Archbishop James Butler I of Cashel and Emly between 1757 and 1774: walls of stone or mud, whitewashed; thatched roofs; altars made of boards or stone, some raised on steps and others with a canopy over them; no seating or other furnishings.[11]

In the towns the building of more substantial churches, and the celebration of a more elaborate liturgy, was possible. The Liffey Street Chapel in Dublin, as early as 1749, had

> on the altar... a gilt tabernacle, with six large gilt candlesticks... the altar piece carved and embellished with four pillars, cornices and decorations gilt and painted. The picture of the Conception of the B.V.M. to whom the chapel is dedicated fills the altar piece; and on each side are paintings of the apostles Peter and Paul.[12]

10   I. Murphy, *The Diocese of Killaloe in the Eighteenth Century*, Blackrock 1991, pp 148-9, 176-7.

11   See C. O'Dwyer (ed), 'Archbishop Butler's Visitation Book', *Archivium Hibernicum*, xxxiii (1975), pp 1-90, and xxxiv (1977), pp 1-49.

12   J. Kelly and D. Keogh (eds), *A History of the Catholic Diocese of Dublin*, Dublin 2000, p 226.

From 1779 the Francis Street Chapel in Dublin employed a Neapolitan musical director, Tommaso Giordani, who composed a new *Te Deum* for the special service held to mark the recovery of George III in 1789. At Wexford in 1820, both Roman Catholic churches had excellent choirs, processions on Palm Sunday and on the Feast of Corpus Christi, Stations of the Cross on Sundays in Lent and Benediction of the Blessed Sacrament on all festivals. By that date most Dublin churches had Benediction at least once a month, Stations of the Cross and public recitation of the rosary. By the early years of the nineteenth century an ambitious programme of church building had begun to have an impact on the standards of worship in the rural areas as well. Eleven new churches were built in the diocese of Cloyne between 1775 and 1785, thirty in that of Clogher between 1786 and 1814 and eighty in that of Cork between 1805 and 1848. The new church at Callan (Co. Kilkenny) cost £4000 in 1810, though the average cost of a new building before 1845 was only £400. By 1844 every thatched mass-house in County Wexford had been replaced by a new church.

Before the early part of the nineteenth century many Roman Catholic churches in Ireland had no seating. One of the first to be fitted with seats was the new South Chapel in Cork in 1766, where the pews were inscribed with the names of those who had subscribed to the building costs. Seating was also provided in galleries. Most seats appear to have been allocated, as in the Cork example, to the subscribers to the new building, or else rented out. Other seating was paid for by individual families and reserved for their exclusive use. Attempts by reforming bishops, such as Blake of Dromore at Lurgan in 1833, to abolish private or rented seating, were generally resisted by congregations. Other bishops, such as Doyle of Kildare and Leighlin, were able to enforce some constraints on such seating by preventing the owners or renters of pews from selling or transferring their seats to others. Some galleries were built very cheaply; that at Longford collapsed on Christmas Day 1823, injuring several members of the congregation beneath it.

Among the new churches erected by the Roman Catholic Church in Ireland in the late eighteenth and early nineteenth centuries were the first cathedrals of the revived dioceses. The costliest was the one in Waterford in 1793-6, designed by the same local architect, John Roberts, as the earlier Church of Ireland cathedral (1774-9), but costing £20,000 compared with the latter's £6000. This was followed by the cathedrals in Cork and Dublin. The latter was styled the pro-cathedral, in the vain hope that one day the Roman Catholics would be permitted to re-occupy one of the two Church of Ireland cathedrals in the city. It was begun in 1814, furnished by 1823, with a portico erected in 1834, and was one of the most handsome neo-Classical buildings in Ireland (Illustration 5.5). Six of the new cathedrals were built in the 1820s and 1830s: at Ballina for the diocese of Killala, at Carlow for that of Kildare and Leighlin, at Ennis for that of Killaloe, at Newry for that of Dromore, at Skibbereen for that of Ross and at Tuam. That at Skibbereen was another neo-Classical building but the others were all in the antiquarian 'Gothick' Style.

The new, especially town, churches of the late eighteenth and early nineteenth centuries, such as those at Ardkeen (1777), which preserves most of its liturgical furnishings intact, Cashel (1792-1804) and Youghal (1796), had their altars in the short wall opposite the entrance, an arrangement shown very clearly in the plan of St Paul's, Arran Quay, Dublin, designed by Patrick Byrne in 1835-44 (Figure 5.1). This was, however, a reorientation of the earlier Roman Catholic arrangement in Ireland

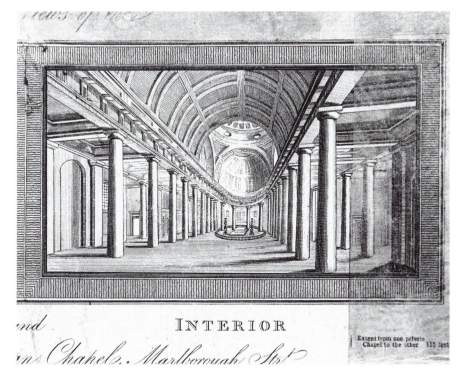

Illustration 5.5   Design for the interior of the Pro-Cathedral in Dublin, 1815
(Dublin Diocesan Archives)

in which the altar had normally been placed on one of the long walls, often with galleries across the two short walls. An excellent survival of this earlier arrangement, built in 1783 and refurnished in 1831, is the Church of St John Baptist at Drumcree (Co. Armagh), now re-erected at the Ulster Folk and Transport Museum (Illustration 5.6). Others, though now substantially refurnished, survive at St Malachy's, Belfast (1841-4), Navan (1836-46) and Rosslea (1834). All have galleries around three sides of the interior and at Rosslea (Co. Fermanagh) the original altar piece survives intact. Some of these rectangular churches were extended, by the addition of a transept opposite the altar, to form a T-plan interior, a good example being the church at Grange (Co. Louth), now refurnished (Figure 5.2). Others were built as T-plans, usually with transepts flanking the sanctuary. Normally such churches, as at Grange, had galleries or lofts in all three projections. Excellent examples of churches with transepts flanking the sanctuary survive at Corofin (Co. Clare) of 1822-3, Fethard (Co. Tipperary) of 1829 and Dunmanway (Co. Cork) of 1834. At Corofin and Fethard the original gallery seating survives, and at Dunmanway both the gallery seating and the original reredoses of both the high and the transeptal side altars remain intact. There were also some L-plan Roman Catholic churches in Ireland, such as that at Keash (Co. Sligo), where the two projections, at right angles to each other, were of equal length with the sanctuary constructed at the point where the two projections met.

Figure 5.1   Ground plan of St Paul's, Arran Quay, Dublin, 1835-44

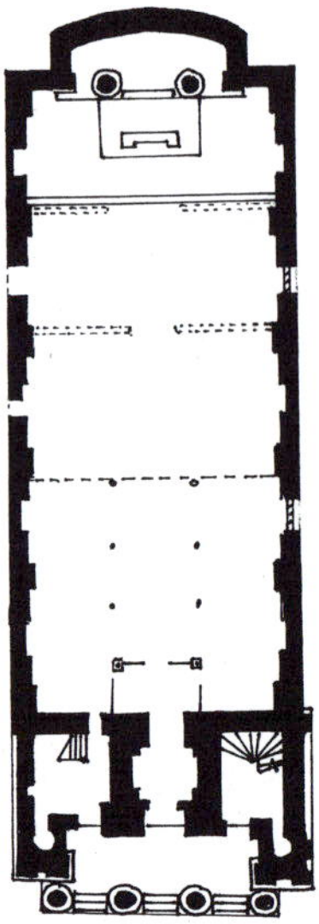

Figure 5.2   Ground plan of St James, Grange, 1762, showing the extensions of
c.1818 and c.1852

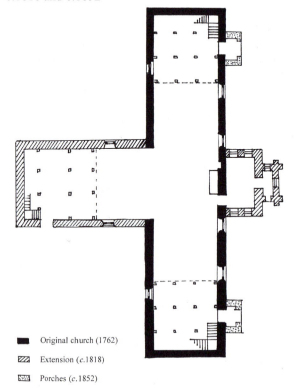

■ Original church (1762)

▨ Extension (*c.*1818)

▦ Porches (*c.*1852)

Illustration 5.6   St John the Baptist's Church at Drumcree, Co. Armagh, refitted in
1831 (Ulster Folk and Transport Museum)

Although Roman Catholic church buildings, both in countries with established
Roman Catholic churches as well as those in which Roman Catholics were only
tolerated, needed to provide for a particular form of liturgical worship, the eucharistic
rite of the Tridentine missal, there were many respects in which Roman Catholic
buildings shared common characteristics with their Protestant counterparts of the
same period and for exactly the same pragmatic reasons. As has been noted earlier,
pulpits were frequently placed well down the nave so that the preacher could be heard
by the whole congregation; seating was frequently arranged so that as many people
as possible could follow the liturgical action at the altar; galleries were erected as the
cheapest method of enlarging existing buildings; and seating was assigned so that it
reflected the social composition of the congregation. Doctrinal differences were not
always reflected in architectural ones.

Chapter 6

Ecclesiology and Neo-Medievalism

During the second half of the eighteenth century there were the beginnings of a movement in Europe to try to recapture the spirit of the Middle Ages. There is no doubt that the centre of this movement was the British Isles, though there were parallel developments in France and Germany. By the end of the nineteenth century the influence of what was known as the 'Gothic Revival' had spread across the whole of Europe, though it was weakest in what might be termed its 'fringes', especially southern Catholic Europe and Lutheran Scandinavia. In some churches, notably the Roman Catholic ones, the changes were primarily architectural, but in others, especially the Anglican ones, they were also liturgical. The precise relationship between architectural and liturgical change was a complicated one, and there has been a good deal of argument between religious historians of the nineteenth century about which influenced the other. The views expressed in this chapter, which I have argued in more detail elsewhere, are still controversial in some quarters and have not to date been generally adopted by architectural historians in Britain. Nevertheless I reiterate them here as offering a more balanced account of developments in the nineteenth century, and as an antidote to the more popular view that the Gothic Revival swept all before it and transformed the nature of religious worship almost overnight.

Just as the 'Gothic Revival' had its origins and its core in the British Isles, so the misconceptions about its success and its development have been perpetrated by several generations of British architectural historians since the first major study of the topic by the late Lord Clark in 1928. Since then the received orthodoxy has been that by 1840 Gothic was seen to be the only acceptable style of religious architecture in Britain and Ireland, that most denominations leapt on to this bandwagon, and that British and Irish church interiors were transformed within a matter of one or two decades from functional buildings into ones in which the symbolism of the Middle Ages was offered afresh to a new and enthusiastic generation of clergy and laity. Much British and Irish architectural history, and to a lesser extent a good deal of that in Europe as well, has been written from the standpoint that this interpretation of the nineteenth century still holds good and that architectural history can be seen as a series of, fairly closely defined, periods in which one style was dominant. The difficulty with the prevailing interpretation of the 'Gothic Revival' is that it is simply not borne out by the evidence. The fact that this particular model for the design of church buildings should have been promoted by contemporary writers, whether it was Pugin in Britain and Ireland, or Viollet-le-Duc in France, or Stieglitz in Germany, does not mean to say that it was adopted either speedily or universally. Both clergy and laity in the nineteenth century, as at most periods in history, tended to be conservative, and preferred more traditional forms of church architecture and liturgical arrangement. The evidence from contemporary documentation – plans, photographs, minutes, correspondence – shows this only too clearly. The 'ecclesiological revolution' of the nineteenth century was one that moved at a much slower pace than has been recognised. It is true that by the end of the nineteenth century there was a general acceptance by both Catholics and Protestants across Europe that Gothic was the preferred style for church architecture, and even a good deal of consensus about the way in which churches should be arranged liturgically, but this situation had not been achieved without a good deal of vigorous debate within the churches. This needs to be recognised and unfortunately too many architectural historians have failed to do so.

The Origins of the Gothic Revival

This is a topic on which there is now a substantial literature.[1] In England an early supporter of the Gothic Revival was Dr John Milner (1752-1826), Roman Catholic parish priest of Winchester and later Vicar-Apostolic of the Midland District. Milner had built a new church at Winchester in the Gothic style in 1792 and, six years later, published his *History, Civil and Ecclesiastical, and a Survey of the Antiquities of Winchester*, the second volume of which appeared in 1801. In 1809 the researches of a young Cambridge scholar, G.D. Whittington, were published posthumously as *An Historical Survey of the Ecclesiastical Antiquities of France with a View to Illustrate the Rise and Progress of Gothic Architecture in Europe*. Even more influential was the publication in 1817 by a practising architect, Thomas Rickman, of *Attempts to Discriminate the Styles of English Architecture, from the Conquest to Reformation*. It was Rickman who pioneered the popular use of the terms 'Norman', 'Early English', 'Decorated' and 'Perpendicular' to refer to the principal styles of church architecture in this period. There followed, through the 1820s and 1830s, a spate of books on Gothic architecture culminating in the work of A.W.N. Pugin, a controversial theorist and a practising architect. Pugin (1812-52) regarded Gothic as the only style fit for the building of churches, or indeed any buildings. His defence of Gothic and his detestation of 'modern' architecture was dramatically advocated, with accompanying illustrations, in *Contrasts: or a Parallel Between the Noble Edifices of the Fourteenth and Fifteenth Centuries, and Similar Buildings of the Present Day*, published in 1836. This was followed by a number of other publications in similar vein: *The True Principles of Pointed or Christian Architecture* (1841), *The Present State of Ecclesiastical Architecture in England* (1843) and *An Apology for the Revival of Christian Architecture* (1843). Although Pugin had left the Church of England to become a Roman Catholic, well before the flood of Tractarian converts in the 1840s, his influence was certainly greater, at least initially, on the church that he had left than the one that he had joined.

By the first quarter of the nineteenth century a similar interest in Gothic architecture was being pursued in France. Auguste le Prévost translated Whittington's study of

---

1   See especially Ian Ousby, *The Englishman's England*, Cambridge 1990, pp 92-129; Rosemary Sweet, *Antiquaries: The Discovery of the Past in Eighteenth-Century Britain*, London 2004, pp 231-76; and David Watkin, *The Rise of Architectural History*, London 1980, pp 1-33, 49-93.

French Gothic architecture, noted above, into French and in 1823 was one of the co-founders of the Société des Antiquaires de Normandie. In 1833 the government of Louis-Philippe appointed Prosper Merimée as the first Inspecteur Général des Monuments Historiques and it was he who was to offer the first important commission to the young French architect and Gothicist Eugène-Emmanuel Viollet-le-Duc (1814-79). In 1839 Viollet-le-Duc was commissioned to restore the important basilica at Vézelay; in 1840 he began work on the restoration of the Sainte-Chapelle in Paris, and in 1844 the cathedral of Notre Dame de Paris. Strongly influenced by the work of Pugin in England, he published, in ten volumes between 1854 and 1868, his *Dictionnaire Raisonné de l'Architecture Française du XIe au XVIe Siècle*. In Germany the first study of the nation's medieval architecture was C.L. Stieglitz's *Von Altdeutscher Baukunst*, published in two volumes at Leipzig in 1820. One of the first fruits of this new interest was the project to complete the great Gothic cathedral at Köln (Cologne). Sulpiz Boisserée (1783-1854) and Georg Moller (1784-1852) discovered plans of the cathedral, which had been lost, and used them to complete the unfinished cathedral according to what were thought to have been the original intentions.

Ecclesiology and Ritualism in the Church of England

The new interest in Gothic architecture in England coincided with much questioning by some radical high churchmen in the Church of England of the state of the church in the early nineteenth century. From 1833 a series of *Tracts for the Times* was published at Oxford and in 1839 two Cambridge undergraduates, John Mason Neale and Benjamin Webb, founded the Cambridge Camden Society. The revival of Gothic architecture was not new in England in the 1830s. Large numbers of churches had been built in a sort of romantic Gothic style, frequently termed 'Gothick', since the last quarter of the eighteenth century, and, as we have already noted, there were significant changes in Anglican liturgical attitudes well before the 1830s, with a new emphasis on the importance of the altar and the breaking-up of the old three- and two-decker pulpits. Ecclesiologists, however, such as those in the Cambridge Camden Society or the Oxford Society for Promoting the Study of Gothic Architecture, founded at about the same time, were highly critical of such churches as making far too many concessions to practical liturgical needs.

> The ecclesiologists carried their theory that medieval churches should be precisely imitated… They also required long chancels, so that the altar was separated from the congregation, and formed the focus of attention. The pulpit was not to be near the altar, which was to lie due east, with a middle aisle forming the chief approach to it. The sittings should be so placed that the people might kneel. Such rules had, for the most part, been long observed… but the ecclesiologists based them on symbolism.[2]

Some were decidedly impractical. What was one to do with the long gap between the altar and the congregation? Pre-Reformation churches had had stalls in their chancels, so these were to be replicated. Since they had been designed for monks,

---

2   M.H. Port, *Six Hundred New Churches*, London 1961, p 123.

or colleges of secular priests, or just those in minor orders who took part in pre-Reformation services, who was to sit in them now? The first answer was children who, since they now sat in full view of the congregation, would behave themselves better in church. It was not long, however, before these stalls began to be occupied by the choir, moved out of the west gallery and now vested in surplices to replicate the vested clergy of the Middle Ages.

In the first four years of its existence the Cambridge Camden Society issued a series of publications designed to promote the building of new churches and the restoration of old ones along ecclesiological lines. In *A Few Words to Church Builders*, published in 1841, it was clearly set out that

> there are two parts, and only two parts, which are absolutely essential to a church – Chancel and Nave. If it have not the latter, it is at best only a chapel; if it have not the former, it is little more than a meeting house... A very magnificent appearance may be given to the Chancel by raising it on a flight of nine or ten steps.[3]

Also advocated were stone altars, altar candlesticks, reredoses, *sedilia*, credence tables, aumbries, rood screens, faldstools and lecterns. Box pews were to be replaced by open benches or chairs, galleries and reading desks to be removed completely. At the same time that the Cambridge Camden Society was advocating a new approach to church buildings, and some architects were following them, some Tractarian clergy were introducing new ceremonial into the services of the Church of England. In addition to vesting choristers in surplices, already noted, other innovations in the late 1830s and early 1840s included the use of embroidered stoles and lighted candles, the introduction of credence tables and litany desks, preaching in a surplice rather than the traditional black gown and turning to the east for certain parts of the service. Tractarian clergy also introduced, even in village churches, daily services of Morning and Evening Prayer and a weekly communion service, frequently early in the morning, and detached from Morning Prayer, so as to encourage fasting beforehand. Other changes were slower in coming but churches regarded as 'ritualist' by the 1860s were generally observing some or all of what were known as the 'Six Points': the celebration of Holy Communion by the priest with his back to the people rather than at the north end of the altar; the lighting of two or more candles on the altar; the mixing of water with wine in the chalice; the use of the traditional pre-Reformation eucharistic vestments (alb, amice, girdle, stole, maniple and chasuble); the use of unleavened (wafer) bread at Holy Communion; and the use of incense during the service.

Although many Anglican high churchmen, though not themselves ritualists, were sympathetic to ritualism (even when they criticised it publicly) the press, the politicians and large sections of the British laity were generally hostile. The publication of liturgical manuals, such as the *Directorium Anglicanum* in 1858, which showed how medieval ceremonial could be introduced into Anglican services (Illustration 6.1), were deeply disturbing. The publication in magazines of illustrations of fully-blown ritualist services, employing all the ceremonial of contemporary Roman Catholic worship (Illustration 6.2), were positively horrifying.

---

3   Christopher Webster (ed), *'Temples Worthy of His Presence': the Early Publications of the Cambridge Camden Society*, Reading 2003, pp 137, 143.

Illustration 6.1   'An Altar Vested', 1858 (Purchas, *Directorium Anglicanum*, plate 7)

From the 1850s measures were taken to control ritualism in the Church of England. Suits were brought against ritualist clergy in the ecclesiastical courts under the terms of the Church Discipline Act of 1840. The vicar of St Paul's, Knightsbridge, Robert Liddell, was taken to court by his own churchwarden, Charles Westerton, in 1854 for the introduction of a stone altar, credence tables, altar crosses and candles, a chancel screen with gates, coloured altar frontals and altar cloths edged with lace. After three hearings in different courts, Liddell won on most points but lost on four: the use of lighted candles, an altar cross, a credence table and coloured frontals. During the 1860s suits were brought against three other clergymen (A.H. Mackonochie of St Alban's, Holborn; R.H.E. Wix of St Michael's Swanmore in Ryde; John Purchas of St James, Brighton, the original editor of the *Directorium Anglicanum*) for various ritual innovations. The cases revealed the inconsistencies in the judgements. The Dean of the Arches, Sir Robert Phillimore, ruled in both 1868 and 1870 against the use of incense, but in 1868 in favour of lighted candles (*Martin v. Mackonochie*) and in 1870 against them (*Sumner v. Wix*) The uncertain state of the law, and the gradual increase in the number of ritualist churches, led to Parliament setting up a Royal Commission on Ritual in 1867, but it failed to agree on any of the major points at issue, its high church members issuing minority reports disagreeing with majority recommendations in favour of making lighted candles, vestments and incense illegal. In 1874 a new Parliament passed, despite strong opposition from several bishops, peers and MPs, the Public Worship Regulation Act, which was designed to make it easier for suits to be taken against clergy thought to be introducing illegal ceremonial.

Illustration 6.2   High Mass at St Augustine's, Haggerston, as illustrated in *The Graphic*, 5 March 1881

Illustration 6.3   The interior of Wilton Church as illustrated in *The Illustrated London News*, 4 August 1849

Although several clergy were prosecuted under the provisions of the Act, and a few went to prison for contempt of court, such prosecutions were quickly abandoned. By the 1880s a popular press, which had vilified Anglican ritualists two decades earlier and generally supported the new legislation, had decided that it was not acceptable to send clergy, who felt that they were obeying their consciences in ritual matters, to prison. From then on any serious attempt to regulate the worship of the Church of England was abandoned, despite protests, sometimes violent, from anti-ritualists. The most extreme high church practices were never widely adopted in Anglican churches, though some of the more modest ones became widespread. By the end of the nineteenth century about 40% of Anglican clergy took the eastward position, with their backs to the people, at Holy Communion, about a quarter had lighted candles on their altars and mixed water with wine in the chalice, but only 10% wore the full eucharistic vestments. During the twentieth century a large number of clergy began to wear vestments but comparatively few adopted the use of incense.

Although in the 1840s there was quite a correlation between ecclesiology and ritualism this quickly ceased to be the case. In 1841-5 the moderate Tractarian Secretary of State for War, the Rt. Hon. Sidney Herbert, paid for an elaborate Italian Romanesque style church at Wilton (Wilts). An illustration of the interior in 1849 (Illustration 6.3) shows a very traditional pre-Tractarian high church arrangement, with pulpit and reading desk placed at the east end of the nave, and a raised sanctuary in which the altar is vested with a velvet altar carpet and cushions, but without either an altar cross or candlesticks. The idea that large numbers of fully ecclesiological and quasi-ritualist Anglican churches were erected in the 1840s and 1850s is simply not borne out by the evidence, either of contemporary plans and illustrations, or of the surviving buildings. The ecclesiological revolution was a very gradual affair, many new church buildings or restorations adopting some, mostly the safer, ecclesiological ideas, and eschewing those that might have been considered to have had overtones of ritualism about them. There were still examples of churches being built in the 1850s and the 1860s in which the ideas of the ecclesiologists had been totally disregarded, and in which even box pews and two- or three-decker pulpits were installed.

The initial impact of the ecclesiologists on Anglican church architecture was both limited and conventional. In 1843-4 the Cambridge Camden Society was almost destroyed by a furore over its involvement in the restoration of Holy Sepulchre, Cambridge, where a stone altar was introduced without the sanction of the, non-resident, incumbent. W.F. Hook, a traditional high churchman sympathetic to Tractarianism, incorporated much that was ecclesiological into his rebuilding of Leeds parish church in 1839-41, with the result that the Camdenian's organ, *The Ecclesiologist*, described it as 'the first great instance of the catholic feeling of a church' in the Church of England. There were two candlesticks on the altar and no reading desk. The officiating clergy sat in stalls in the chancel, along with a surpliced choir, and read the lessons from an eagle lectern and the litany from a faldstool in the middle of the chancel. At Kilndown (Kent), the new church, begun in 1839, had open benches, a rood screen, clergy and choir stalls and an eagle lectern. Yazor (Hereford), built in 1843-51, also had open benches for the laity and stalls for the clergy. One of the finest of the early Tractarian churches, in which an elaborate ritual was maintained from the beginning, was William Butterfield's

All Saint's, Margaret Street, St Marylebone, completed in 1859. Opposition from traditionalists resulted in many churches permitting compromises on ecclesiological principles, even when the buildings were designed in the Gothic style. At Jesmond parish church, in Newcastle upon Tyne, galleries were still built across the aisles as late as 1858-61. Box pews were introduced into two Isle of Man churches, Kirk Arbory and Kirk Christ Rushen, as late as 1885-6. In many churches there was an attempt to combine the traditional reading desk with the new clergy stall, by having a seat for the officiating minister at the west end of the chancel or the east end of the nave with desks facing both west into the nave for reading the lessons, and either north or south towards the pulpit, for reading the prayers. The slow progress of ecclesiology was dramatically illustrated in W.A. Delamotte's drawings, in 1853, of the sixteen Anglican churches in Brighton. Only one, the ritualist St Paul's, built in 1846-8, had a fully ecclesiological interior. Six had pulpits and reading desks placed on either side of the entrance to the sanctuary, the arrangement that had long been favoured by both the Church Building Commission and the Incorporated Church Building Society. Four churches still retained the eighteenth-century arrangement most popular in town churches with pulpit and reading desk directly in front of the altar. Two churches still had two-decker pulpit and reading desks at the east end of the nave, and a third had a three-decker pulpit half-way down the fully-pewed interior. At St Margaret's, built in 1824, the pulpit was placed over the altar and entered from the gallery behind it. At St Stephen's, built as late as 1851, the altar occupied a recess in the middle of one of the long walls, with pulpit and reading desk placed on opposite sides of the recess arch.[4] When F.R. Wilson published his *Architectural Survey of the Churches in the Archdeaconry of Lindisfarne* in 1870, and reproduced plans of all their interiors, he found that, of the 75 churches in the archdeaconry, only 43 were new buildings or restorations which were substantially ecclesiological in character, and 32 still had largely non-ecclesiological interiors. In Staffordshire, where there are surviving water-colours of the interiors of all 307 Anglican churches in the county, painted between 1857 and 1860, only seventeen had stalls in the chancel, whereas 160 still had box pews, 133 had two- or three-decker pulpits (of which 43 were placed centrally at the east end of the nave or in front of the altar) and 42 had substantial galleries.[5]

After 1870 the pace of church restoration in England quickened and it is virtually impossible to find either a restoration or a new building which does not observe ecclesiological principles. By this date many of the leading church architects were prepared to break away from the rather rigid principles that the early ecclesiologists had imposed on church design in an effort to achieve 'correctness'. Excellent examples of much less constrained neo-medievalist building will be found in the later work of G.E. Street and J.L. Pearson, or in that of William Burges and G.F. Bodley. The lesser, more local, architects preferred to continue with the Camdenian model, in which space could be as severely constrained as in those churches crammed with

---

4   The original Delamotte drawings are held in Brighton Museum and Art Gallery, but several have been reproduced in A. Dale, *Brighton Churches*, London 1989.

5   S.A. Jeavons, 'Staffordshire Church Interiors during the Years 1857-60', *Transactions of Lichfield Archaeological and Historical Society*, ii (1960-1), pp 7-26, 65-76.

box pews and galleries which the ecclesiologists had so violently condemned. Even Sir George Gilbert Scott's design for the rebuilding of St Mary Abbots, Kensington, in 1872 showed a building in which open benches or stalls were crammed into virtually every part of the building, even though the rules of ecclesiology, in relation to the respective positions of the font, altar and pulpit were strictly applied (Figure 6.1). Gothic, even if in a fairly free form, was, however, the only style that most church architects were prepared to consider building in for the best part of a century after the 1830s. Neo-Norman had a brief vogue in the 1840s. A brave architect might occasionally attempt 'neo-Perp' or 'Tudoresque', but it was 'neo-Dec' that reigned supreme after 1850. Whilst architects of 'Arts and Crafts' or 'Art Nouveau' churches, such as those at Brockhampton-by-Ross (Hereford) of 1901-2, Kempley (Glos) of 1903, Great Warley (Essex) of 1904 or Roker (Sunderland) of 1906-7, might provide a variant on traditional Gothic design, their liturgical arrangements preserved those that had been pioneered by the ecclesiologists. Indeed from the 1890s a new phase of neo-medievalism, with screens, hanging pyxes for the reservation of the Blessed Sacrament and 'English altars' with curtains and riddle posts, was introduced by architects such as Sir Ninian Comper. Churches such as Holy Redeemer, Clerkenwell, built in 1887-8 without choir stalls, and St Aidan's, Leeds, built in 1891-4 in an Italian Romanesque style, though still with choir stalls in a raised chancel, screened from the congregation by a mosaic *cancelli*, were very much the exception.

Figure 6.1   Seating plan of St Mary Abbotts, Kensington, 1872

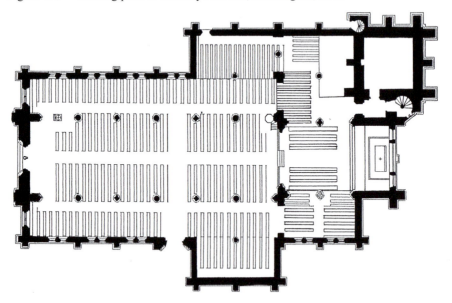

The ecclesiological and ritualist innovations, which transformed the Church of England, albeit gradually, in the second half of the nineteenth century, were exported to other parts of the Anglican Communion. They had a substantial impact in Scotland, rather less of one in Wales and hardly any in Ireland. In Scotland there were early

Tractarian churches, both wholly ecclesiological in their design, at Jedburgh (1841-3) and Dalkeith (1843-7). The first Tractarian and ecclesiological church in Edinburgh was St Columba's, completed in 1848. Another early Tractarian venture was the collegiate church on the Isle of Cumbrae, designed by William Butterfield, which became the cathedral for the diocese of Argyll and the Isles in 1876. The appointment of three Anglican ritualists as the first canons of the new cathedral for the diocese of St Andrews, Dunkeld and Dunblane at Perth in 1850 led to severe tensions within the diocese. Despite this conflict virtually every Scottish Episcopal church in Scotland from the 1850s onwards was built in a manner favoured by the ecclesiologists, and by the end of the nineteenth century Scotland was widely, and correctly, seen as the part of the British Isles in which the agenda of the Anglican ritualists was most enthusiastically adopted. In Wales by contrast there were very few ritualist churches before the last quarter of the nineteenth century and even ecclesiological ideas made relatively slow progress in the principality in the 1850s and 1860s.[6] In Ireland the growth of Evangelicalism in the Church of Ireland resulted in strong lay opposition to anything that smacked of 'popery'. Bishop Mant of Down, Connor and Dromore was strongly criticised for his perceived sympathy for both Tractarianism and ecclesiology. No fully ecclesiological churches were built for the Church of Ireland before the 1860s, and even then they were few in number. By that date there were three churches in Dublin in which Tractarian liturgical innovations had been made, but any advance on this was outlawed by the new Irish Canons of the late 1870s. They forbade the use of vestments, lighted candles, altar crosses, wafer bread or incense; the carrying of crosses or banners in processions; taking the eastward position at Holy Communion; and even the traditional Anglican high church practice of bowing to the altar.

Roman Catholic Ecclesiology and Ritual

By contrast with the Church of Ireland, the Irish Roman Catholic Church was much more willing to jump on the ecclesiological bandwagon. The principal Roman Catholic enthusiast for ecclesiology, A.W.N. Pugin, designed cathedrals at Enniscorthy and Killarney, as well as parish churches in the south-east of Ireland at Bree (1837-9), Gorey (1839-42), Tagoat (1841-6) and Barntown (1844-8), and the chapel of St Peter's College, Wexford. Pugin's initiative and style were imitated by a group of Irish ecclesiological architects, chief among whom was J.J. McCarthy, responsible for many of the later Roman Catholic cathedrals in Ireland. Before the 1840s Roman Catholic church design throughout the British Isles included buildings in both the classical and Gothic styles, those in the latter being in the sort of 'Gothick' much despised by the ecclesiologists. Pugin's earliest English Roman Catholic church, in his own 'correct' version of Gothic, was St Marie's, Derby, in 1838-9, slightly later than his earliest work in Ireland. It was followed by his Roman Catholic churches at Macclesfield (1839-41), Cheadle (1840-6) and Ramsgate (1845-51), and the

---

6   See W.N. Yates, 'The Progress of Ecclesiology and Ritualism in Wales', *Archaelogia Cambrensis*, cxlix (2000), pp 59-88.

future cathedrals at Birmingham and Nottingham. After Pugin most Roman Catholic churches in England and Wales were also in the Gothic style, though towards the end of the nineteenth century a number of non-Gothic buildings were built for Roman Catholic worship, such as the Baroque Oratory of St Philip Neri and the Immaculate Heart of Mary at Brompton, begun in 1878, and the Byzantine style cathedral at Westminster, begun in 1894.

Roman Catholic worship throughout the British Isles, which had generally eschewed the lavishness of its counterpart in mainland Europe, either through caution or poverty, began to change from the 1830s. However, there was, as there was among Anglican ritualists in the late nineteenth and early twentieth centuries, a debate over whether the new ceremonial should be medievalist or mainstream European Catholic in character. Pugin naturally favoured the medievalist approach. He was reported to have asked one priest whom he had spotted wearing a pre-Revolution French cope, 'What is the use, my dear sir, of praying for the conversion of England in that cope?'[7] He strongly supported the revival of plainchant, as did many Anglican ecclesiologists. He was as enthusiastic for rood screens as they were, even though they separated the clergy from the congregation. The Anglican convert to Roman Catholicism, Ambrose Phillips de Lisle, introduced a surpliced choir into his private chapel at Grace Dieu. However, many of the Roman Catholic clergy were hostile to the Gothic revival influencing either the liturgy or the ceremonial attached to it. They preferred Baroque church music, continental cassocks and birettas, even the rather hurried and careless manner in which the mass was celebrated in many parts of Catholic Europe. After the restoration of the Roman Catholic hierarchy in 1850, Cardinal Wiseman, despite his interest in attracting Tractarian converts from Anglicanism, made strenuous efforts to promote Roman-style devotions into parishes which had previously not had them. Under one of these Tractarian converts, Frederick William Faber, the London Oratory became a centre for Roman-style Catholic worship. The disputes over whether English Roman Catholic priests should wear Gothic or Baroque vestments were referred to Rome for a decision in 1839-40. The Vicars Apostolic sent in drawings of the two different vestment designs and it was ruled that Gothic vestments, not then used in other parts of Europe, should not be used in England and Wales. The Gothicists were, of course, horrified. Ambrose Phillips de Lisle described 'the censure as a death-blow to the Catholic cause in England... all the rights and privileges of the National Church are to be stamped out forever'.[8] One Roman Catholic bishop who stood apart from most of his colleagues was the Benedictine Bishop Brown of Newport and Menevia. In 1859 he established a monastic pro-cathedral for his diocese at Belmont, near Hereford, on land and with financial resources provided by the Tractarian convert F.R. Wegg-Prosser, and it was agreed that 'no music but Gregorian chant may be used at Solemn Mass or in the solemn liturgical service in the church'.[9] Elsewhere in the British Isles,

---

7   J.D. Holmes, *More Roman than Rome: English Catholicism in the Nineteenth Century*, London 1978, p 69.

8   E.R. Norman, *The English Catholic Church in the Nineteenth Century*, Oxford 1984, p 237.

9   Dom Basil Whelan, *The History of Belmont Abbey*, London 1959, p 18.

including Ireland under the fanatical pro-Roman leadership of Cardinal Cullen, the Roman Catholic Church may have built Gothic buildings, but they certainly did not, as some of their Anglican ritualist counterparts did, use them as the settings for Gothic ceremonial.

Ecclesiology and Ritual in Protestant Nonconformity and the Church of Scotland

As might have been expected, the Oxford Movement, and the ecclesiology and ritualism that flowed from it, tended to enlarge the gulf between Anglicanism and the other Protestant churches in the British Isles, but it would be a mistake to assume that it made no impact on them. Indeed at a very early stage one very small Protestant church in England was deeply influenced by the neo-medievalist movement. The Catholic Apostolic (or Irvingite) church had its origins in the preaching of Edward Irving (1792-1834), a Scottish presbyterian minister, at the Caledonian Church in London. The church was millenarian in its beliefs and ordained twelve 'apostles', some at least of whom were expected to witness the Second Coming of Christ, but in fact the last 'apostle' died in 1902. One of these 'apostles', Henry Drummond, a London banker, built an ecclesiological church on his country estate at Albury (Surrey) at which the church's new liturgy, based on a mixture of Anglican, Eastern Orthodox and Roman Catholic sources, was first used in 1842. This liturgy prescribed the use of traditional pre-Reformation eucharistic vestments and incense; oil lamps were substituted for candles and the Blessed Sacrament was reserved in a tabernacle, as in Roman Catholic churches. In the 1850s the ritual in use in Catholic Apostolic churches was considerably in advance of that in even the most ritualist of Anglican churches. No Anglican church reserved the Blessed Sacrament until the 1880s, and even then the use of a tabernacle, as opposed to an aumbry, was exceptionally rare. Catholic Apostolic churches had, like Tractarian ones, daily services of Morning and Evening Prayer. On Sundays there was a choral celebration of the Holy Eucharist in the morning, with a shorter service in the afternoon at which communion was given from the reserved sacrament to those unable to be present that morning.

Although no other Protestant nonconformist churches were to adopt such elaborate rituals, the adoption of the Gothic style in church buildings was certainly not unknown. Three early examples were the Unitarian churches at Dunkinfield, Gee Cross and Leeds. The first of these, though partly refurnished, retains its original pulpit, suspended over the communion table, as in some Lutheran churches, and entered from the organ gallery behind. Here no attempt was made to alter the centrality of the pulpit, which had always been a feature of the non-Anglican Protestant churches in the British Isles, but the two later examples, both of 1848, certainly did so. At both the Hyde chapel in Gee Cross and the Mill Hill Chapel in Leeds, the building style was indistinguishable from that of Anglican or Roman Catholic churches built by ecclesiologically-minded architects. They had separate chancels, with the communion table at the far end, choir stalls and the pulpit placed at one side of the chancel arch. Even if other Protestant nonconformists in England and Wales did not immediately adopt the Gothic style, they did make important liturgical changes to their buildings which, like many pre-ecclesiological Anglican ones, had been crammed with box pews focusing on a tall pulpit. There were two schools of thought: the minority one which adopted ecclesiological ideas as fully as was consistent with their liturgical needs; and the majority one which created a new, but essentially Protestant, type of liturgical model. This was the pulpit-platform arrangement. It dispensed with the box pews, the long communion tables and the small pulpits. New sets of benches, often but not always with doors, replaced the box pews, and the galleries were generally retained, but the short wall opposite the entrance was made the focus of the building. A platform was provided against the wall, at the back of which was a lower but much larger pulpit, suitable for walking around in and preaching the more emotional extempore sermons that were popular in many nonconformist churches. In front of the pulpit was the communion table and, either behind or to each side of it, seats for the minister and the deacons or elders. Generally behind the pulpit was a gallery for the organ and choir. It was an arrangement not that dissimilar to the one pioneered at the Dukinfield Unitarian Chapel in 1840-5. This type of chapel will be found all across England and Wales, though some have been modified in recent years for new forms of worship. They could be, and were, built in either a classical style, such as the Congregationalist chapel of 1858-9 at Saltaire (Yorks), or a Gothic one, such as the King's Weigh House Chapel of 1889-91 in Mayfair.

Nonconformist chapels built, not just in the Gothic style, but with a quasi-Anglican ecclesiological arrangement, were not unknown, except in Wales where the pulpit-platform arrangement was almost universally adopted. Good examples of later-nineteenth- and early-twentieth-century buildings in this fully ecclesiological style included the Unitarian Church of 1869 at Todmorden,[10] the Immanuel Congregational Church at Southbourne (Hants) and the Albion Congregational Church at Ashton-under-Lyne (Lancs).[11] At Otley (Yorks) the Congregational chapel of 1825 was replaced by a new church in 1899. The old chapel was a classical building with an elliptical galleried interior, a central block of pews and a pulpit in front of the organ gallery. The new church, a handsome Gothic structure with a spire, had a quasi-Anglican interior, with a stalled chancel and stained glass in the window behind the communion table.[11] By the last quarter of the nineteenth century ecclesiological influences on nonconformist architecture were being matched by high church influences in liturgical matters. As early as the 1850s chanting was introduced at the Union Chapel in Islington. Cheetham Hill Congregational Church in Manchester had in 1869 adopted *A Form of Morning and Evening Service* based on the Anglican *Book of Common Prayer*. The Wesleyan Methodist Chapel at Blackheath had Tallis's responses and chanted canticles in 1885. At Trinity Congregational Church in Glasgow, the high church minister, John Hunter, had introduced observance of the major festivals and daily services in Holy Week by 1890. One of the most remarkable of these 'ritualist' nonconformist churches was the Thomas Coats Memorial Baptist Church at Paisley, opened in 1894 (Illustration 6.4). The church was paid for by the Coats family in memory of the Paisley sewing-

---

10   Graham Hague, *The Unitarian Heritage*, Sheffield 1986, p 93.

11   M.S. Briggs, *Puritan Architecture and Its Future*, London 1946, Plates VII and VIII.

Illustration 6.4   The interior of the Coats Memorial Baptist Church in Paisley, opened in 1894

thread manufacturer. It was designed by Hippolyte Blanc with a pulpit of marble and alabaster, an extravagant brass lectern, pews with kneeling boards and stalls for a surpliced choir. Its only concession to the Baptist liturgical tradition was the total immersion font, in veined marble with a brass rail, placed in front of an elaborately carved communion table.

The pattern of architectural and liturgical development in the Church of Scotland in the late nineteenth and early twentieth centuries was not dissimilar from that of the English and Welsh nonconformists, or indeed of the Baptists and Congregationalists in Scotland, as noted above. By the end of the nineteenth century Gothic had become the preferred style of church building but some churches had adopted the pulpit-platform arrangement and others the quasi-Anglican model with a proper chancel. Good examples of the former were Barclay Church in Edinburgh and the West Church in Alloa, whereas the latter arrangement was adopted at the Colinton and Reid Memorial Churches in Edinburgh.[12] In some respects the Church of Scotland was a pioneer in liturgical revolution. It appears, though further research needs to be done on this point, to have been the first of the European Protestant churches to have abandoned the use of box pews for open benches, though largely, one suspects, on grounds of economy rather than liturgical philosophy. In 1824, St John's, Glasgow, became the first established church in Scotland to abandon the traditional practice of receiving communion at long tables in favour of distributing the elements to people seated in their pews, which were draped with linen houseling cloths for the purpose. Although this new practice was condemned by the General Assembly of the Church of Scotland, which believed that the traditional practice of receiving at tables should be retained, it quickly gained ground since it had the practical advantage of reducing the length of the communion service by several hours. From the middle years of the nineteenth century some churches, such as Greyfriars in Edinburgh, began installing organs and stained glass windows. By the 1890s several churches had also introduced surpliced choirs. The Church Service Society, founded in 1865, and the Scottish Church Society, founded in 1892, were established by high church Presbyterian ministers to explore ways of returning to set forms of worship and abandoning the extempore forms which had been adopted in the Church of Scotland since the late seventeenth century. One of the major innovators was James Cooper (1846-1922), successively minister at Broughty Ferry and St Nicholas East, Aberdeen, before his appointment to the professorship of ecclesiastical history at Glasgow in 1898. At Broughty Ferry he introduced Christmas services in 1874 and Holy Week services in 1878; he also presented the church with a brass lectern and a set of communion vessels in the Gothic style. At Aberdeen he introduced daily services in 1881, used an intoned liturgy at special services for children and led the prayers kneeling at a desk that faced the east end of the church, with his back to the congregation. At Coatdyke in 1906 another high church minister, Cromarty Smith, introduced a weekly communion service at an early hour, deliberately imitating the practice of some Tractarians sixty years earlier.

High church ministers in Scotland were controversial. Like ritualists in the Church of England or the Scottish Episcopal Church, their innovations were frequently construed as 'popery' by a Protestant laity, or even fellow clergy. John

---

12   Drummond, *loc. cit.*

Macleod of Duns and Govan, John Charleson of Thornliebank and T.N. Adamson of Barnhill were subjected to opposition at the level of either the kirk session or the presbytery. At Duns there were complaints against Macleod's introduction of the organ, weekday services, the observance of festivals and monthly communion. At Govan he had more support and complaints against him were rejected by both the kirk session and the presbytery. Once again he introduced monthly communion, an organ, kneeling and Holy Week services. He also rebuilt the parish church. The new church, opened in 1888, had a separate chancel with a communion table at the far end, the pulpit to one side of the chancel arch, a prayer desk for the minister and a side chapel for daily services. By 1893 Holy Communion was celebrated seventeen times a year. The *Te Deum* was sung at the morning service on non-communion Sundays. At the communion service the *Gloria*, Creed, *Sanctus* and *Agnus Dei* were sung, and on Sunday evenings the *Magnificat* and *Nunc Dimittis*. At Thornliebank complaints were made against the minister from 1890, John Charleson, that he had introduced a service book with congregational responses, encaustic tiles and stained glass in the chancel and the erection of a communion table with a tabernacle. Even the Scottish Church Society, which assumed that the tabernacle must be for the reservation of the sacrament, thought this was a step too far. In 1901 Charleson resigned the charge to become a Roman Catholic. The Barnhill case was even more celebrated. Here the minister, T.N. Adamson, had introduced an 'altar' with a cross and candlesticks, had celebrated the Holy Communion with his back to the people and had communicated the congregation kneeling around the altar. He also mixed water with wine in the chalice, elevated the elements after consecration and used a communion rite based on the English Prayer Book of 1549. All these practices were ruled to be unacceptable by the presbytery in 1905. Although few Church of Scotland churches ever became as ritualistic as Barnhill, the more modest innovations that had been made by John Macleod at Duns and Govan were emulated by other ministers, such as G.W. Spott at North Berwick and H.J. Wotherspoon at St Oswald's, Edinburgh.

Even more popular than ritualist innovations was the building of ecclesiological churches. After the pioneering example of John Macleod at Govan, advanced ecclesiological churches were built at Crathie (Aberdeenshire), opened in 1893, and St Cuthbert's, Edinburgh, rebuilt in 1894, with a marble communion table in a chancel decorated with marble and mosaic. Crathie was designed with an apsidal chancel raised four steps above the level of the nave, a stone pulpit and a brass lectern; in 1913 the original oak communion table was replaced by one of marble. A good example of the ecclesiological restoration and reordering of an existing church was that undertaken at Holy Trinity, St Andrews, in 1907-9 under the direction of P.M. Chalmers. Before this date the interior of this church had been very similar to that which still exists at St Nicholas West, Aberdeen. There was a gallery around four sides of the aisled interior with a canopied pulpit placed in the middle of one of the long sides. After its restoration the church had a stalled chancel and a pulpit placed to one side of the entrance to the chancel, separated from the nave by a new open-work screen.[13] Chalmers was responsible for the design of many other ecclesiological, and some Celtic revival, churches throughout Scotland and had the sort of influence on

---

13   *Ibid.*, Plate II.

Scottish Presbyterian church architecture that A.W.N. Pugin had had on Anglican and Roman Catholic church architecture sixty years earlier. The ultimate expression of ecclesiology in the Church of Scotland was St Conan's, Loch Awe. Here, in the remoteness of North Argyll, Walter Douglas Campbell, younger brother of the first Lord Blythswood, had built a small church in 1881-6. Between 1907 and 1930 it was extended and refurbished. At the west end is a cloister garden and small chapel dedicated to St Brigid and St Conval. The apsidal chancel has canopied choir stalls and the font is in the form of an angel bearing a Breton fishing boat. The whole interior is reminiscent of those erected by high church Anglican ecclesiologists in the 1840s and 1850s.

European Gothic, Catholic and Protestant

Although the British Isles remained the epicentre of the Gothic revival throughout the nineteenth century, and indeed well into the twentieth century, Gothic churches were built throughout Europe, Catholic and Protestant, from the 1830s. In Belgium, where the revival had a substantial impact on Roman Catholic architecture, a total of 174 neo-Gothic churches were built between the 1830s and 1930s, peaking between 1850 and 1880, but with a second wave of new buildings in the first decade of the twentieth century, including the especially handsome church of St Peter and St Paul at Ostend, designed by Louis Delacenserie, and built between 1905 and 1907. Early examples of Gothic revival churches in France were St Nicholas at Nantes and the churches of St Eugene and Ste Clothilde in Paris. The church of St Joseph at Roubaix, built in 1876-8, is a handsome Gothic revival building, though it still had its canopied pulpit placed well down the nave in the traditional eighteenth-century position, rather than at the east end, favoured by the ecclesiologists. However, the high altar was a very correct ecclesiological composition of three carved panels and there was a medievalist painting of the last judgement over the chancel arch. In the Netherlands an early example of Gothic revival architecture was the Roman Catholic church of St Peter and St Paul at Amsterdam, opened in 1848. Although it still had galleries across the side aisles, the tall canopied pulpit was placed, in the correct ecclesiological position, against the south-east pier of the nave. In Belgium and the Netherlands the leading neo-Gothic architects of Roman Catholic churches were Albert Tepe and P.J.H. Cuÿpers. Tepe designed the churches of St Nicholas at Jutphaas in 1874, St Willibrord at Utrecht in 1876 and St Francis Xavier at Amsterdam in 1880. The Utrecht church, which preserves all its original furnishings intact and has not been adapted for modern Roman Catholic worship, exudes the influence of A.W.N. Pugin. The church at Jutphaas has an excellent neo-medieval altarpiece, canopied pulpit and rood beam with supporting figures of Our Lady and St John. It is quasi-Anglican in atmosphere, replicating to a large extent the work of architects such as G.F. Bodley and J.L. Pearson in the British Isles. Cuÿpers was exceptionally prolific. Early works included St Lambert's at Veghel (1853-4) and St Catherine's at Eindhoven (1859-67). In addition to new buildings in Belgium and the Netherlands some existing ones received neo-Gothic makeovers. Our Lady's Cathedral at Antwerp was fitted with neo-Gothic canopied choir stalls, incorporating much statuary, in 1839.

Although Protestants also built Gothic Revival churches they were, on the whole, less confident about doing so than Roman Catholics. In the Netherlands there were a few examples before 1850, such as the Zuiderkerk at Rotterdam, designed by A.W. van Dam in 1845-8, but thereafter, especially following the controversial decision to revive a Roman Catholic hierarchy in the Netherlands in 1853, the Reformed churches there eschewed Gothic which they considered 'popish'. Unlike Reformed churches in the British Isles, they also never adopted the pulpit-platform arrangement, but retained the traditional style of pulpit enclosure throughout the nineteenth century.[14] In Germany there was more support for the Gothic revival among both Protestants and Roman Catholics. Probably the most important individual work was the completion of Cologne cathedral but there were other significant buildings: St Apollonaris at Remagen, designed by E.F. Zwirner in 1839-57; St Nicholas, Hamburg, of c.1870 from designs by the English architect, Sir G.G. Scott; Christ Church, Hanover, designed by K.W. Hase in 1867. The design by G.G. Ungewitter for the Lutheran church at Hundelshausen in 1863-7 was much influenced, like all of Ungewitter's work, by ideas of church design that he had borrowed from another English architect, G.E. Street. F.A.L. Hellner (1791-1862) was an architect whose early work was overwhelmingly in the classical style, mostly adopting the pulpit-altar arrangement internally. However, from the 1840s he was beginning to design in a rather incorrect Gothic. His early 1850s church at Molzen, though it still had galleries, had abandoned the pulpit-altar arrangement for a tall pulpit placed against the side wall at the entrance to an apsidal sanctuary, which had an elaborate Gothic altarpiece. At his slightly later church at Gross Lobke the arrangement was similar though here he even introduced a small prayer desk for an officiating pastor.[15]

Scandinavian Lutherans were less minded to adopt the Gothic style than their German counterparts, though there were strenuous efforts to restore the medieval cathedrals of Denmark, Norway and Sweden to something approaching their pre-Reformation internal arrangement. A good example was the nineteenth-century restoration of Lund Cathedral. Before the restoration began the ground plan shows box pews in the nave with the altar placed in front of the chancel screen. The choir stalls were in the western part of the chancel, which was used for university lectures, returned against the chancel screen. The post-restoration ground plan shows the box pews and chancel screen removed, the latter being replaced by a series of steps. The altar was placed in the middle of the chancel and the choir stalls had been rearranged in the eastern apsidal part of the chancel.[16] Later on further alterations took place whereby the choir stalls were reinstated in their earlier position and with the altar further east (Illustration 6.5). In northern Sweden churches were still being built in the classical style until well into the nineteenth century. A good surviving example is the church of 1849 at Örträsk. By the last two decades of the nineteenth century Gothic had finally taken over, even in wooden buildings such as those at Stensele (1886), Edefors (1888), Jokkmokk (1889) and Robertsfors (1898), though

---

14   C.A. van Swigchem et al, *Een Huis voor Het Woord: Het Protestantse Kerkinterieur in Nederland tot 1900*, The Hague 1984, pp 170-207.

15   Müller (ed), *Hellner*, pp 135-6, 145-7.

16   Otto Rydbeck, *Lunds Domkyrka Byggnadshistoria*, Lund 1923, Plates V and VI.

Illustration 6.5   The interior of the restored Lund Cathedral in 1923 (Rydbeck,
                     Lunds Domkyrka, opposite p 6)

they were far from being ecclesiological internally. The church at Stensele still had galleries across the side aisles and the traditional semi-circular altar rails. No attempt was made to lengthen chancels or install choirs in them. The chancels at Stensele and Robertsfors were shallow apses; that at Edefors was rectangular but still very shallow.[17]

By contrast, and particularly compared with the hostility of Reformed churches in the Netherlands to the Gothic revival, Calvinists in both Switzerland and Hungary were much more prepared to embrace neo-medievalism. St Elizabeth's at Basel was rebuilt in the Gothic style in 1857-64. The church had an apsidal sanctuary with a free-standing communion table. However, some compromises were made. There were galleries across the two aisles with entrances at each end. A canopied stone pulpit was placed on one side of the entrance to the sanctuary but there was another, wooden, pulpit half-way down the nave, and all the seating in the nave was focused on this second pulpit.[18] Gothic revival churches in Hungary were somewhat later than those in Switzerland. The Little Church at Debrecen was rebuilt in the Gothic style in 1886-7 though it was not ecclesiologically arranged. The organ and choir occupied a gallery at one end of the building. At the other there was a shallow chancel, also galleried, and the communion table was placed, in the middle of the seating, at the junction of the chancel and the nave. The canopied pulpit was, however, placed against the outer wall at the same junction, to the side of, but slightly behind, the communion table. The neo-Gothic church at Kaposvár, built in 1906-8, had a similarly unecclesiological interior with an organ gallery in the apsidal chancel and a round communion table placed under it. The canopied pulpit was placed on one side of the communion table but over the seat for the minister, the retention of a traditional Hungarian arrangement, which has already been noted.[19] As in the Netherlands, the popular British arrangement of the pulpit-platform was never adopted in the reformed churches of either Hungary or Switzerland. By the early twentieth century Art Nouveau and neo-Romanesque churches were also making an appearance in both countries. The Art Nouveau Fasor Church in Budapest, built in 1911-13, had a gallery around three sides, and on the fourth side a pulpit approached by a double staircase with the communion table in front and the organ in a gallery behind. The pulpit was, in effect, placed in an internal apse beneath this gallery. The arrangement was almost identical to that in the neo-Romanesque St Paul's Church in Basel, built in 1898-1901. Here the apse was fitted up with a stone pulpit raised up behind a stone communion table. Also in the apse was a gallery, with a central arch behind the pulpit, in which the organ and choir were placed.[20] These two arrangements had much more in common with the pulpit-altar composition of churches in Lutheran Germany than the pulpit-platform arrangement in many British non-Anglican Protestant churches.

---

17   M. Järnfeldt-Carlsson, 'Träkyrkobyggandet i Övre Norrland från 1870-tal till 1920-tal' in Anders Åmen and Marta Järnfeldt-Carlsson (eds), *Övre Norrlands Kyrkor*, Uppsala 1991, pp 147-80.

18   Klaus Speich and H.R. Schläpfer, *Kirchen und Klöster in der Schweiz*, Zurich 1978, pp 326, 336.

19   Dercsényi et al, *Calvinist Churches in Hungary*, pp 14-16, 148-50.

20   *Ibid.*, pp 115-19; Speich and Schläpfer, *Kirchen und Klöster*, p 328.

The Ethos of the Gothic Revival

Although some Protestants undoubtedly saw the Gothic revival and neo-medievalism as something that compromised their liturgical purity, it was, as we have seen, possible to build in Gothic and ignore liturgical attitudes that some of those who built in Gothic regarded as essential. Nevertheless it is not without significance that the most widespread adoption of neo-Gothicism was in those churches that were most willing to accept a degree of pre-Reformation ceremonial: those belonging to Roman Catholics, Anglicans and a few high church Protestants. There was tension within Roman Catholicism between neo-medievalism and the retention of Baroque ceremonial favoured by the Vatican. Though many Roman Catholic churches were built in the Gothic style, few adopted Gothic ceremonial. The most enthusiastic supporters of both Gothic architecture and a liturgy to match that style were Anglican high churchmen. Even in the Anglican outposts in Europe, such as Christ Church, Naples, opened in 1862, buildings were designed in a manner that reflected both the architectural ideals of the ecclesiologists and the liturgical ideals of the more advanced Tractarians. For Anglicans ecclesiology and neo-medievalism, despite the gradual nature of their introduction and expansion, represented the biggest change ever to impact on their communion, far greater one suspects than the liturgical changes of the late twentieth century. For others the changes were less momentous and the Gothic revival was more architectural than it was liturgical. Nevertheless it was a movement that had some impact on virtually all the mainstream churches of Western Europe, whatever their doctrinal dispositions.

Chapter 7

Liturgical Renewal and Church Design in the Twentieth Century

The changes that had taken place in the design and ethos of church buildings since the 1840s across all the nations, and most of the denominations, of Western Europe had so much impact on worshippers that they were still being aggressively defended in the second half of the twentieth century. Much of the writing on liturgical reform or modern church design has come from the pens of those committed to new ideas and, not surprisingly, the opposition to them has not been treated very sympathetically. The truth, of course, is that traditional patterns of worship are difficult to break. The liturgical reformers of the last fifty years have had to confront precisely the same type of opposition that confronted the sixteenth-century reformers, or those that wanted to return to more medieval notions of worship and church design in the nineteenth century. They have, however, had to confront one difficulty that their forbears did not have to face: the very strong conservationist movement in many parts of Europe since the 1960s. Between the 1550s and the 1950s churches were reordered with little thought given to the preservation of the architecture and furnishings of the past. If the existing furnishings did not meet the requirements for worship or the latest architectural ideas they were, quite ruthlessly, destroyed and replaced. By the 1960s many architectural historians and planning authorities were expressing serious concern that the architectural quality of many cities, towns and villages was being compromised by unsuitable new buildings or the loss of existing ones. In recent years the debate over liturgical reordering has not just been one between the reformers and those who want to preserve traditional forms of worship and the furnishings that go with them. Liturgical reformers and their architects have also had to take account of planning and other controls which have restricted the changes that can be made to existing buildings.

These restrictions have not had exactly the same effect across Europe. They vary to some extent according to the planning legislation. In Britain and Ireland there has been a general reluctance to mix modern and traditional. Buildings are expected to be one or the other and legislation that seeks to preserve buildings of importance has usually included elements that prevent alteration to both their external and internal appearance. In fact churches have generally been exempt from the stricter appliance of such rules, but it has been expected that they would exercise their own controls on inappropriate alterations. The Anglican churches have generally done so and, indeed, exercised through the process known as faculty jurisdiction[1] exceptionally

---

1   See *The Continuing Care of Churches and Cathedrals: Report of the Faculty Jurisdiction Commission*, London 1984. This commission was chaired by Bishop Eric Kemp

strict controls over the alteration of church buildings. Some other denominations have been less rigid in maintaining such controls and many furnishings have been unnecessarily destroyed in misguided attempts to make buildings more functional. This was particularly the case in Roman Catholic churches throughout Britain and Ireland in the late 1960s and early 1970s, where the requirements to meet new liturgical directives was not balanced by the establishment of proper advisory bodies. By the time these bodies had been set up the damage had been done. Enthusiastic parish priests, with or without the support of their congregations, had removed screens, altars, pulpits and other furnishings of high architectural quality, whereas in many cases they could have been retained as part of a more enlightened and carefully-considered reordering scheme. In mainland Europe there has been a much greater willingness, in both secular and religious buildings, to mix ancient and modern in a way that can be extremely effective. This has particularly been the case in Scandinavia and there are excellent examples of reordered Swedish Lutheran cathedrals, in which modern furnishings have been incorporated in historic buildings, as at Karlstrad and Växjö, those of the latter being illustrated on the cover of this volume.

The Survival of Traditional Buildings

Throughout much of the twentieth century ideas of modern church design and liturgical arrangement have had to compete with much more traditional views. Although this has been particularly so in Britain and Ireland, mainland Europe has certainly not been free of such competition. Attention can easily be drawn to the Gothic rebuilding of Ieper Cathedral in the 1920s, the neo-Romanesque ossuary chapel of 1927-32 at Douaumont, near Verdun, or the neo-Byzantine basilica of St Theresa at Lisieux, begun in 1929. In the north of Sweden there are interesting churches in a revival of the Swedish national style at Bureå (1917-20) and Skellefteå (1925-7). In Hungary there are important but very traditional churches at Miskolc (1938) and Pápa (1931-41). The former is an *Art Nouveau* wooden building with a long canopied pulpit against the end wall of the chancel and the communion table in front. The latter is a neo-Classical building with a galleried interior. The pulpit is placed over the door to the vestry with seats for the minister and elders on each side of the door. The traditional wooden communion table has an equally traditional velvet cover.[2] At All Saints, Millbrook, in Jersey, an undistinguished church of 1840 was transformed in 1934. The transformation did not relate to the liturgical arrangement, which was wholly traditional, but to the installation of glass furnishings by the contemporary Parisian artist, René Lalique (Illustration 7.1). Between 1935 and 1963, the cathedral at Luxembourg, the former seventeenth-century Jesuit church, was substantially enlarged by the addition of a Gothic sanctuary and transepts, traditional in style yet more contemporary in ethos, with its Art-Deco furnishings and stained glass (Illustration 7.2).

---

of Chichester.

2   Balázs Dercsényi *et al*, *Calvinist Churches in Hungary*, Budapest 1992, pp 78-9, 155-7.

Illustration 7.1   Glass furnishings by René Lalique installed in Millbrook Church, Jersey, in 1934

In Britain and Ireland there was little in the way of modern church design before the 1960s. The Gothic style in England and Wales was maintained by architects such as Sir Charles Nicholson, W.H.R. Blacking and Stephen Dykes-Bower. Their churches attempted to combine, as those of Sir Ninian Comper had pioneered in the 1890s, neo-Medievalism with neo-Classicism or at least neo-Jacobeanism. For Peter Anson they reflected 'the spirit of the Caroline Divines. Both Archbishop Laud and Bishop Andrewes would feel quite at home in them'.[3] A splendid example was the new cathedral at Guildford, begun to a design by Sir Edward Maufe in 1932, but looking decidedly old-fashioned by the time it was completed in 1966. Such traditional stances had not disappeared even by the 1950s. It was not assisted by the view of the War Damage Commission that churches destroyed in the Second World War should only be funded by the commission if they re-used the ground-plan of the destroyed building and attempted, as far as practicable, to recreate the destroyed interior. Although some latitude was permitted in the way in which this guidance could be interpreted, it effectively precluded the much more exciting reconstruction of destroyed churches that had taken place in some other parts of Europe, especially Germany. Good examples of such conservative rebuildings are St Mary's, Swansea (1955-9) and Holy Spirit, Southsea. The latter, reopened in 1958 after a rebuilding supervised by Stephen Dykes-Bower, is the more successful of the two. Whilst it preserves the aisled nave and chancel of the previous building, and other features

---

3   Peter Anson, *Fashions in Church Furnishings*, 2nd edn, London 1965, p 348.

Illustration 7.2   The east end of Luxembourg Cathedral, begun in 1935 and
                     completed in 1963

such as the raised Lady Chapel, it has a much more spacious sanctuary and a far less cluttered interior than its predecessor on the same site. The judicious use of appropriate furnishings and stained glass from other churches, damaged in the war and not subsequently rebuilt, enhances the ethos of the building.

It was not just Gothic forms that were retained in the 1950s. There was also an interesting revival in neo-Classical buildings. Perhaps the most interesting is the church at Bawdeswell, Norfolk, built in 1955. It comprises a broadish nave, apsidal chancel, south porch and balancing north vestry, and unashamedly attempts to replicate, in a modern way, the interior of an Anglican Georgian church. The altar is free-standing in the apse and there is a three-decker pulpit in the north-east part of the nave, with the font placed under a west gallery for the organ and choir. Whilst this is the most complete Georgian revival church in England, neo-Classical buildings with sanctuaries arranged to evoke the ethos of Laudianism were also designed by the Yorkshire architect, Francis Johnson, at Hilston (1956-7) and St Michael's, North Hull (1957-8). Similar neo-Classical and, in the former case neo-Laudian, interiors were created for the Church of Scotland at the Canongate Kirk in Edinburgh (1946-54) and Bellie Kirk at Fochabers (1954). In Ireland the preference was for neo-Celtic, neo-Romanesque or neo-Byzantine. The first of these had been pioneered at Kilcar, Co. Donegal (1903-4) and Newport, Co. Mayo (1909-18), but was repeated by Ralph Byrne at St Patrick's, Donegal, in 1931-5. Byrne also designed the neo-Classical cathedral at Mullingar in 1933-9 and there are later neo-Classical cathedrals at Cavan (1939-42) and Galway (1957-65). The church at Gortahork, Co. Donegal, is another late example of a neo-Classical building, designed by W.J. Doherty in 1950-3. Neo-Byzantine Roman Catholic churches were designed in many parts of the British Isles, following the pioneering example of Westminster Cathedral, between 1920 and 1960. There is a good Irish example at Westport, Co. Mayo, of 1930-2.

Liturgical Renewal in the Inter-War Period

Although the most active period of liturgical reform in the churches of Western Europe was that inaugurated by the Second Vatican Council of 1962-5, it should not be thought that the earlier years of the century were ones of liturgical complacency. It was for example a period of considerable, though often frustrated, activity in the Anglican churches. All these churches, in or outside Europe, entered the century in a very difficult liturgical position. The Tractarians, ecclesiologists and ritualists had transformed the way in which Anglican services were conducted and the manner in which Anglican church buildings were ordered, yet these changes had no official sanction. All Anglican churches had an official liturgy which, apart from a few minor modifications in Scotland and America, was the *Book of Common Prayer* as authorised in 1662. In practice very few, if any, clergy used this liturgy exactly as composed. Most left bits out or added bits in. Anglican high churchmen had, from the 1890s, interpolated, initially silently, and latterly audibly, sections of the Roman Catholic Mass. The unsatisfactory nature of these compromises, and the lack of authority for them, had been recognised by the Royal Commission on Ecclesiastical Discipline in 1906, and it was as a result of that Commission's recommendations that 'letters of business' were issued which authorised the bishops of the Church of England to set up appropriate mechanisms to consider a reform of the prayer book. A number of committees were established but little was achieved before 1920. Thereafter progress was more rapid and three suggestions for reform were put forward by independent pressure groups. *The Green Book* (1922) was produced by the English Church Union and proposed a reform that would have brought Anglican services much closer to Roman Catholic practice. *The Grey Book* (1923) was produced by a group of broad churchmen with the support of Bishop Temple of Manchester, and was described by Canon Cuming as 'a remarkable combination of sound liturgical craftsmanship, modernist theology, and high-flown liberal sentiment'.[4] *The Orange Book* (1924), compiled largely by the leading contemporary liturgist, Bishop Frere of Truro, a moderate Anglo-Catholic, attempted to blend the best characteristics of the Green and Grey Books. What is noticeable about these three drafts is that none of them were promoted by Evangelicals. Evangelicals were happy with the 1662 *Book of Common Prayer* and were fearful that any revision would make concessions to Anglo-Catholics. It was Evangelical opposition to liturgical reform, and the fact that the reformers were divided over what sort of reform they wanted, that eventually frustrated these attempts at prayer book revision, finalised in 1927-8.

In fact, although Evangelical propaganda was eventually successful in preventing the necessary parliamentary approval for liturgical reform, the Church of England's National Assembly did adopt the final draft of the revised prayer book, by a significant majority, 517 votes for to 133 against. It was approved by the House of Lords by 214 votes to 88, but was defeated in the House of Commons by 238 votes to 205. This majority was only achieved by the votes of Scottish and Welsh members, mostly non-Anglicans, but Protestants for whom the anti-Romanist lobbying of Anglican Evangelicals had proved sufficiently persuasive. The bishops thought that if they made some concessions to the Evangelicals they might get the revised prayer book adopted. These concessions, which included watering down the earlier provisions for reservation of the Blessed Sacrament, simply resulted in fewer Anglo-Catholics, including Bishop Frere, supporting the modified version, without gaining any support from Evangelicals. It now passed the Assembly by 396 votes to 153, with many former supporters abstaining. The House of Commons also maintained its opposition to prayer book revision, by a slightly higher margin, 266 votes to 220. The bishops decided that it was impossible to proceed with revision officially but agreed that they would not take action against clergy who used the provisions of the rejected revision, even though they were technically as illegal as the much more advanced irregularities of the extreme Anglo-Catholics. Although Anglicans in England, and in Wales, where the Anglican Church had been disestablished in 1920, continued to have only the 1662 *Book of Common Prayer* as their official liturgy, this was not the case in either Ireland or Scotland. The Church of Ireland made some minor changes to its official liturgy in 1926 and a more comprehensive revision was undertaken by the Scottish Episcopal Church in 1929.

---

4   G.J. Cuming, *A History of Anglican Liturgy*, 2nd edn, Basingstoke 1982, p 169.

The failure to revise the prayer book in 1927-8 meant that liturgical revision was off the official agenda of the Church of England for more than three decades. It did not, however, mean that liturgical revision was off the unofficial agenda, and the 1930s and 1940s produced a considerable flowering of Anglican thought on liturgical matters, much of it designed to make the eucharist the central act of Anglican worship. Prior to that date Anglican churches generally followed one of three different types of service provision on Sundays. In Anglo-Catholic churches there would usually be one or more said celebrations of Holy Communion early in the morning attended by those who wished to communicate, who would normally do so having fasted from the previous midnight. The main Sunday morning service would be a sung celebration of Holy Communion at which only those who were medically unable to receive fasting would be permitted to communicate; those who had communicated earlier would not do so at this service though they would still attend. In 'middle-of-the-road' Anglican churches there would be an early morning said celebration of Holy Communion. The main Sunday service would normally be Morning Prayer but this was often replaced by a sung celebration of Holy Communion once a month. Evangelical Anglicans would never have a sung celebration of Holy Communion. In some churches it was still celebrated only twice a month, once after Morning and once after Evening Prayer. In others there would be a weekly said celebration either early in the morning or after one of the main services. The intention of those that launched what eventually became known as the Parish Communion Movement was that all the different Sunday morning services should be replaced by a single service of Holy Communion, but that it should be conducted according to the ceremonial and ritual with which that congregation was already familiar: a Solemn High Mass with deacon and subdeacon, but with everybody communicating, in Anglo-Catholic churches; a more simple celebration, perhaps incorporating the canticles from Morning Prayer or hymns which could be sung rather than settings of the communion service itself, in Evangelical ones.

The origins of the Parish Communion Movement have been much debated and the scanty nature of the evidence makes it impossible to state where and when the first examples of a genuine Parish Communion, in the later definition of the term referred to above, took place. A Sung Eucharist with general communion followed by a 'congregational breakfast' was introduced at All Saints, North Street, York in 1912 and, at about the same time, similar services were introduced at St James, Milton, Portsmouth and Temple Balsall, near Birmingham. A Parish Communion was introduced at Holy Trinity, Sneyd, Stafford in 1925 and at St John's, Newcastle upon Tyne, in 1927. In their earlier days these Parish Communions did not always replace the earlier and later services but were introduced alongside them in the hope, often realised, that they would gradually disappear. The movement was popularised in 1937 by a volume of essays edited by Father Gabriel Hebert, SSM, on *The Parish Communion*, and containing accounts of its introduction at Temple Balsall and St John's, Newcastle upon Tyne. It was further promoted by the establishment of the Parish and People Movement, and the holding of its first conference, in 1949. The periodical, *Parish and People*, followed in 1950. The conferences and the periodical were used as vehicles for promoting the adoption of Parish Communion services as the core of Anglican worship. By the late 1950s an increasing number of Anglican churches had abandoned their 11am Sung Eucharists or Morning Prayers, and often their 8am Holy Communions as well, for a Parish Communion at 9.30am. That number increased thereafter, greatly assisted by the first experimental eucharistic services officially approved by the Church of England in the 1960s. It was only in the 1980s, with the rise of charismatic Evangelicalism, that some parishes began to abandon the Parish Communion, feeling that it was now too exclusive, and not a focus for mission. The main Sunday morning service was now more likely to be a non-eucharistic family service, often called All Age Worship, with the Holy Communion more likely to be celebrated for the more committed on a Sunday evening.

Some other Protestants also developed interests in liturgical reform in the inter-war period. In 1929 the union of the Church of Scotland with most members of the United Free Church meant that, for the first time in more than eighty years since the Disruption of 1843, when the original Free Church was formed, the vast majority of Scottish Presbyterians belonged to the same church. As part of this Act of Union a committee was set up to consider matters relating to public worship and aids to devotion in the re-united church. The committee included a number of members of the high church Church Service Society. One of these was the distinguished liturgist, W.D. Maxwell, who produced the first edition of his *Outline of Christian Worship* in 1936. Maxwell was the main influence behind a number of liturgical texts produced by the committee, which culminated in the production of a new *Book of Common Order* in 1940. The intention was not that the new book would be mandatory but that it should seek to influence ministers and their kirk sessions in adopting particular forms of worship for their own use. There were orders for morning and evening services, adapted from those used by the Anglicans, and a new eucharistic order with a number of variants. This was not just influenced by Anglican liturgical thinking but was, in many respects, closer to the Roman Catholic or Eastern Orthodox models than any of the revised Anglican prayer books. It began with a psalm or hymn and a call to prayer, followed by a further canticle, psalm or hymn, an Old Testament lesson, another psalm, epistle, gospel, creed, intercessory prayer, another psalm or hymn and the sermon. After the sermon a further psalm or hymn was to be sung during which the elements of the bread and wine were to be 'brought into the church and laid on the Holy Table'. After the minister had unveiled the elements he was to say the consecration prayer which included the *Sanctus* and *Benedictus*, invocation of the Holy Spirit, Lord's Prayer, and words of institution incorporating the fraction and the *Agnus Dei*. The order was slightly unusual but all the essential elements of the eucharistic action and traditional prayers were provided for. The minister and congregation then communicated and the service concluded with a prayer of thanksgiving, another psalm or hymn and the blessing; 'as the elements are being removed from the church, *Nunc dimittis...* may be sung'.[5]

The new *Book of Common Order* had some influence on the English Free Churches. In 1948 four English Congregationalists, John Marsh, Romilly Micklem, John Huxtable and James Todd, published *A Book of Public Worship Compiled for the Use of Congregationalists*. It contained five alternative orders for Sunday worship, four alternative orders for Holy Communion, separate orders for the baptism

5   *The Liturgy in English*, ed. B.J. Wigan, 2nd edn, London 1964, pp 192-200.

of children and believers' baptism and a service for the ordination of ministers. It was supplemented in 1951 by James Todd's *Prayers and Services for Christian Festivals*, and both volumes came to be widely used in Congregational churches. A movement for liturgical reform in the Methodist churches was inaugurated with the establishment of the Methodist Sacramental Fellowship in 1935. Although some Methodists were suspicious of its alleged 'Romanising' tendencies, it was formally cleared of such in an investigation by the Methodist Conference in 1938, and was able to attract such distinguished Methodists as A.E. Whitham, J.E. Rattenbury and Donald Soper, the first Methodist minister to become a life peer, as successive presidents. Initially its membership remained small, 320 in 1939 of which one third were ministers and two thirds members of the laity. Members were required to say a daily office and to receive Holy Communion at least once a month. By the 1950s a small number of Methodist churches with MSF ministers had established a weekly communion service. Other Methodist initiatives of the inter-war period were the revival of the traditional love feasts and covenant services of the early Methodists. The love feast, or *agape*, provided an opportunity for ecumenical activity at a time when open communion was not permitted in the Church of England. At Hilgay in Norfolk the first Anglican-Methodist *agape* took place on Maundy Thursday 1949, the broken bread being distributed by an Anglican churchwarden and a Methodist local preacher.

Perhaps the most remarkable liturgical initiative undertaken from within one of the Reformed churches before the 1960s was that at Taizé in south-east France. Here, not far from the remains of the great Benedictine abbey of Cluny, a Swiss Protestant, Roger Schutz-Marsauche, set up a religious community in 1940. In 1949 the initial brothers took life vows and the community became fully ecumenical, with the inclusion of Roman Catholic members, in 1969. In its early years the community developed a eucharistic liturgy which borrowed quite eclectically, as the Catholic Apostolic church had done a century earlier, from Protestant, Roman Catholic and Eastern Orthodox sources. The basic form is the western High Mass with celebrant, deacon and subdeacon, though all apart from the celebrant are frequently lay persons. The eucharist begins with an introit psalm, confession, *Kyrie eleison* and absolution. *Gloria in excelsis* is sung, except in Advent and Lent, followed by the collect, Old Testament lesson, gradual psalm or hymn, epistle, alleluia and gospel. Then follows a hymn before the sermon and another hymn afterwards, creed and intercessions. The offertory prayer is said silently during the singing of a psalm and is followed by the preface, *Sanctus* and *Benedictus*, a four part eucharistic prayer (*epiclesis*, institution, memorial, invocation), Lord's Prayer, fraction, *Agnus Dei*, kiss of peace and communion. The eucharist ends with the thanksgiving prayer and the blessing. The Taizé rite has been enormously influential in the work of liturgical revision throughout Western Europe since the 1960s. This has not only been in terms of the texts and the psalm and hymn arrangements, widely adapted in both Protestant and Roman Catholic churches, but in the whole ethos of the eucharist and its emphasis on the involvement of the whole worshipping community, clerical and lay, in the liturgical action at the altar.

A move towards liturgical renewal also took place within the Roman Catholic Church. At a conference at Malines in 1909, a Belgian Benedictine monk, Dom

Lambert Beauduin, delivered a paper in which he argued that the Roman Catholic Mass had become divorced from what ought to be the corporate worship of the local community. The cause was taken up by the German abbey of Maria Laach under the leadership of Dom Ildephonsus Herwegen, abbot from 1913 until 1946. In England a notable landmark was Dom Anscar Vonier, the French-born abbot of Buckfast's, *Key to the Doctrine of the Eucharist*, published in 1925. In this, and in *The People of God* (1937), Vonier argued, through a reinterpretation of the doctrine of eucharistic sacrifice, that the eucharist must be a corporate liturgical action involving all those present. Contemporary Roman Catholic practice was very different. The Mass was a service in which the laity were little more than spectators and encouraged to perform their own devotions whilst the priest and servers carried out the liturgical action in the sanctuary. In England most services were low masses, largely inaudible and, in large churches, barely visible, with neither singing nor sermon. The larger churches would have a sung, possibly high, mass on Sundays at 11am, with a sermon. On Sunday evenings there would be a service of devotions in English, usually with a sermon, and Benediction in Latin. At Ampleforth by the 1920s the boys in the school had been permitted to join with the monks in the singing at the services they attended. By that date in Belgium some parishes had introduced a dialogue mass, in which the congregation joined with the servers in making the responses and with the priest in saying the *Gloria*, Creed, *Sanctus*, *Benedictus*, Lord's Prayer and *Agnus Dei*. In 1935 the Congregation of Rites, the Vatican body responsible for overseeing the liturgical practice of the Roman Catholic Church, gave formal approval, and indeed encouragement, for the dialogue mass, but many Roman Catholic bishops, especially those in Britain and Ireland, were at best unenthusiastic and at worst implacably hostile. One exception was the new archbishop of Westminster, Cardinal Hinsley, who, through the influence of the Society of St Gregory, established in 1929 as a pressure group for liturgical reform and the adoption of plainsong as a vehicle for congregational singing, permitted the holding of an annual Mass for Peace in his cathedral in the years 1937-9, at which the whole congregation joined in singing the ordinary of the mass in plainsong.

The Earliest Modern Churches

By the inter-war period there was a recognition in some church circles that the prevailing style for church buildings, Gothic as interpreted by the ecclesiologists, was liturgically impractical. The long naves and chancels, crammed with pews and stalls, were not conducive to a more corporate style of worship and a better design would be achieved by churches with much broader naves and chancels, by the replacement of aisles used for seating with much narrower ones used solely as passageways, and by placing the choir in a west gallery in the nave, rather than in the chancel. An even more radical response to making the liturgy more corporate would be to design churches in a cruciform style, with a central altar placed under the crossing and a Lady Chapel in the chancel.[6] A number of churches that adopted

---

6   Richard Mellor, *Modern Church Design*, London 1948, pp 23-7, 104.

at least some of these principles were beginning to be built by the 1920s and 1930s, though they remained the minority. The Lutheran Stahl Kirche at Essen was built in 1928. It had an apsidal sanctuary and walls comprised almost wholly of windows with coloured glass. The altar was raised eight steps above the level of the nave and the pulpit placed below the altar and set into the altar steps. However, in the roughly contemporary Hoffnungskirche in Pankow the pulpit was placed in the traditional position, raised up behind the altar. At the Swiss Reformed church at Alstetten, designed in 1938 and built in 1942, the sanctuary, raised three steps above the nave, has the pulpit on one side with the font in front of it and the communion table on the other side with a large free-standing cross behind it.[7] In several British nonconformist churches in the 1930s the traditional pulpit-platform was abandoned in favour of a sanctuary in which pulpit and lectern were placed on opposite sides of a central communion table.[8] An early Anglican example of a church that completely rejected the ideas of the ecclesiologists was N.F. Cachemaille-Day's Church of the Epiphany, Gipton, Leeds, of 1938. A central altar was balanced on opposite sides by two ambos serving as lectern and pulpit, with the organ and choir placed in transeptal galleries. The Lady Chapel formed a separate small church, raised sixteen steps behind the main altar.

On the whole it was the Roman Catholics rather than the Protestants who contributed most to radical church plans in the inter-war period. Good examples are Christ the King, Turner's Cross, Cork and the church at Ringenberg. At a time when every other architect in Ireland was designing neo-Celtic, neo-Classical, neo-Romanesque or neo-Byzantine buildings, Barry Byrne, a Chicago-based architect and former pupil of Frank Lloyd Wright, was designing one of the earliest modern churches in Europe for this new parish in a working-class suburb of Cork (Figure 7.1). Although the church, opened in 1927, still had its altar at the east end, and was flanked by two side altars, the seating was angled to face them in four blocks. In England interesting experiments took place at the Church of the First Martyrs in Bradford, a circular building of 1935 in which the pulpit was placed behind a central altar, and at St Peter's, Gorleston-on-Sea, a cruciform building of 1939 in which the congregation was seated on four sides of a central altar. The church at Ringenberg was part of a more widespread movement for the building of radically-designed churches in France, Germany and Switzerland. One of the earliest was Notre Dame du Raincy, designed by Auguste Perret in 1922-3. As at Cork, the main altar was still placed at the east end of a broad nave, but the side altars were placed behind it in separate chapels. In 1927 Karl Moser provided a similar type of building for the parish of St Antony at Basel. In Germany the pioneering architect was Rudolf Schwarz, who designed the churches of Corpus Christi, Aachen (1930), Riehl (1930) and Ringenberg (1935). The first two still have the main altars at the end of the building, even though the church at Riehl was circular. At Ringenberg (Figure 7.2) Schwarz produced what was essentially a T-plan interior in a cruciform building,

---

    7   Albert Christ-Janer and M.M. Foley, *Modern Church Architecture*, New York 1962, pp 132, 225; Drummond, *Church Architecture of Protestantism*, Plates XV and XVI.

    8   Briggs, *Puritan Architecture*, pp 86-8.

Figure 7.1   Seating plan of Christ the King, Turner's Cross, Cork, 1927

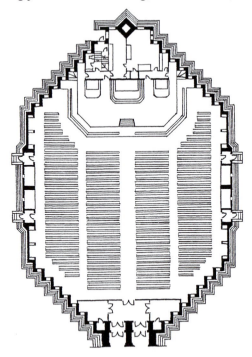

Figure 7.2   Seating plan of new Roman Catholic church at Ringenberg, 1935

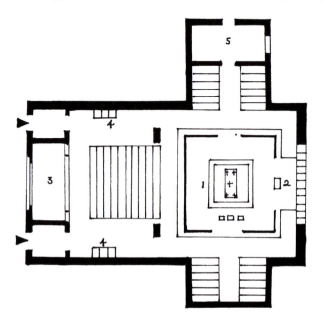

with the altar placed centrally, seating in nave and both transepts and a free-standing tabernacle, thirty years ahead of its time, behind the altar. Fritz Metzger's church of St Charles at Lucerne, consecrated in 1933, has an exceptionally broad nave and an apsidal sanctuary raised well above it, with seating for the clergy and servers against the walls of the apse and a free-standing high altar. There were also two important inter-war churches built for Scandinavian Lutherans: the Högalid Church in Stockholm (1918-23) and Grundtvig's Church in Copenhagen (1921-6). Although both had strikingly modern exteriors, the Copenhagen church designed by P.V. Jensen Klint 'plainly showing the architect's intention to create a cathedral in the style of the Danish village church with late Gothic gables... made to remind [one] of the front of a giant organ',[9] their internal arrangements were wholly traditional.

Liturgical Reform Since 1945

The end of the Second World War did not make an immediate impact on the liturgical reform agenda. Indeed for much of the 1950s little advance was made on the experiments that had begun in the two decades before that war. One event in particular has transformed the liturgical agenda for most of the churches of Western Europe – Anglican, Lutheran, Reformed and Roman Catholic – and that was the Second Vatican Council of 1962-5 and the subsequent reform of the Roman Catholic liturgy. The impact of this event can be seen in the comparison in Figures 7.3 and 7.4 between the modern and traditional Roman Catholic rite, the modern and traditional Anglican rite in England, and, most importantly, that between the two modern rites, one Catholic and the other Protestant. Today it is possible to see remarkably minimal variants on an agreed eucharistic order and text across Europe in churches which had previously had very different eucharistic rites. This is especially so in the case of Anglican, Lutheran and Roman Catholic rites but an increasing number of churches in the Reformed tradition have adopted similar eucharistic rites. Even issues such as vestments and ceremonial, that once provided major liturgical differences between Catholics and Protestants, are becoming increasingly irrelevant. Both Roman Catholic priests and Reformed ministers are prepared to discard their traditional chasubles or Geneva gowns for a cassock-alb and coloured stole.

---

9   Plate caption in *The Danish Church*, ed. Poul Hartling, Copenhagen 1964.

Figure 7.3   Comparison of the eucharistic rites of the Tridentine and modern
                     Roman Catholic missals

Tridentine Missal	Vatican II Missal
Asperges	
Introit/Preparation	Introit/Preparation
Kyrie	Penitential Rite
Gloria	Gloria
	Collect
	First Reading
	Responsorial Psalm
Epistle	Second Reading
Gradual	Alleluia
Gospel	Gospel
Sermon	Sermon
Creed	Creed
	Intercessions
Offertory	Offertory
Orate Fratres	Orate Fratres
Preface	Preface
Sanctus/Benedictus	Sanctus/Benedictus
Canon	Eucharistic Prayer
Lord's Prayer	Lord's Prayer
	Peace
Agnus Dei	Agnus Dei
Confession	
Communion	Communion
Post-Communion	Post-Communion
Dismissal	
Blessing	Blessing
	Dismissal
Last Gospel	

Figure 7.4   Comparison of the eucharistic rites of the *Book of Common Prayer* and *Common Worship*

Book of Common Prayer	Common Worship
Lord's Prayer	
Collect for Purity	Collect for Purity
Ten Commandments	Penitential Rite
	Gloria
Collect for the Day	Collect
Epistle	Readings
	Psalm or Hymn
Gospel	Gospel
Creed	
Sermon	Sermon
	Creed
	Intercessions
	Peace
Offertory	Offertory
Confession	
Comfortable Words	
Preface	Preface
Sanctus	Sanctus/Benedictus
Prayer of Humble Access	
Prayer of Consecration	Eucharistic Prayer
	Lord's Prayer
	Agnus Dei
Communion	Communion
Lord's Prayer	
Prayer of Thanksgiving	Post-Communion
Gloria	
Blessing	Blessing
	Dismissal

The most surprising feature of liturgical reform in the Roman Catholic Church was its rapid nature. A church, which in 1960 had made little progress on the matter, had been totally transformed ten years later. In some parts of Europe, especially Germany, the laity had already been encouraged to participate in the Mass and there was pressure for at least some parts of it to be in the vernacular language. Another innovation was the celebration of Mass facing the people, and even the head of the Holy Office, Cardinal Ottaviani, a theological conservative, celebrated westwards in 1953 at a newly-consecrated church in Lugano. In Britain and Ireland there was strong resistance to such changes from the Roman Catholic hierarchies, though a number of priests were much more amenable to the idea of change. Conferences on liturgical reform held at Spode House, Staffordshire, every year between 1962 and 1968 attracted good attendances. The pressure for liturgical reform resulted in some concessions being made by the Vatican. In 1953 permission was given for mass to be celebrated in the evening and modifications were made to the fasting requirements for such masses; the prescribed fast was initially three hours, later reduced to one hour, but fasting from midnight remained the norm for early morning masses. In 1951 the liturgy for Easter Eve was revised and this revision was, in 1955, incorporated into a more extensive revision of the full liturgy for Holy Week; these revisions permitted the profession of faith and renewal of baptismal promises on Easter Eve to be said in the vernacular rather than Latin. In 1958 a set of instructions issued by Pope Pius XII encouraged the reading of the epistle or lesson at mass in the vernacular and permitted it to be read by a lay person; encouragement was also given for the use of vernacular hymns during the mass.

The draft Constitution on the Sacred Liturgy was first considered by the Second Vatican Council on 4 December 1963. It stated 'that full and active participation by all the people is the primary and indispensable source from which the faithful are to derive a true Christian spirit'; that, whilst private masses remained legitimate, all future emphasis should be placed on 'the preference to be given to communal celebration'; that there must be a proper role for the congregation in the liturgy and that, at sung celebrations, 'the role of the choirs... must never be taken to obliterate or minimise the participation of the people in the common song'; 'that there should be more reading from holy scripture in sacred rites and that the selection should be more varied and suitable'; and that where there are many priests attached to a single church, for example in monasteries, it shall be normal 'to extend the practice of ritual or sacramental concelebration beyond the medieval and modern instances to which we have become accustomed (the occasion of the ordination of priests and consecration of bishops)'.[10] By far the most important provision of the Constitution, however, was its assumption that, though the use of Latin might continue on certain occasions, the bulk of the mass, certainly all those parts in which the congregation were expected to participate, would be in the vernacular. Of course this could not happen overnight since individual national hierarchies had to approve appropriate translations. The first thing that most Roman Catholics noticed, therefore, were some changes in the continuing Latin rite approved by the Council. The introductory prayers at the front of the altar were to be omitted, the prayer over the offerings, the former 'secret prayer' and the doxology at the end of the Canon of the Mass were to be said or sung aloud, the Lord's Prayer was to be said or sung by the whole congregation and not just the celebrant, the formula for the reception of communion was shortened to the phrase *Corpus Christi* to which the communicant now replied *Amen*, and the last gospel was to be omitted so that the mass concluded with the dismissal and blessing. It was also permissible for High Mass to be celebrated without a subdeacon, the deacon taking over most of his liturgical functions but

10   F.R. McManus, *Sacramental Liturgy*, New York 1967, pp 20, 35-6, 38, 71, 101.

with the epistle being read by a lay person. A number of other modifications were made to certain parts of the ceremonial such as bowing to and censing the clergy, and all kissing of the celebrant's hands or objects presented to him were to be discontinued.

In England and Wales the bishops gave their first instructions to the clergy on the requirements for liturgical change on 20 October 1964. This simply set out which parts of the service could be sung at Low, High or Sung Mass. On 10 March 1965 a further instruction was given that the whole of the mass from the beginning to the 'secret prayer', except for the *Kyrie*, and from the Lord's Prayer to the end, except for *Domine, non sum dignus*, *Ite missa est* and the blessing, should be said or sung in English, according to a provisional translation authorised by the English, Welsh and Scottish bishops, with effect from Palm Sunday, 11 April 1965. The Canon of the Mass continued to be said silently in Latin. It was just over four years before a final English version of the new Roman Catholic Mass, including the Canon, was authorised for use from the first Sunday in Advent 1969. A new calendar of feasts was authorised for use from 1 January 1970, a new baptism rite from Easter Sunday 1970 and a complete English Breviary from July 1970. Whereas the Constitution on the Sacred Liturgy had envisaged that Latin would remain the language of the liturgy in some churches, many national hierarchies issued instructions that made this virtually impossible. As a result pressure groups were set up for both the celebration of the new rites in Latin, where there was demand for this, and for certain churches to be permitted to retain some use of the Tridentine Mass, in the same way that Pope Pius V had permitted certain congregations in Spain to retain use of the Mozarabic rite at the time that the Tridentine mass had been introduced.

Although Anglican liturgical revision proceeded quite independently of that in the Roman Catholic Church it was strongly influenced by the new Roman Catholic rites from the 1960s, especially amongst some Anglo-Catholics. The first official move since the *débacle* of 1927-8 was the passing of the Vestments of Ministers Measure 1964 which for the first time made legal the wearing of the eucharistic vestments which some Anglican churches had been familiar with for more than a century, and which had been widely worn in Anglican churches since the 1920s. This was followed in 1966 by the publication of *Alternative Services: First Series*, which officially permitted the experimental use of new liturgies, though they were not much of an advance on what had been put forward in 1927-8. It was followed in due course by much more radical experimental services in Series Two and Three. The Order for Holy Communion in the former, published in 1967, replaced the formal Prayer for the Church by much more informal intercessions for the first time, and introduced a new text to accompany the fraction. The Series Three Communion Service, in experimental use between 1973 and 1980, largely retained the text of the Series Two revision but in a modern language translation, parts of which were identical to those used by English Roman Catholics. A minor, but significant, innovation was the introduction, again from the new Roman rite, of the versicle 'This is the Word of the Lord' after the first two scripture readings. The liturgical revisions in the Church of England were paralleled by revisions in Ireland, Scotland and Wales. The Irish Experimental Liturgy of 1967 was the most conservative. It did not permit the substitution of *Kyrie eleison* for the Ten Commandments and retained *Gloria in excelsis* in the 1662 prayer book position, after communion. There was, however, provision for an Old Testament lesson, for informal intercessions in place of the Prayer for the Church and for a prayer at the offertory, but the core of the service remained that enshrined in the 1662 prayer book and it is hard to detect much desire to engage with the modern liturgical movement. Apart from a decision made in the 1960s to rescind the 1878 canon which had forbidden the placing of a cross on the communion table, all the other restrictive canons of that date, designed to prevent the Church of Ireland from adopting any 'Romanising' ceremonial, such as lighted candles or eucharistic vestments, remained in place. The Scottish Experimental Liturgy of 1966, though still conservative in character, brought the Scottish Episcopal Church further into line with the pre-Vatican Council Roman Catholic Church. It included a preparation and confession at the beginning of the service, *Kyrie eleison* followed by *Gloria in excelsis*, *Benedictus* and *Agnus Dei*. There was also provision for an Old Testament lesson and a short litany could be used as an alternative for the Prayer for the Church. The Church in Wales also published an experimental liturgy in the same year. This permitted the use of *Kyrie eleison* as an alternative for the Ten Commandments and restored *Gloria in excelsis* to its traditional position before the Ministry of the Word. There was provision for an Old Testament lesson and the Prayer for the Church was broken up by the petition 'Hear us, good Lord' at appropriate points. There was also provision for an offertory versicle and response, *Benedictus*, another set of versicles and responses at the fraction, *Agnus Dei* and a post-communion prayer with congregational participation.

All these Anglican liturgies were designed to be experimental and short-lived, to be used alongside the official authorised prayer books. This experimental phase was finally resolved by the authorisation of new official liturgies in England (1980), Scotland (1982), Wales and Ireland (both 1984). Mostly these finalised the drafts of the experimental liturgies. That for Scotland permitted a freer form of intercession than that which had been permitted in the experimental liturgies of 1966 and 1977, but it enshrined officially the major innovation of the latter which was to render the text in modern English. The Irish book of 1984 was also a modern language liturgy and, for the first time, brought the Church of Ireland into the mainstream of liturgical revision. *Gloria in excelsis* was said or sung before the Ministry of the Word and could be omitted in Advent and Lent. The sermon could be preached either after the gospel or after the creed. There were two alternative forms of intercession, both involving congregational participation. This was followed by the penitential rite, which began with either the summary of the law or the Ten Commandments, followed by confession, absolution and the Prayer of Humble Access. This was followed by the sign of peace and the offertory, the latter retaining the formula of 1967 rather than one based on the modern Roman rite adopted by most other Anglican churches. Again for the first time the Lord's Prayer was to follow the Prayer of Consecration and there was provision for both the *Benedictus* and the *Agnus Dei* to be sung as communion antiphons. The Welsh book of 1984 was by far the most conservative of the three Anglican rites outside England and provided little advance on the experimental rite of 1966. The standard text for the communion service remained in traditional English; although a translation into modern English was permitted as an alternative, few congregations used it; the only concession to the modern liturgical movement was the permission to use informal intercessions instead of the formal intercessions provided in the text. It was not until the 1990s that a further experimental rite, bringing the Church in Wales more into line with the Scottish and English Anglican churches and the Roman Catholic Church, was authorised for use. Even so the evidence is that most Welsh congregations still prefer the 1984 book.

Within the context of the British Isles, by far the most advanced of the new official Anglican liturgies was the *Alternative Service Book* authorised by the General Synod of the Church of England for use from 1 May 1980. *ASB* provided two alternative eucharistic rites, one in modern and one in traditional English, with a substantial number of permitted variations and each having four alternative Eucharistic prayers. The modern language rite could be celebrated in such a manner that it was virtually identical to a celebration according to the modern Roman rite, which also has a choice of eucharistic prayers, or the traditional language rite could be celebrated in a manner that met the needs of those who valued the *Book of Common Prayer*, or disliked excessive ritual. It was the ultimate flexible liturgy. It is worth noting that, whereas the Roman Catholic Church, at least in the 1970s, did its best to consign the Tridentine rite to the dustbin of history, the Church of England never officially disowned the *Book of Common Prayer*, and there are many churches in which a version of the 1662 communion service is still celebrated, especially at early morning Sunday communion services. *ASB* could have remained the culmination of Anglican liturgical revision in England, since it brought that church entirely into line with the liturgical thinking of the Roman Catholic Church and those Protestants, especially in the Lutheran and Reformed churches of Europe, which had also been strongly influenced by the liturgical reforms of the Second Vatican Council. In fact *ASB* had only been authorised for ten years, though this authorisation was subsequently extended for a further ten. In 1986 the church's Liturgical Commission produced a new series of services for Lent, Holy Week and Easter. Previously Anglicans who had wished to observe this period with traditional ceremonial had had to use Roman Catholic texts. The new Anglican services provided rites for the imposition of ashes on Ash Wednesday, the blessing and procession of palms on Palm Sunday, washing feet on Maundy Thursday, the veneration of the cross on Good Friday and the blessing of the new fire and paschal candle, as well as the renewal of baptismal vows, on Easter Eve. By 1993, when Bishop David Stancliffe of Salisbury became chairman of the Liturgical Commission, the need to consider what, if anything, should replace *ASB* was becoming urgent. One of the Commission's concerns was that *ASB* permitted too much variation in the Eucharistic rite, which could be very different in ethos, language and text from one Anglican church to another. Perhaps those Anglican churches in Ireland, Scotland and Wales that permitted far less variation were better models to follow. The final result was the publication of *Common Worship* to replace *ASB* in 2000. As in *ASB* two orders are provided for Holy Communion, but with far fewer permitted variants than previously. Order One follows a form which, as Figures 7.3 and 7.4 above show, is entirely consistent with that of the modern Roman rite and with the extensive use of identical texts. This order offers a choice of eight eucharistic prayers; although there are also choices of texts at other points in the service, *Common Worship* avoids the variations in the location of prayers or liturgical actions in the service that could make *ASB* very confusing to the occasional worshipper. Order One can also be used in either modern or traditional language, as can Order Two. This is essentially a reprint of the text of the eucharist published more than thirty years previously in *Alternative Services: Series One*. It is a rite based very firmly on the 1662 prayer book but with permission for the addition or omission of certain prayers. The evidence is that most Anglican churches are currently using Order One for the main eucharist on Sundays and festivals, with Order Two being used for some early morning communion services. Variable eucharistic prayers are now as much the norm in Anglican as in Roman Catholic celebrations throughout Europe.

The extent to which different Protestant denominations have responded to the liturgical agenda of the Second Vatican Council has varied considerably. German and Scandinavian Lutherans have been deeply influenced. Many have abandoned the traditional manner of celebrating with their backs to the people in favour of westward celebration at a free-standing altar. Both the Danish and Swedish Lutheran churches have revised their liturgies to bring them more into line with current Roman Catholic (and Anglican) practice. Note has already been made of the importance of the new liturgy of the Taizé community in stimulating liturgical reform generally, and particularly showing Reformed Protestants that it is possible to adopt traditional liturgical models without sacrificing theological purity. In the British Isles there has been a very positive response to the liturgical agenda of the Second Vatican Council by some non-Anglican Protestants, though there are some churches, such as the Calvinistic Methodists in Wales, the Pentecostalist churches, or some of the more extreme Presbyterian churches in Ireland and Scotland, in which the emerging consensus on eucharistic belief and practice has had no impact whatsoever. The Church of Scotland published a new version of the *Book of Common Order* in 1994. It was based on the earlier version of 1940 but used gender-inclusive language and provided five orders for Holy Communion. The first is in line with the core liturgical developments since the Second Vatican Council with three alternative eucharistic prayers. The second is an order inspired by Celtic sources. The other three are for special occasions: a short order that can be added to a main Sunday service, an order for when children are present and one for use in hospitals or for the private communion of the sick. In 1991 the Baptist Union of England and Wales published *Patterns and Prayers for Christian Worship*. It is not a mandatory liturgy but merely a series of liturgical forms for the guidance of ministers including three orders for Holy Communion, some of which incorporate material from Anglican and Roman Catholic sources. This was complemented in the same year by a new hymn book, *Baptist Praise and Worship*, which incorporated charismatic Evangelical choruses and material from the Taizé and Iona communities, as well as traditional hymns. In 1974 the newly-formed United Reformed Church, a merger of the former Congregational and English Presbyterian churches, published a *Book of Order for Worship*. The eucharistic rite it contains was strongly influenced by that of the *Anglican Alternative Services: Series Three*. This 1974 rite was included in *A Book of Services* published by the United Reformed Church in 1980. A further revision of this rite, including prayers from the modern Roman Catholic rite, was included in a revised URC *Service Book*, published in 1989. The Methodist Church published a new *Service Book* in 1975, the first since the *Book of Offices* published in 1936. The Sunday service was designed in two parts so that it could be either eucharistic or non-eucharistic. As a result an increasing number of congregations saw the value of using the whole service, rather than truncating it, with the result that communion services became more frequent. A new, experimental, communion service was authorised for use in 1991, and in 1998 a revised *Service Book* offered three alternative eucharistic rites for ordinary Sundays, and special ones for Advent, Christmas and Epiphany, Lent and Passiontide, Easter and Ascensiontide and Pentecost. All these new Protestant rites have been influenced by Anglican and Roman Catholic liturgical thinking since the Second Vatican Council and attempts have also been made to incorporate appropriate features from the worship of the Eastern Orthodox churches. It would be foolish to say that there was complete unanimity on liturgical matters across all the main churches of Western Europe, but equally it is the case that the cross-fertilisation of liturgical ideas across the different denominations has been very noticeable and has generally enriched the worshipping experience for Christian communities.

New Churches and Liturgical Reordering

The agreement between liturgists on the essential core of Christian worship has been shared by those responsible for the building of new churches and the adaptation of existing ones to modern liturgical needs. The degree to which the needs of liturgists 'to cleanse worship from the excessively individualistic… to restore the corporate aspect',[11] has been realised in the design of church buildings has, however, differed across Europe with Britain and Ireland being amongst the most conservative nations in their appreciation of modern buildings and the creation of better-ordered space. Peter Hammond, editing a collection of essays produced by members of the New Churches Research Group which he had co-founded in 1957, was scathing in his criticism of church architecture, not just in Britain, but more widely.

> If anything that can properly be described as modern church architecture exists at all today it does so only in embryonic form. There are plenty of new churches: they have been going up in their hundreds during the last few years all over the world… How many of these churches can really be called *modern* buildings is another matter altogether. The great majority are essentially backward-looking; they merely take the formal concepts of the past and deck them in a new brightly coloured wrapper.[12]

What Hammond and his colleagues tried to do was to draw attention to those buildings, mostly in mainland Europe, in which an attempt had been made to design churches in which the liturgical action was placed centrally within the building rather than at one end of a rectangular, and preferably aisled, structure. A good example, designed by two members of the New Churches Research Group, Robert Maguire and Keith Murray, and opened in 1960, was the Anglican church of St Paul's, Bow

---

11   Turner, *From Temple to Meeting House*, p 311.
12   *Towards a Church Architecture*, ed. Peter Hammond, London 1962, p 15.

Common. It had a central altar and the choir stalls were incorporated in the seating which surrounded the altar on three sides. In France there was the pioneering work of Le Corbusier in the pilgrimage chapel at Ronchamp, consecrated in 1955; the churches designed by André Le Donné at Mulhouse (Sacred Heart, 1959) and Porte de Pantin, Paris (St Clare, 1959); and those of Rainer Senn at Pontarlier (Our Lady of Lourdes, 1959), Pelousey, near Besançon, and Villejuif, Paris (both 1961). In Germany there were the most recent churches by the pioneering inter-war architect, Rudolf Schwarz: St Michael, Frankfurt-am-Main (1954); St Andrew, Essen (1957); Holy Family, Oberhausen (1958); St Antony, Essen (1959); St Christopher, Cologne-Niehl (1960). Even more impressive than these was the remarkable parochial centre designed by Emil Steffann and Klaus Rosiny, *Maria in den Benden* at Düsseldorf-Wersten in 1959. This was a series of buildings built around a central courtyard: presbytery, school, meeting rooms and a flexible worship space with a central altar and seating on three sides.

Although the lead in radical church design before the late 1960s was taken by Roman Catholics, with the occasional Anglican contribution, a few modern buildings were designed for Protestant congregations in Europe. There was the Finnish Lutheran church at Orivesi (1961); even though altar, font and pulpit were still placed in a separate, railed, apsidal sanctuary, the seating was angled so that the whole congregation had a clear view of the sanctuary. The Danish Lutheran church at Stengård had a free-standing brick altar with steps behind to reach the pulpit, and the font in front of the pulpit. Seats faced the sanctuary from two different directions if the adjacent hall was opened to provide for a large congregation. The Dutch Reformed churches at Aardenhout and Nagele had sanctuaries that gave a separate and balanced emphasis to both the pulpit and the communion table, and at Aardenhout the congregation faced the pulpit from two different directions. The Swiss Reformed churches at Reinach and Effretikon were L-shaped buildings with their pulpits and communion tables placed in the angle of the building with seats facing them from two different directions. The church of the Taizé community, built in 1962, had a central altar and no fixed pulpit. In Scotland the pioneering Presbyterian contribution to modern church architecture was St Columba's, Glenrothes (1960), which had seating for the congregation on three sides of a central platform and seating for the elders and choir on the fourth side behind the pulpit. The pulpit was placed at the back of the platform, towards one corner, with a free-standing communion table at the front and the font between the pulpit and the altar.

Apart from St Paul's, Bow Common, there was little Anglican architecture that met the tough criteria of Peter Hammond or Frederic Debuyst, who thought that 'the great mass of the faithful, Catholics as well as Protestants' were 'not yet disturbed' by the fact that the church architecture of the 1950s and 1960s was still largely 'unauthentic... a compromise between the old medieval, symbolic and monumental concept of church buildings, and the new vision of things'. Indeed he suspected that they were 'probably not even aware of it'.[13] A typical example was St Oswald's, Tile Hill, Coventry, designed by Sir Basil Spence in 1957-8, a rectangular building

13   Frederic Debuyst, *Modern Architecture and Christian Celebration*, London 1968, p 9.

with the altar still at the east end and a tapestry on the east wall, separated from the congregation in the nave by the customary choir stalls.[14] The same was true of Spence's new Anglican cathedral at Coventry, begun in 1951 and completed in 1962. In terms of its individual furnishings it was thoroughly modern: the stained glass by John Piper and Patrick Reyntiens, the tapestry by Graham Sutherland, the eagle lectern by Elizabeth Frink, the altar cross by Geoffrey Clarke and candlesticks by Hans Coper; but the liturgical arrangement was wholly traditional and not designed for the forms of worship that Anglicans were to adopt within a few years of its completion. Indeed the only Anglican cathedral in the British Isles that makes such provision for modern worship is the one at Portsmouth, where the long-planned extension of a very cramped building was eventually achieved during the provostship of the future Bishop David Stancliffe between 1982 and 1993. This new extension took the form of a

> large assembly place for penitence and preparation, proceeding to initiation around the font... then advances to the Ministry of the Word... And so to Eucharist, the table fellowship of thanksgiving... at the extreme east end the pyx with the reserved sacrament, housed in an arch which symbolises the ascent into heaven, the goal and confirmation of the Christian life and of God's purpose in the universe.[15]

An early indication of Anglican church design responding to the contemporary movement for liturgical reform was the plan of the new church of St Swithun's Kennington, Oxford, in 1958 (Figure 7.5). This was a cruciform building with a central altar, the seating facing it from three directions in the short nave and transepts. The pulpit, lectern, choir stalls and seats for the clergy were all placed behind the altar.

There is no doubt that in the British Isles, as in the rest of Europe, the principal protagonists of modern church design were architects designing buildings for Roman Catholic worship. One of the earliest was the circular church of St Mary at Leyland, designed in 1959 and built in 1962-4 for the Roman Catholic population of this expanding Lancashire town (Figure 7.6). The design was strongly influenced by buildings that the parish priest, Edmund Fitzsimons, had seen on his travels through Europe, ideas he communicated to the project architect, Jerzy Faczynski of Weightman and Bullen. As at Coventry Anglican Cathedral, a number of specialist craftsmen were involved in the project. The ceramic tympanum of the Last Judgement over the entrance and the figure of Christ the King suspended over the altar were provided by Adam Kossowski, the stained glass by Patrick Reyntiens and the bronze Stations of the Cross by Arthur Dooley. St Mary's, Leyland, was followed by two other dramatic circular buildings, the new cathedrals for the Roman Catholic dioceses of Liverpool and Clifton. The former, built in 1962-7 over the completed crypt of Edwin Lutyens's unfinished cathedral, designed in 1932, is a vast building, popularly known as 'Paddy's wigwam'. Over the central altar is a funnel-like lantern with stained glass designed by John Piper and executed by Patrick Reyntiens.

---

14   Colin Cunningham, *Stones of Witness: Church Architecture and Function*, Stroud 1999, p 200.

15   G.S. Wakefield, *An Outline of Christian Worship*, Edinburgh 1998, pp 199-200.

Figure 7.5   Seating plan of St Swithun's, Kennington, Oxford, 1958

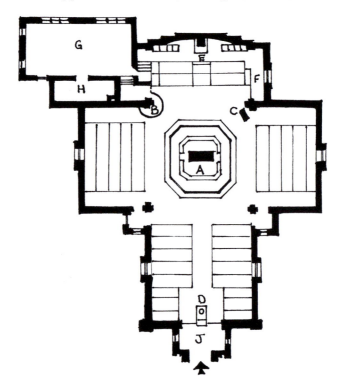

Figure 7.6   Ground plan of new Roman Catholic Church at Leyland, 1959

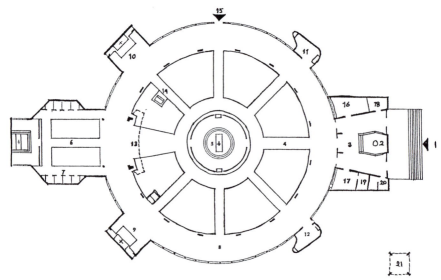

The altar itself was a single block of Macedonian marble on which was a tall crucifix by Elizabeth Frink. Unfortunately the architect, Sir Frederick Gibberd, was unaware of the liturgical changes being contemplated by the Second Vatican Council, and most of the thirteen side chapels he designed for the building quickly became redundant. In some ways the cathedral at Clifton, built in 1969-73, after the liturgical agenda of the Council was being implemented, is the more satisfactory building pastorally, though of admittedly lesser architectural quality. Although the building was basically circular, part of the interior was screened off to serve as the one side chapel in which the Blessed Sacrament was reserved. The main altar was placed on a platform backing on to this chapel and with the congregation arranged in a fan shape on three sides of the altar.

After almost half a century of unremittingly revivalist Roman Catholic architecture in Ireland, the liturgical movement began to have an impact there in the 1960s, most notably in the work of the Donegal architect Liam McCormick. He designed his churches so that they blended with the landscape and were built, as far as possible, of local materials. The influences upon his designs were eclectic, so that no McCormick church is ever the same as another. His church of St Aengus at Burt (1967) was a circular design inspired by the nearby stone fort, the Grianán of Aileach (Figure 7.7, Illustration 7.3). Another church, St Michael's at Creeslough (1971), was strongly influenced by Le Corbusier's Notre Dame de Ronchamp. A third, St Columbcille's at Glenties (1974), had seating at different levels. In some parts of Europe, whilst the debates about the future of Roman Catholic worship were in full flow, architects deliberately designed churches that were flexible and with as few permanent furnishings as possible. A group of such churches was built in Belgium by the architect Marc Dessauvage: Willebroek (1963), Ezemaal (1964), Aarschot (1965) and Westmalle (1967). They were provided with free-standing square altars and free-standing tabernacles for the reservation of the Blessed Sacrament. All other furnishings were designed to be 'mobile, so that their position can be changed according to the different kind of celebration'.[16]

Changing liturgical attitudes and priorities have not just created opportunities for the architects of new churches. They have also been instrumental in the reordering of existing buildings, or provided opportunities for more flexible structures in buildings destroyed during the Second World War or subsequent disasters. In Europe some architects took advantage of damaged buildings to provide far better replacements. At St Roch, Duisdorf, a new nave and chancel were placed at right angles to the existing nave and apsidal chancel, the latter being used as the new baptistery. At St Maurice's, Cologne, the ruins of the former church were used as an open courtyard in front of the new fan-shaped building. The Protestant church at Trier, which had occupied the fourth-century throne room of the former Roman imperial palace since 1856, was severely damaged during the war. Afterwards advantage was taken to replace the heavy nineteenth-century furnishings with a much lighter and more spacious interior, one of the features of which was a sunken baptistery at the west end of the building. The impact of this successful modern interior in one of the city's most ancient buildings was not lost on the Roman Catholics of Trier, who took

---

16   Debuyst, *Modern Architecture and Christian Celebration*, p 66.

Figure 7.7   Seating plan of St Aengus, Burt, 1967

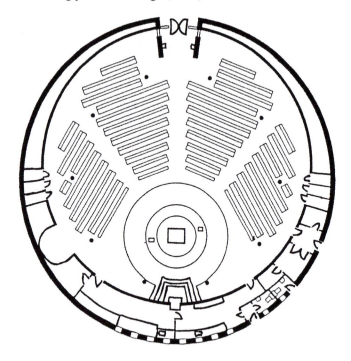

Illustration 7.3   The interior of St Aengus, Burt, 1967

advantage of the liturgical reforms required by the Second Vatican Council to reorder some of their own buildings in a similarly successful and contemporary manner. A particularly impressive example of this reordering is the new circular sanctuary under the crossing of the thirteenth-century Liebfrauenkirche. A rare British example of an attempt to achieve something innovative as a result of damage to an existing building was at Llandaff cathedral, where the work of post-war reconstruction was undertaken under the direction of George Pace between 1949 and 1957. The medieval fabric was restored but the building was given a new chapel off the north aisle and the choir was separated from the nave by a new organ loft on concrete arches, the front of which was used to display Sir Jacob Epstein's *Christ in Majesty*. Another successful post-war rebuilding is that of the London City Temple. Before the war the church had a very traditional late-nineteenth-century nonconformist interior, with a gallery around four sides and the organ in that part of the gallery behind the platform with its large pulpit and communion table. The seating on the ground floor was provided by three blocks of pews with narrow passageways between them. When the church was reopened for worship only one of the four former galleries was replaced. The communion table was placed in a recess with seats for the choir on each side. The seating in the body of the church was separated by a broad central passageway with steps leading up to the sanctuary. On one side of the sanctuary the pulpit projected from the wall and was entered by the staircase built into the wall. On the other side of the sanctuary was a lectern from which the minister could conduct the service. Vases of flowers were placed on pedestals either side of the communion table. On the wall behind the table was a large illuminated cross and above it a small rose window, containing stained glass illustrating the Holy Spirit in the form of a dove.[17]

The liturgical reordering of existing, undamaged, churches in both Britain and Europe has seen a very mixed record of success and failure. Sometimes the architectural importance of the building has frightened architects into being unduly cautious. Sometimes alliances between clergy and congregations, only interested in current pastoral needs, and architects with no academic understanding of the development of church buildings, have produced reorderings of appalling unsuitability. Nowadays the advice given by all conservation bodies is to ensure that work carried out is reversible so that, when fashions change, the worshipping community is not left with a building which no longer meets its needs or one that simply reflects the iconoclasm of a previous generation. A salutary lesson in experience here is provided by the Irish Roman Catholic cathedrals at Enniscorthy and Killarney, both designed in the 1840s by one of the leading early Gothic revivalists, A.W.N. Pugin. At Enniscorthy most of Pugin's furnishings were removed in the reordering of the interior after the Second Vatican Council. The result was not considered satisfactory and in 1994 some of the Pugin furnishings, which had been safely stored, such as the canopied pulpit and episcopal throne, were reinstated, and much of the original decoration of the interior restored or replicated. At Killarney all the Pugin furnishings were not just removed but destroyed. The bleak and featureless interior of what had been a magnificent building cannot now be returned to anything resembling its original splendour. Some enhancing of existing

---

17   Victor Fiddes, *The Architectural Requirements of Protestant Worship*, Toronto 1961, pp 52, 81.

Illustration 7.4   Late-twentieth-century reordering at Waha Church, Belgium

buildings through re-orderings have, however, been very successful. Although it was considered very controversial at the time, the radical reordering of the Wren church of St Stephen's, Walbrook, in the City of London, has subsequently been widely praised. The eighteenth-century pulpit and reredos were retained *in situ*, but all the fixed seating was removed and replaced by flexible chairs, to be arranged as required around a new circular free-standing altar. Radical reorderings of the early medieval churches at Waha in Belgium (Illustration 7.4) and Jelling in Denmark (Illustration 7.5), the former Roman Catholic and the latter Lutheran, have been similarly successful in architectural terms whilst making the buildings liturgically and pastorally flexible.

Illustration 7.5   Late-twentieth-century reordering at Jelling Church, Denmark

Whilst many existing buildings can be successfully adapted to the requirements of a modern liturgy, there are those which retain such complete interiors of a particular period that they are difficult to reorder without severely compromising their architectural integrity. In recent years all Christian churches across Europe have become aware of these problems and devised mechanisms for dealing with them. One of the difficulties is, that faced with the proposal that a particular church should be reordered, it is not always easy to identify how important the building is in the context of the architecture of that period as a whole. This is because basic inventories of religious buildings and their contents have either not been produced or are inadequate. The absence of research on the architectural and liturgical history of church buildings is variable and, in some parts of Europe, virtually non-existent. The countries of Scandinavia, especially Denmark and Sweden, are exceptionally well documented with major series of regional publications on church architecture. The majority of churches in England are listed, and many discussed in considerable detail, in Nikolaus Pevsner's *Buildings of England*, published in 46 volumes between 1951 and 1974, an average of two volumes a year. Many of the earlier volumes have been subsequently revised and the series has been extended to cover Ireland (three volumes to date), Scotland (now more than half complete) and Wales, where only the volume on Gwynedd, covering the historic counties of Anglesey, Caernarfonshire and Meirionydd, remains to be published. The publication of such inventories, and a few more specialist ones such as those in my own *Buildings, Faith and Worship* or *The Religious Condition of Ireland*, enable each surviving building to be contextualised and some sort of informal grading applied to it. At a time when Christianity is in decline across Europe, and when the churches need to adapt existing buildings to new modes of worship, not every building can be preserved intact and it is important that judgements for or against preservation are made on the basis of an adequate knowledge of each building's status in the history of architectural and liturgical development.

Where buildings cannot be adapted or even demolished, because of their architectural or liturgical importance, there are now an increasing variety of satisfactory options. A number of important buildings across Europe have been preserved by dismantling them and re-erecting them at open-air museums. The Ulster Folk and Transport Museum has three such churches, one Anglican, one Presbyterian and one Roman Catholic, reflecting the principal religious divisions of Northern Ireland. There are now two religious buildings, one pre-Reformation and another an eighteenth-century chapel, re-erected at the Museum of Welsh Life. Churches have also been dismantled and re-erected at open-air museums in England, Hungary, the Netherlands, Norway and Sweden. Occasionally original buildings have been adapted as museums *in situ* with the majority of their original furnishings preserved. A particularly good example is the museum at Ullapool in the Scottish highlands, where some seating has been removed to permit the installation of displays on the natural and social history of the local community, but the pulpit and precentor's desk, complete with their original hangings, the gallery fronts, the long communion table and a representative section of seating, have been preserved. Another very satisfactory conversion has been that of the former Countess of Huntingdon's Chapel at Worcester, built in 1804, extended in 1815 and partially refurnished in 1840, which was adapted to serve as a concert hall between 1977 and 1987. The insertion of a stage required the removal of a few box pews, but otherwise the remarkable furnishings, including the two eagle lecterns flanking the pulpit and panels inscribed with the Ten Commandments, Creed and Lord's Prayer on the back wall of the communion enclosure, remain intact. The fact that the chapel's secondary buildings have been adapted to serve as a coffee shop means that the chapel can be visited by the general public even when concerts are not taking place. Another option that has been widely adopted across England, and is being extended to Scotland and Wales, is the vesting of important churches no longer required for worship in bodies such as the Churches Conservation Trust, the Historic Chapels Trust or the Friends of Friendless Churches, funded from a mix of government, church and charitable sources. When this has not been possible a number of churches and chapels have been vested in local trusts set up to secure their preservation.

The principal problem for churches in the modern world is still how to marry pastoral and liturgical adaptation to sensible policies of conservation and preservation. These demands are often conflicting and achieving a balanced response to them is not always easy. It has not been assisted by the way in which some church leaders have openly disparaged the work of conservation bodies or the blinkered approach that some of these bodies themselves have taken towards the preservation of buildings or furnishings of relatively little importance. An essential mechanism in getting the balance right is a controlled and expert planning process. Whilst it has not always been wholly successful, the faculty jurisdiction process of the Church of England, and particularly the important role of the diocesan advisory committees and the Council for the Care of Churches, has provided a model that some other churches have begun to emulate, and which can generally be commended. Even so, some serious mistakes have been, and continue to be, made. Despite strong specialist advice urging that such changes should not be permitted, the parish of St Peter's, Congleton, was granted a faculty after a consistory court hearing in September 1985 to remove its rare central pulpit (one of only four surviving examples) and convert some of the box pews, in a little-altered Georgian interior, into choir stalls. A faculty was granted, in this case without even a consistory court hearing or referral to the Council for the Care of Churches, for the relocation and insensitive repair of a three-decker pulpit and the complete destruction of a set of early-nineteenth-century box pews in the Shropshire church of St Martin's. At Great Gidding Baptist chapel complete furnishings of 1790 were removed and destroyed in a wholly insensitive restoration of the interior that took no account of, and did not even consult on, its historical importance.

Even when churches have been vested in some of the major conservation bodies this has not always, usually for lack of specialist liturgical knowledge, guaranteed satisfactory interpretation or treatment. At Rycote (Oxon) one of the finest of surviving seventeenth-century church interiors has been placed in the guardianship of English Heritage. Although the furnishings were carefully repaired, the altar table was allowed to remain uncovered by an appropriate 'carpet' or frontal, contrary to the express directions of the Canons of 1604, or the manner in which it would have been vested in the late seventeenth century. A significant number of important private chapels in large houses, and even a few free-standing churches and chapels, belong to the National Trust. Again, despite the attention that the trust has paid to making sure that secular furnishings are appropriate, and that fabrics and wallpapers are carefully preserved, it has shown a distinct lack of liturgical expertise in the treatment of some of its ecclesiastical buildings, and in some cases it appears to be unaware of the importance of the ecclesiastical buildings it now administers. This is certainly the case at Calke Abbey in Derbyshire. The house, which is an important time capsule, is extensively described and inventoried in the guidebook. The church in the park gets a bare page of description and nothing that suggests it is one of the most remarkable of all the surviving early-nineteenth-century churches in England. Built in 1826 its interior is completely unaltered, right down to the hangings of the pulpit, reading desk and clerk's seat and the hassocks in the box pews and benches. It is indeed a living relic of the type of church promoted at the time by Bishop Richard Mant: pulpit and reading desk placed on opposite sides of a visible altar table, railed on three sides; music provided by a barrel organ in the west gallery; seating facing eastwards and provided with facilities for kneeling. A church of this importance deserves to be better promoted by those responsible for it, especially when it is one of the major conservation bodies.

The buildings that have been discussed in this volume are representative of the different liturgical traditions that have existed in Western Europe over the last five hundred years. They bear witness to the fact that the liturgy of the western Christian churches have never become totally fossilised. Each new generation brings its new understanding of liturgy and new ideas on how existing buildings can be adapted to meet these new requirements. In an age where we place greater emphasis than previously on the preservation of the past, we need to develop policies which will allow representative examples of a previous liturgical dispensation to be preserved intact as lessons from history, but which also permits other buildings, still needed for worship, to be reordered sensibly, so that their architectural qualities are maintained, or even enhanced. That is the concluding message of this book. It is the author's hope that it will be acted on with an appropriate mix of discretion and enthusiasm.

Guide to Further Reading

General Surveys

The best general guide to the history of Christian worship, which also includes a chapter by Peter Cobb on its architectural setting, is Cheslyn Jones, Geoffrey Wainwright and Edward Yarnold (eds), *The Study of Liturgy*, 1978, and its subsequent revised editions. A shorter, but still useful, introduction is Gordon Wakefield, *An Outline of Christian Worship*, 1998. Also extremely useful is Yngve Brillioth, *Eucharistic Faith and Practice Evangelical and Catholic*, 1930, but with many subsequent reprintings. This is an English translation of the Swedish original by A.G. Hebert, the distinguished English liturgist. Another classic text, though one that needs to be treated with some caution, is Gregory Dix, *The Shape of the Liturgy*, 1945.

There are several good studies showing the impact of the liturgy on the design of church buildings across the centuries of which the best are Colin Cunningham, *Stones of Witness: Church Architecture and Function*, 1999; J.G. Davies, *Temples, Churches and Mosques: A Guide to the Appreciation of Religious Architecture*, 1982; Richard Kieckhefer, *Theology in Stone: Church Architecture from Byzantium to Berkeley*, 2004; Basil Minchin, *Outward and Visible*, 1961; H.W. Turner, *From Temple to Meeting House: The Phenomenology and Theology of Places of Worship*, 1979; and John Wilkinson, *From Synagogue to Church: The Traditional Design*, 2002.

The Legacy of the Pre-Reformation Church

The leading modern authority on early Christian worship is Paul Bradshaw; see especially *The Search for the Origins of Christian Worship*, 1992, and *Early Christian Worship*, 1992. There are good chapters on Eastern Orthodox worship and church buildings in Timothy (Kallistos) Ware, *The Orthodox Church*, 1963, and Nicholas Zernov, *Eastern Christendom*, 1961. For more specialist studies see H-J. Schultz, *The Byzantine Liturgy*, 1986, and Hugh Wybrew, *The Orthodox Liturgy*, 1989. The best introductions to early church buildings are R. Krautheimer, *Early Christian and Byzantine Architecture*, 1965, and K. Painter (ed.), *Churches Built in Ancient Times*, 1994.

For the historic development of the liturgies of the medieval Western church see J.A. Jungman, *The Early Liturgy to the Time of Gregory the Great*, 1959; A.A. King, *Liturgies of the Past*, 1959; S.J.P. van Dijk and J.H. Walker, *The Origins of the Modern Roman Liturgy*, 1960; and C. Vogel, *Medieval Liturgy: an Introduction to the Sources*, 1986. There are very good chapters on medieval English church services in J.R.H. Moorman, *Church Life in England in the Thirteenth Century*, 1946.

Most studies of medieval Romanesque and Gothic architecture are written from the standpoint of the architectural rather than the liturgical or social historian.

Valuable exceptions are Justin Kroesen and Regnerus Steensma, *The Interior of the Medieval Village Church/Het Middeleeuwse Dorpskerkinterieur*, 2004, a beautifully illustrated bilingual text in English and Dutch, and Colin Platt, *The Parish Churches of Medieval England*, 1981.

The best overviews of the Reformation in Europe are Euan Cameron, *The European Reformation*, 1991, and Diarmaid McCulloch, *Reformation: Europe's House Divided, 1490-1700*, 2003. An excellent account of late medieval piety in Britain, and the impact on it of the Reformation, is Eamon Duffy, *The Stripping of the Altars*, 1992. The liturgical rites of the early Reformers – Luther, Zwingli, Bucer, Calvin, Cranmer and Knox – are published in Bard Thompson, *Liturgies of the Western Church*, 1962. The implications of Reformed worship for the adaptation of pre-Reformation church buildings are considered in A.L. Drummond, *The Church Architecture of Protestantism*, 1934 (still useful), J.F. White, *Protestant Worship and Church Architecture*, 1964, and Bernard Reymond, *L'Architecteure Religieuse des Protestants*, 1996.

The Lutheran Churches of Germany and Scandinavia

Because there is virtually no Lutheran presence in the British Isles there are few works on Lutheran worship or church buildings in English. The most useful guide to the former is Chapters IV and VII of Brilioth's *Eucharistic Faith and Practice* (see above). The best modern survey of German and Scandinavian Lutheranism is Nicholas Hope, *German and Scandinavian Protestantism 1700 to 1918*, 1995. This can be supplemented by material in Lars Österlin, *Churches of Northern Europe in Profile*, 1995. Poul Hartling's, *The Danish Church*, 1964, part of a series entitled 'Danish Culture' published by Det Danske Selskab, also contains very useful material on worship and church buildings, and there is a substantial consideration of modern Lutheran worship in the Nordic countries in L.S. Hunter (ed.), *Scandinavian Churches*, 1965. For Icelandic churches see G. Kristjánsson, *Churches of Iceland*, 1988. The literature on Swedish church architecture has been exceptionally comprehensive but it is only available in Swedish. The following can be particularly recommended: P.G. Hamberg, *Norrländska Kyrkoinredningar*, 1974, a general study; S. Fernland, *Kyrkor in Skåne*, 1980, covering the southern province that belonged formerly to Denmark; and Anders Åman and Marta Järnfeldt-Carlsson (eds), *Bebyggelsehistorisk Tidskrift Nr. 22, Övre Norrlands Kyrkor*, 1991, covering the northern provinces of Norrbotten and Västerbotten, including the area of Swedish Lappland.

The Calvinist and Reformed Churches

Chapter V of Brilioth's *Eucharistic Faith and Practice* is still useful. For the Reformed traditions in England see the relevant chapters in Horton Davies's monumental work in six volumes, *Worship and Theology in England*, 1996, largely a reprint of the five volumes published by Princeton University Press between 1961 and 1975. Davies was Henry W. Putnam Professor of the History of Christianity at Princeton.

See also Stephen Mayor, *The Lord's Supper in Early English Dissent*, 1972. There is a good literature on the history of worship in Scotland. Still valuable is W.D. Maxwell, *A History of Worship in the Church of Scotland*, 1955, and G.B. Burnet, *The Holy Communion in the Reformed Church of Scotland*, 1960. These two works have been updated by Duncan Forrester and Douglas Murray (eds), *Studies in the History of Worship in Scotland*, 1984, reprinted with minor revisions in 1996, and, for the late sixteenth and early seventeenth centuries, by Margo Todd, *The Culture of Protestantism in Early Modern Scotland*, 2002. A more general study that covers the worship of Presbyterian churches in England, Ireland and Scotland is J.M. Barkley, *The Worship of the Reformed Church*, 1966. There is a significant section on Irish presbyterian worship in Andrew Holmes, *The Shaping of Ulster Presbyterian Belief and Practice 1770-1840*, 2006.

On the architecture of the Reformed traditions in England and Wales see M.S. Briggs, *Puritan Architecture and its Future*, 1946; Kenneth Lindley, *Chapels and Meeting Houses*, London 1969; Graham Hague, *The Unitarian Heritage*, 1986; and Anthony Jones, *Welsh Chapels*, 1996. The authoritative study of Scottish church buildings in the post-Reformation period is still George Hay, *The Architecture of Scottish Post-Reformation Churches 1560-1843*, 1957. There is also useful material in Peter Galloway, *The Cathedrals of Scotland*, 2000, and Ian Lindsay, *The Scottish Parish Kirk*, 1960.

There is, perhaps surprisingly, now a good literature in English on the Reformed Church in Hungary, in respect of both worship and buildings. See Graham Murdock, *Calvinism on the Frontier 1600-1660: International Calvinism and the Reformed Church in Hungary and Transylvania*, 2000, and Balázs Dercsényi, Gábor Hegyi, Ernö Marosi and Béla Takács, *Calvinist Churches in Hungary*, 1992. Unfortunately such publications do not exist for either the Netherlands or Switzerland, and one needs to rely on material in Dutch, French or German. For the Netherlands see Joris van Eijnatten and Fred van Lieburg, *Nederlandse Religiegeschiedenis*, 2005, and C.A. van Swigchem, T. Brouwer and W. van Os, *Een Huis voor Het Woord: Het Protestantse Kerkinterieur in Nederland tot 1900*, 1984. For Switzerland see Georg Germann, *Der Protestantische Kirchenbau in der Schweiz von der Reformation bis zur Romantik*, 1963, Klaus Speich and H.R. Schläpfer, *Kirchen und Kloster in der Schweiz*, 1978, and Bernard Reymond, *Temples de Suisse Romande*, 1997. The worship of the French Calvinists, both in seventeenth-century France and in exile, is excellently covered in Tessa Murdoch (ed.), *The Quiet Conquest: The Huguenots 1685 to 1985*, 1985. For a good historical overview of the Reformed churches generally in Europe before c.1700 see Philip Benedict, *Christ's Churches Purely Reformed: A Social History of Calvinism*, 2002, and Andrew Spicer, *Calvinist Churches in Early Modern Europe*, 2007, the latter being particularly angled towards worship and church buildings.

The Buildings of the Anglican 'Via Media'

As might be expected there is an extensive literature on both Anglican worship and the buildings in which it took place. An early seminal work, still of great value, is

G.W.O. Addleshaw and F. Etchells, *The Architectural Setting of Anglican Worship*, 1948, though this has been substantially revised and updated, especially for the period after 1700, by Nigel Yates, *Buildings, Faith and Worship: The Liturgical Arrangement of Anglican Churches 1600-1900*, rev. ed. 2000.

The best guide to the development of Anglican worship since the Reformation is G.J. Cuming, *A History of Anglican Liturgy*, 2nd ed. 1982. An older work, still of value, is W.K.L. Clarke (ed.), *Liturgy and Worship*, 1932. The high church Anglican liturgies of the seventeenth and eighteenth centuries have been edited with an authoritative commentary by W.J. Grisbrooke, *Anglican Liturgies of the Seventeenth and Eighteenth Centuries*, 1958.

Detailed studies of Anglican architecture between the seventeenth and early nineteenth centuries are Marcus Whiffen, *Stuart and Georgian Churches*, 1948; B.F.L. Clarke, *The Building of the Eighteenth Century Church*, 1963, and *Church Builders of the Nineteenth Century*, rev. ed. 1969; and M.H. Port, *Six Hundred New Churches*, rev. ed. 2006, a detailed study of the work of the Church Building Commission between 1818 and 1856. Mark Chatfield, *Churches the Victorians Forgot*, 1979, is beautifully illustrated but the text needs to be treated with caution as his fundamental hypothesis on the nature of the 'Prayer Book' interior has been significantly undermined by recent research. Graham Parry, *The Arts of the Anglican Counter-Reformation*, 2005, provides a general overview of Anglican high church architecture, literature and music in the early seventeenth century.

Useful background material on the historic development of Anglicanism between the late sixteenth and early nineteenth centuries will be found in Judith Maltby, *Prayer Book and People in Elizabethan and Early Stuart England*, 1998; Kenneth Fincham (ed.), *The Early Stuart Church 1603-42*, 1993; John Spurr, *The Restoration Church of England, 1646-1689*, 1991; W.M. Jacob, *Lay People and Religion in the Early Eighteenth Century*, 1996; John Walsh, Colin Haydon and Stephen Taylor (eds), *The Church of England c.1689-1833: From Toleration to Tractarianism*, 1993; and Frances Knight, *The Nineteenth Century Church and English Society*, 1995. For Ireland see Alan Ford, *The Protestant Reformation in Ireland*, rev. ed. 1997; F.R. Bolton, *The Caroline Tradition of the Church of Ireland*, 1958; and Nigel Yates, *The Religious Condition of Ireland 1770-1850*, 2006. For Wales see Glanmor Williams, W.M. Jacob, Nigel Yates and Frances Knight, *The Welsh Church from Reformation to Disestablishment 1603-1920*, 2007.

Counter-Reformation Roman Catholicism

The best guide to the development of Roman Catholic liturgy is George Every, *The Mass*, 1978. The most authoritative studies in English of the Tridentine rite of 1570, which remained, with some minor alterations, the liturgy of the Roman Catholic Church until the reforms of the Second Vatican Council, remain those of Adrian Fortescue: *The Ceremonies of the Roman Rite Described*, 1917, and *The Mass: A Study of the Roman Liturgy*, rev. ed. 1926. For a more recent but more limited study see J. Harper, *The Forms and Orders of the Western Liturgy from the Tenth to the Eighteenth Centuries*, 1991.

There is surprisingly little material available in English on the Roman Catholic Church in mainland Europe. Two recent studies of French Roman Catholicism contain good sections on religious practice: Timothy Tackett, *Priest and Parish in Eighteenth Century France*, 1977, and John McManners, *Church and Society in Eighteenth Century France*, 2 vols, 1998. There is similar material for one of the German dioceses in Marc Forster, *The Counter-Reformation in the Villages: Religion and Reform in the Bishopric of Speyer, 1560-1720*, 1992, and for Spain in Helen Rawlings, *Church, Religion and Society in Early Modern Spain*, 2002.

There is a more extensive literature available on Roman Catholicism in Britain and Ireland. The best overview is Michael Mullett, *Catholics in Britain and Ireland, 1558-1829*, 1998. Still authoritative on England and Wales are John Bossy, *The English Catholic Community 1570-1850*, 1975, and Eamon Duffy (ed), *Challoner and His Church: A Catholic Bishop in Georgian England*, 1981. Roman Catholic architecture in England and Wales is surveyed in Bryan Little, *Catholic Churches since 1623*, 1966, and Christopher Martin, *A Glimpse of Heaven: Catholic Churches in England and Wales*, 2006. There is less available material on Scotland but C. Johnson, *Developments in the Roman Catholic Church in Scotland 1789-1829*, 1983, is useful.

There is a very good recent literature on Roman Catholicism in Ireland. This includes S.J. Connolly, *Priests and People in Pre-Famine Ireland*, rev. ed. 2001; P.J. Corish, *The Catholic Community in the Seventeenth and Eighteenth Centuries*, 1981, and *The Irish Catholic Experience: A Historical Survey*, 1985; M. Elliott, *The Catholics of Ulster: A History*, 2000; I. Murphy, *The Diocese of Killaloe in the Eighteenth Century*, 1991, and *The Diocese of Killaloe 1800-1850*, 1992; G. O'Brien and T. Dunne (eds), *Catholic Ireland in the Eighteenth Century: Collected Essays of Maureen Wall*, 1989; T.P. Power and K. Whelan (eds), *Endurance and Emergence: Catholics in Ireland in the Eighteenth Century*, 1990; O.P. Rafferty, *Catholicism in Ulster 1603-1983: An Interpretative History*, 1994; and Nigel Yates, *The Religious Condition of Ireland 1770-1850*, 2006.

Ecclesiology and Neo-Medievalism

Although there is a substantial literature in English on the British Isles, that for mainland Europe is much less extensive. This major gap has recently been filled by Jan de Maeyer and Luc Verpoest (eds), *Gothic Revival: Religion, Architecture and Style in Western Europe 1815-1914*, 2000. A slightly older but still useful book is Georg Germann, *Gothic Revival in Europe and Britain: Sources, Influences and Ideas*, 1972. A valuable comparative study is Nikolaus Pevsner, *Ruskin and Viollet-le-Duc: Englishness and Frenchness in the Appreciation of Gothic*, 1969.

For the British Isles, and especially England and Wales, the still authoritative study, which sets ecclesiology and neo-medievalism in church architecture in its broader cultural and social context, is Kenneth Clark, *The Gothic Revival*, first published in 1928 and substantially revised by the author in 1962. The major Victorian church architects are surveyed in B.F.L. Clarke, *Church Builders of the Nineteenth Century*, rev. ed. 1969. A very useful collection of essays is Chris Brooks and Andrew Saint (eds), *The Victorian Church: Architecture and Society*, 1995. The pioneering study of early ecclesiology in England is J.F. White, *The Cambridge Movement*, 1962. All these studies tend to simplify the process of the adoption of ecclesiological opinions and styles, particularly in relation to furnishings and liturgical arrangement, in the British Isles; for a revisionist approach see Nigel Yates, *Buildings, Faith and Worship: The Liturgical Arrangement of Anglican Churches*, rev. ed. 2000, especially chapters 7 and 8.

For guides to surviving buildings see especially Peter Howell and Ian Sutton (eds), *The Faber Guide to Victorian Churches*, which covers England, Scotland and Wales, but not Ireland, and J.C. Curl, *Victorian Churches*, 1995. Two very good regional studies are D.R. Elleray, *The Victorian Churches of Sussex*, 1981, and Roger Homan, *The Victorian Churches of Kent*, 1984. Reference should also be made to Michael Fisher, *Pugin-Land: A.W.N. Pugin, Lord Shrewsbury and the Gothic Revival in Staffordshire*, 2002. When it comes to furniture and ornaments, rather than the buildings themselves, P.F. Anson, *Fashions in Church Furnishings 1840-1940*, rev. ed. 1965, remains unsurpassed.

There are also a substantial number of biographies of nineteenth- and early-twentieth-century architects who specialised in church design: Jill Allibone, *Antony Salvin 1799-1881*, 1988; J.M. Crook, *William Burgess and the High Victorian Dream*; Anthony Quiney, *John Loughborough Pearson*, 1979; Andrew Saint, *Richard Norman Shaw*, 1976; Phoebe Stanton, *Pugin*, 1971; Anthony Symondson and Stephen Bucknall, *Sir Ninian Comper*, 2006; Paul Thompson, *William Butterfield*, 1971.

On religious architecture in Ireland in the nineteenth century see D.S. Richardson, *Gothic Revival Architecture in Ireland*, 1983; J. Sheehy, *The Rediscovery of Ireland's Past: The Celtic Revival 1830-1930*, 1980; and P. Galloway, *The Cathedrals of Ireland*, 1992.

For the historical and liturgical background to all these developments, especially, though not exclusively, in Anglican churches, see Nigel Yates, *Anglican Ritualism in Victorian Britain 1830-1910*, 1999. Also useful are A Härdelin, *The Tractarian Understanding of the Eucharist*, 1965; Owen Chadwick, *The Victorian Church*, 1966-70; Edward Norman, *The English Catholic Church in the Nineteenth Century*, 1984; and Derek Holmes, *More Roman than Rome: English Catholicism in the Nineteenth Century*, 1978.

Liturgical Renewal and Church Design in the Twentieth Century

By far the best introductory reading is Hugh McLeod (ed.), *World Christianities c.1914-c.2000*, 2006. This includes chapters on the Pentecostal and Charismatic movements by Allan Adamson, the religious ferment of the 1960s by Michael Walsh, liturgy by Bryan Spinks, music by Andrew Wilson-Dickson, art by Julia Vincent and architecture by Nigel Yates. It can be supplemented for the British Isles by Adrian Hastings, *A History of English Christianity, 1920-2000*, 2001.

The texts of Anglican liturgies in this period are printed in Bernard Wigan (ed.), *The Liturgy in English*, 2nd edn 1964, and three volumes edited by Colin Buchanan:

Modern Anglican Liturgies 1958-1968, 1968; *Further Anglican Liturgies 1968-1975*, 1975; and *Latest Anglican Liturgies 1976-1984*, 1985. Paul Bradshaw (ed.), *Companion to Common Worship*, 2001, is an excellent commentary on the texts most recently authorised for use in the Church of England. For the Anglican background to the liturgical movement see A.G. Herbert, *Liturgy and Society*, 1935; A.G. Herbert (ed.), *The Parish Communion*, 1937; Peter Jagger, *A History of the Parish and People Movement*, 1978; and Donald Gray, *Earth and Altar*, 1986.

For Roman Catholic worship the comparable studies are those by Frederick McManus, *Sacramental Liturgy*, 1967; J.D. Crichton, H.E. Winston and J.R. Ainslie (eds), *English Catholic Worship: Liturgical Renewal in England Since 1900*, 1979; and Allen Bouley (ed.), *Catholic Rites Today: Abridged Texts for Students*, 1992. For liturgical developments in English nonconformity see the last two volumes of Horton Davies's *Worship and Theology in England* (see above) and for the Church of Scotland the chapter by Duncan Forrester on 'Worship since 1929' in Forrester and Murray's *Studies in the History of Worship in Scotland* (see above). For the exceptionally interesting liturgy of the ecumenical Taizé community see M. Thurian, *The Eucharistic Liturgy of Taizé*, 1962. A broad perspective on liturgical developments within the Reformed tradition is provided by Bryan Spinks and Ian Torrance (eds), *To Glorify God: Essays on Modern Reformed Worship,* 1991.

On the relationship between liturgy and architecture since 1945 the most fundamental studies are those by Peter Hammond: his *Liturgy and Architecture*, 1960, and the collection of essays by architects and liturgists he edited, *Towards a Church Architecture*, 1962. Both books set the issue in a fully cross-denominational and European perspective. Also fundamental is Frederic Debuyst, *Modern Architecture and Christian Celebration*, 1968. Other useful books are Gilbert Cope (ed.), *Making the Building Serve the Liturgy*, 1962, and W.E.A. Lockett (ed.), *The Modern Architectural Setting of the Liturgy*, 1964. Richard Giles, *Re-pitching the Tent: Re-ordering the Church Building for Worship and Mission*, 1999, is an important contribution to the current debate on reordering issues but tends to emphasise the pastoral side of the argument, sometimes at the expense of the conservationist one.

There are a number of useful works on modern church building of which the following can be strongly recommended: E.S. Heathcote, *Church Builders*, 1997; Richard Hurley, *Irish Church Architecture in the Era of Vatican II*, 2001; G.E. Kidder-Smith, *The New Churches of Europe*, 1964; and Robert Maguire and Keith Murray, *Modern Churches of the World*, 1965. Bryan Little's *Catholic Churches Since 1623* (see above) contains a good section on the middle years of the twentieth century in England and Wales.

Guide to Buildings to Visit

One of the best introductions to the design and contents of churches from the Middle Ages to the present day will be found in the displays of the Rijksmuseum Het Catharijneconvent, the national museum of the religious history of the Netherlands in Utrecht. Other national museums and some diocesan museums contain displays of religious objects but none are so comprehensive. The best religious displays in the British Isles will be found at St Mungo's Museum in Glasgow.

The Legacy of the Pre-Reformation Church

An interesting reconstruction of a late medieval church has recently been opened at the Museum of Welsh Life in St Fagan's on the outskirts of Cardiff. There are no complete surviving medieval church interiors anywhere in Europe though many churches preserve individual medieval furnishings. There are excellent survivals of medieval altar-pieces in Germany at Creglingen, Mühlhausen and Tiefenbronn; in Italy at Niedelana and San Ingenuino; in Spain at Aneuto, Artziniega and Gumiel de Hizán; and at Heiligenblut (Austria), Sahl (Denmark) and Sankt Olof (Sweden). The finest surviving examples of tabernacles or sacrament houses will be found in Germany (Audorf, Datteln, Everswinkel, Kalchreuth, Lichtenhagen, Ottensoos, Petersdorf, Stiepel), and at Fresnes and Vieux-Thann in France, Bocholt in Belgium and Haraldsted in Denmark. Several churches in England have good sets of surviving choir stalls, good examples being those of Salle (Norfolk), Stowlangtoft (Suffolk) and Tong (Shropshire). They will also be found in Germany at Ditzingen, Ennetach and Oberlenningen and in Sweden at Gothem. Rood screens, complete with their lofts, can be seen at Patricio (Wales) and at several churches in Brittany (Kerfons, Le Roche-Maurice, Lambader-en-Plouvorn, Le Faouët, Loc-Envel, Melrand, Plélauff). Stone pulpits are frequent survivals in Italy (Brancoli, Gropina, San Gennaro, Santa Maria a Monte), England (Bovey Tracey, Harberton, Swimbridge) and Germany (Eglosheim, Hernsheim, Mertloch, Pipping, Ruppertsberg). Wooden ones are also common in England (Burnham Norton, Castle Acre, Horsham St Faith, South Burlingham). Complete sets of medieval benches can be seen in both England (Abbotsham, Altarnun, Brent Knoll, Fressingfield, Trull, Wiggenhall St Germans, Wiggenhall St Mary) and Germany (Bechtolsheim, Kiedrich, Ruffenhofen), but not generally elsewhere in Europe, the complete set of backless benches at Rhäzüns (Switzerland) being an exceptionally rare survival. The most common survivals throughout Europe, are pre-Reformation baptismal fonts, mostly of stone, though there are surviving lead fonts in England at Ashover and Brookland and in France at St Evrault-de-Montfort and bronze fonts in Germany at Büsum, Eilsum, Groothusen and Wiegboldsbur.

The Lutheran Churches of Germany and Scandinavia

The conservatism of the Lutheran churches has meant that there are many substantially unaltered buildings throughout Germany and Scandinavia, especially in the Nordic countries, in which seventeenth to nineteenth century furnishings have been preserved, a modest selection of which are included in the list below in addition to two interesting buildings outside this area.

Denmark

There are substantially complete seventeenth century interiors in the town churches of Køge and Ringsted; Holmen's Church of 1641-8 and Our Saviour Church of 1682-96 in Copenhagen also have largely unaltered contemporary interiors. Christian's Church, Copenhagen, was designed by the theatre architect Nicholas Eigtved in 1755-9, and is a rare Danish example of the pulpit-altar arrangement with three sets of galleries and box pews. The church at Varde has a T-plan interior refitted in 1812 with painted box pews and galleries in three projections.

England

The former St George's Lutheran Church in Stepney, now vested in the Historic Chapels Trust, was built in 1762-3 and has a well-preserved galleried interior with box pews and the altar placed in front of a raised pulpit.

Germany

There are two well-preserved pre-1800 interiors in Lübeck. At St Giles the box pews are tiered in the aisles and there are a handsome eighteenth-century reredos, pulpit and organ-case. At St James there are seventeenth-century stalls, box pews and gallery and a Baroque altar-piece and pulpit of 1717.

Netherlands

St Ursula's Lutheran Church in Utrecht has a T-plan interior of 1743 with a central pulpit, box pews, galleries in all three projections and loose benches in the middle of the church.

Norway

Austre Moland, on the south coast, has a delightful wooden church of 1673 with virtually complete early-nineteenth-century furnishings: galleries, box pews, canopied pulpit, chancel screen and a reredos incorporating a picture of the Last Supper. The church at Kongsberg, built in 1740-61, is an excellent Norwegian example of the pulpit-altar arrangement with the organ placed over the pulpit, contemporary candlesticks and altar frontal, box pews and three sets of galleries.

Sweden

Genarp, in Skåne, has an excellent example of an early post-Reformation church, built in 1593-6; the pulpit is contemporary with the building but most of the other furnishings – galleries (one containing a family pew), reredos and numbered box pews – date from the seventeenth and eighteenth centuries. The church at Kristianstad, built in 1626-58, has largely contemporary furnishings, including the seating. Kalmar cathedral, designed by Nicholas Tessin the Younger and consecrated in 1682, has an exceptionally well-preserved contemporary interior with box pews, galleries, organ case, canopied pulpit and elaborate altar-piece. The church at Habo, near Jönköping, is one of many eighteenth-century wooden churches in Sweden, with an elaborately painted interior and completely unaltered furnishings. The church at Nordingrå, on the Baltic coast, is a fine neo-Classical building of 1825-9 with contemporary box pews, altar-piece and a canopied pulpit with tromp l'oeil 'hangings'.

Calvinist and Reformed Churches

A number of examples of such churches in England, Wales and Scotland are listed in W.N. Yates, *Buildings, Faith and Worship: The Liturgical Arrangement of Anglican Churches 1600-1900*, rev. ed., Oxford 2000, pp 193-226, and for Ireland in W.N. Yates, *The Religious Condition of Ireland 1770-1850*, Oxford 2006, pp 358-70. The examples listed here for the British Isles, as well as those for Hungary, the Netherlands and Switzerland, are therefore extremely selective.

England

There are well-preserved interiors in the former Baptist chapels of 1859 at Cote (Oxon), of c.1800 at Goodshaw (Lancs) and of the early nineteenth century at Loughwood (Devon), administered respectively by the Historic Chapels Trust, English Heritage and the National Trust. The best-preserved Independent or Congregational interior is the early nineteenth century one at Walpole (Suffolk), now in the care of the Historic Chapels Trust. There are completely preserved interiors of 1809 at the Providence Chapel, Chichester, and of 1805-23 at the Jireh Chapel, Lewes, both belonging to the strict Calvinist sect established by William Huntington in Kent and Sussex. The best-preserved Unitarian chapel is the Old Meeting House at Ipswich, built by a local carpenter, Joseph Clarke, in 1699-1700. The Methodist New Room at Bristol, built in 1739 and enlarged in 1748, also preserves all its original furnishings.

Hungary

The Kálvin Square Church in Budapest has a well-preserved interior of 1816-51, with side galleries designed to resemble boxes in a theatre, organ over the entrance and a pulpit-altar on the opposite wall. This is in the form of a Classical reredos with the pulpit placed behind the communion table, the whole composition being in marble with a gilded chalice incorporated in the table's front panel. One of the great features of Hungarian Calvinist churches is their painted interiors and furnishings: there are good examples of such buildings at Adorjás (1836), Csaroda (which still preserves its thirteenth-century wall paintings and has later texts and furniture), Egerlövö (a thirteenth-century church with a transept, making it a T-plan, added in 1828), Kórós (1793-1834) and Sajószentpeter (a medieval church refitted in 1752), where the painted pulpit has a seat for the bishop underneath incorporated into its columns; opposite is a canopied seat for the minister and the apsidal chancel is filled with a gallery for the organ and seating underneath. The church at Túrkere is a handsome Classical building of 1845-7 with a canopied pulpit in the middle of one of the long walls, canopied seats on either side, a railed communion enclosure in front of the pulpit and the font placed between the pulpit and the communion table; the seating is arranged so that it faces the pulpit from three separate directions.

Ireland

Excellent nineteenth-century Presbyterian interiors have been recreated in the re-erected Omagh Meeting House at the Ulster Folk and Transport Museum and the replica Mountjoy Meeting House at the Ulster-American Folk Park. Of Presbyterian churches in use that at Rathneeny (Co. Donegal) preserves its early nineteenth century furnishings intact. The best survival of late-eighteenth- and early-nineteenth-century Presbyterian interiors in Northern Ireland will be found among the meeting houses of the Non-Subscribing Presbyterian Church: Banbridge (1844-6), Crumlin (1835-7), Downpatrick (1787), Dunmurry (early-nineteenth-century furnishings) and Rademon (1787-9). In most of these churches no permanent communion table has been installed and the long tables, covered with white cloths, are still put out on communion Sundays.

Netherlands

The medieval village churches at Aduard, Kimswerd, Marssum and Zuidlaren preserve excellent seventeenth- and eighteenth-century furnishings including canopied pulpits and family pews, benches and organ cases. Among town churches that at Gouda, as well as its magnificent array of sixteenth- and seventeenth-century stained glass, has also retained its mid-nineteenth-century tiered seating, pulpit and precentor's desk in the nave. The church at Metslawier, built in 1776, retains complete contemporary furnishings including pulpit, a family pew, box pews painted red, long communion table, organ and psalm boards. In the town church at Sneek the box pews of 1872 are arranged in a semi-circle to face a canopied pulpit of 1626 in the middle of the south nave arcade. The organ case dates from 1710 and there is a late-seventeenth-century magistrate's pew and painted Commandments board.

Scotland

The best-preserved urban interior is that of St Nicholas West, Aberdeen, rebuilt in 1752-5 by James Gibbs, and preserving most of its original furnishings. The earliest complete rural interiors are those at Glenbuchat (Aberdeenshire) of 1792 and

Croick (Highland) of 1825-7; both retain their long communion tables, pulpits and precentor's desks, the communion table at Glenbuchat incorporated into one of the rows of box pews. Other Scottish churches preserving their long communion tables are Ardchattan (Argyll and Bute), Durisdeer (Dumfries and Galloway), Ceres and Kilmany (Fife), Rogart (Highland) and South Ronaldsay (Orkney). Very complete late-nineteenth-century interiors of the traditional Scottish type will be found at Kinneff (Aberdeenshire, refitted 1876) and Sleat (Highland, rebuilt 1876-7), the latter still with a precentor's desk in front of the pulpit and square communion table in the front pew of the central block of seating.

Switzerland

The church at Wädenswil, rebuilt in 1764-7, has the pulpit placed on one of the long walls with the font placed in the middle of two passageways separating the four blocks of box pews that are angled to focus on the pulpit. The church at Uster, built in 1823-4, has a quasi-Lutheran type of pulpit-altar arrangement in the middle of one of its long walls; the marble pulpit is entered through the wall built over the marble communion table, with a marble font placed in the open space in the middle of the church, and seating facing the pulpit from three different directions.

Wales

Despite the strength of Protestant nonconformity in the nineteenth century very few chapels have kept their furnishings intact. Although box pews have frequently been retained, the popularity of the pulpit-platform in Wales after 1860 has meant that most earlier chapels have had their earlier pulpits and communion enclosures replaced. Exceptions are the Welsh Baptist Chapel of 1829 at Hengoed (Glam), the re-erected Capel Penrhiw of 1777 at the Museum of Welsh Life, Capel Heol Awst of 1826-7 at Carmarthen, Yr Hen Fethel of 1773 at Glanaman (Carms), Capel Salem of 1850-60 at Cefncymerau (Gwynedd), Capel Newydd of 1769 at Nanhoron (Gwynedd), Capel Caebach of 1715 at Llandrindod Wells (Powys), Capel Beili-du of 1858 at Pentrebach (Powys) and Capel Bethesda'r Fro of 1806-7 at Llantwit Major (Glam). The Pales Quaker Meeting House at Llandegley (Powys) has an exceptionally well-preserved eighteenth-century interior.

The Buildings of the Anglican 'Via Media'

By far the most extensive inventories are those published in Yates's, *Buildings, Faith and Worship* and *The Religious Condition of Ireland* (see previous section). The suggestions made here are therefore highly selective and designed to give both a chronological and a geographical balance across England, Ireland, the Isle of Man and Wales. There are no examples of unaltered pre-ecclesiological Anglican buildings in Scotland, Europe or the Channel Islands.

England

The earliest surviving substantially complete interiors are those of the late sixteenth and early seventeenth centuries at Brooke (Rutland) and Langley Chapel (Salop). There are also substantially complete interiors of 1616 at Leweston (Dorset), 1626-30 at Leighton Bromswold (Cambs) and of 1637 at Wilby (Norfolk). Bramhope Chapel (Yorks) is a rare example of a largely unaltered church built during the Commonwealth, and reflecting Puritan sympathies. The first architectural statement of Laudian high churchmanship is Staunton Harold (Leics) of 1653-65. Virtually contemporary, but illustrating more modest taste, is the simple church of St Ninian at Brougham (Cumb), which dates from 1660-62. Three of the finest eighteenth century churches are those at Shobdon (Hereford) of 1752-6, King's Norton (Leics) of 1757-75, with a central three-decker pulpit placed in front of the altar, and Avington (Hants) of 1768-71. The best surviving example of an eighteenth-century city church is St Swithun's, Worcester, which dates from 1734-6. Teigh (Rutland) of 1782 and Gatton (Surrey) of 1834 are excellent unaltered examples of the collegiate-style interior, the pulpit, reading and clerk's desks at the former being placed over and around the entrance doorway. St John's, Chichester, is a largely unaltered example of an elliptical church of 1812-13, with its three-decker pulpit placed in front of, and its organ over, the altar, and galleries around all four sides of the interior. The churches of 1815-16 at Mildenhall (Wilts) and of 1826 at Calke (Derbys) are among the best surviving examples of the type of church, growing in popularity from the 1780s, in which the pulpit and reading desks were placed on opposite sides of the entrance to the sanctuary. The Gibside Chapel (Durham), fitted up for worship in 1812, has a three-decker pulpit placed behind a central altar table, which is railed on all four sides.

Ireland

The earliest surviving substantially unaltered interiors are those at Ballinderry (Co. Antrim) of 1664-8, the Rotunda Hospital Chapel in Dublin of 1757-62 and Hillsborough (Co. Down) of 1760-73. Good examples of later buildings are Ballymakenny (Co. Louth) of 1785-93, Leckpatrick (Co. Tyrone) of 1816-34 and Dromard (Co. Sligo) of 1817. The last two are T-plan interiors with the pulpit and reading desks placed, respectively, opposite the transept or at the west end of the nave. Ireland is the only part of Britain in which three cathedrals largely preserve pre-ecclesiological interiors: they are those of 1790-1818 at Downpatrick (Co. Down), of 1817, slightly reordered in 1845, at Killala (Co. Mayo) and of 1837 at Kilfenora (Co. Clare).

Isle of Man

The only completely unaltered pre-ecclesiological church is the old church at Kirk Braddan, rebuilt in 1773.

Wales

The earliest substantially unaltered interior is that at Gwydir Uchaf Chapel (Gwynedd) of 1673. There are good eighteenth-century interiors of 1736-9 at Worthenbury (Wrexham) and of 1769 at Llangwyllog (Anglesey). There are also completely unaltered later interiors of 1832 at Ynyscynhaearn (Gwynedd), 1838-9 at Llanddoged (Conwy) and 1840 at Llandygwnning (Gwynedd).

Counter-Reformation Roman Catholicism

Again Yates's *Buildings, Faith and Worship* and the *Religious Condition of Ireland* (see above) are useful guides to surviving examples of substantially unaltered pre-ecclesiological Roman Catholic churches in Britain and Ireland. There is, however, no equivalent guide for other European countries. The liturgical re-ordering of churches required by the reforms of the Second Vatican Council have ensured that very few Roman Catholic churches preserve their original furnishings and liturgical arrangements intact. Individual furnishings, such as the elaborate baroque reredoses of Austria and Southern Germany, as well as those of Southern France, Portugal and Spain, or the lavish pulpits of Belgium and Northern France, have been carefully preserved, and in many cases refurbished, but sanctuaries, and in many cases seating as well, have been altered, often quite radically. The churches listed below are good examples of buildings where liturgical re-ordering has been minimal and virtually all the pre-1850 furnishings have been preserved.

England

There are substantially complete interiors in Dorset at East Lulworth, designed in 1786-7 by John Tasker for Thomas Weld and now vested in English Heritage; in East Yorkshire at Marton, built in 1789 for William Constable of Burton Constable, where the chapel in the house, converted from the former ballroom, dates from 1844; in North Yorkshire at Crathorne (1834) and Leyburn (1835), both of which retain their original box pews; and in Oxfordshire at Milton House Chapel of 1773 and Stonor, designed by James Thorpe in 1796-1800. All these buildings are in strong recusant areas and mostly associated with Roman Catholic landed families. The chapel at Wardour Castle (Wiltshire) begun in 1776 and extended in 1788 also preserves many of its original furnishings including the lavish altarpiece imported from Italy.

France

By far the best-preserved interior, with complete furnishings of the early nineteenth century including numbered box pews and hat pegs, is at the now redundant church of Cheverny in Loire-et-Cher. Box pews also survive at Richelieu (Indre-et-Loire), Souvigny-en-Sologne (Loire-et-Cher) and Thionville (Moselle), though at the last of these the doors have been removed. Among many churches in Northern France which contain large collections of eighteenth-century furnishings one of the most complete is that of St Germain-de-Tallevonde-La-Lande-Vaumont in Calvados, which retains a virtually complete interior of 1745 with contemporary pulpit, lectern, benches, choir stalls, confessionals, chandeliers and three elaborately carved and gilded wooden altar-pieces.

Ireland

The best preserved early Roman Catholic church interior is that formerly at Drumcree and now re-erected at the Ulster Folk and Transport Museum. The church was built in 1783 and refitted in the mid-nineteenth century. It has a simple galleried interior with the two altars placed on one of the long walls. The Tullyallan Mass House, of 1768 and extended in 1830, at the Ulster-American Folk Park has a reconstructed interior, with accommodation for the priest in the extension at the back of the altar. The oldest Roman Catholic church still in use is St Patrick's, Waterford, a former grain store converted to serve as a church in 1764. It preserves its original two-tier galleries and altar-piece, but the seating has been altered. More complete is the church of 1777 at Ardkeen in County Down, which preserves its early-nineteenth-century furnishings virtually intact.

Netherlands

The best example of a former hidden church is that of St Nicholas, more popularly known as Our Lord in the Attic, which now forms part of the Amstelkring Museum in Amsterdam. It dates from 1661-3 and was enlarged in 1735-6. The interior, of the latter date, is complete and includes two sets of galleries. Other largely unaltered, formerly hidden churches, which preserve most of their original furnishings, are the Old Catholic churches of 1743 in Delft and 1722-34 in The Hague.

Scotland

The only substantially complete pre-1850 interiors are the church of 1787 at Tynet in Moray and the chapel of c.1820 at Traquair House in the Scottish Borders.

Ecclesiology and Neo-Medievalism

The vast quantity of surviving ecclesiological and neo-medievalist church buildings across Europe during the late nineteenth and early twentieth centuries means that the examples listed below are highly selective. In every part of Europe it is possible to find buildings, not mentioned below, in which such designs are reflected.

Belgium

The church of St Peter and St Paul at Ostend, rebuilt in flamboyant Gothic style in 1905-7, is comparable to work in England by architects such as J.L. Pearson. The church of Our Lady and St Remaclus at Spa was built in neo-Romanesque style in 1885-6 and has largely contemporary furnishings.

England

There are substantially unaltered examples of early ecclesiological buildings at Arley (Cheshire) of 1845 by Anthony Salvin, with additions of 1856-7 by G.E. Street; at the Roman Catholic church in Warwick Bridge (Cumbria) of 1840-41 by A.W.N. Pugin; at Sowton (Devon) of 1844-5 by John Hayward; at Fretherne (Glos) of 1846-7 by Francis Niblet; at Tetbury (Glos) of 1848 by S.W. Daukes; at Kilndown (Kent) of 1839-45 by Anthony Salvin with furnishings by R.C. Carpenter and William Butterfield; at the Roman Catholic church in Cheadle (Staffs) of 1841-6 by A.W.N. Pugin; at the Catholic Apostolic Church in Albury (Surrey) of 1840 by McIntosh Brooks with advice from Pugin; at Wilmcote (Warws) of 1841, possibly by William Butterfield; at Cholderton (Wilts) of 1840-50 by T.H. Wyatt and David Brandon; at Leigh Delamere (Wilts) of 1846 by James Thompson; at Yazor (Hereford) of 1843-51 by George Moore; at St Peter's, Leeds, of 1839-41 by R.D. Chantrell; at the Mill Hill Unitarian Chapel in Leeds, of 1847 by Bowman and Crowther and strongly influenced by St Peter's; and at the Hyde Unitarian Chapel in Gee Cross (Tameside), also by Bowman and Crowther.

Later ecclesiological or neo-medievalist churches are so plentiful that only a selection of the best and least altered can be attempted: the Roman Catholic cathedrals at Arundel (1870-3 by J.A. Hansom) and Norwich (1884-1910 by G.G. and J.O. Scott); St Philip and St James, Oxford (1860-66) and St John the Evangelist, Torquay (1861-85), both by G.E. Street; Lyndhurst (Hants) of 1858-70 by William White; St Bartholomew, Brighton, of 1872-4 by E.E. Scott; Studley Royal (Yorks) of 1870-78 by William Burges; St Augustine, Kilburn (1870-77) and Truro Cathedral (1880-1910), both by J.L. Pearson; Hoar Cross (Staffs) of 1872-6 and Clumber (Notts) of 1886-9, both by G.F. Bodley; Richard's Castle (Salop) of 1890-93 by Norman Shaw; Holy Trinity, Sloane Street, Chelsea, of 1888-90 by J.D. Sedding; the Unitarian Church at Todmorden (Yorks) of 1869 by John Gibson.

France

There are two very important neo-medievalist churches in Paris: that of Ste Clothilde is an early ecclesiological design of 1846-56 with contemporary furnishings and stained glass; St Jean, Montmartre, is an excellent Art Nouveau design of 1897-1904 with largely contemporary furnishings and stained glass; the nearby church of Sacre Coeur, begun in 1876 and completed in 1919, is a partially neo-Romanesque design modelled on the cathedral of St Front at Périgueux. The cathedral of St Corentin at Quimper was restored in an elaborate neo-medievalist style in 1856 and retains many furnishings of this date including the magnificent Gothic baldichino over the high altar.

Hungary

The Matthias Church in Budapest was remodelled between 1874 and 1896 and contains many sumptuous furnishings of this period including paintings, stained glass, altars, pews and organ case.

Ireland

Relatively few ecclesiological or neo-medievalist churches in Ireland retain their original furnishings substantially intact. Exceptions are the Roman Catholic church at Barntown (Co. Wexford) of 1848 by A.W.N. Pugin, the Roman Catholic cathedrals at Letterkenny (1891-1901 by William Hague and T.F. McNamara) and Loughrea (1897-1903 by William Byrne), the chapel of St Patrick's College, Maynooth (1875 by J.J. McCarthy with an enormous collegiate interior) and the Church of Ireland cathedrals at Cork (1867-79 by William Burges) and Kilmore (1858-60 by William Slater).

Netherlands

The former Roman Catholic church of St Willibrord in Utrecht, designed by Albert Tepe in 1876 and clearly strongly influenced by the work of A.W.N. Pugin, preserves its interior virtually intact with contemporary stained glass, pulpit, rood beams and an elaborate scheme of decoration. There is a similar, largely unaltered, interior, also by Tepe, at the Jesuit Church of St Francis Xavier (1880) in Amsterdam.

Scotland

The Scottish Episcopal Church was an early convert to ecclesiological principles with handsome early examples of such work at St Mary's, Dalkieth (1843-7 by William Burn and David Bryce), the college chapel at Glenalmond (Perthshire) of 1846-51 and the Cathedral of the Isles at Millport of 1850-51, both by William Butterfield, and at St John's, Jedburgh (1844 by Thomas Hayward). Later buildings retaining most of their original furnishings are All Saints, Challoch (Dumfries and Galloway), of 1871-2 by Habershon and Pite, and St Andrew's, Fort William (Highland), of 1876-80 by Alexander Ross. The Church of Scotland began to be influenced by the ecclesiological movement from the late 1870s but most of the best neo-medievalist churches date from the early years of the twentieth century. Good examples of these include the churches designed by P.M. Chalmers at Ardwell (1900-1902) and Colvend (1910-11) in Dumfries and Galloway, and the remarkable church of St Conan on the shores of Loch Awe (Argyll and Bute), begun in 1907 and completed in 1930. Slightly earlier are the churches at Connel (Argyll and Bute) of 1887-8, strongly influenced by Iona Abbey, and St Cuthbert's, Edinburgh, of 1892-5, with its raised sanctuary and marble communion table. Other important ecclesiological buildings in Scotland are the Crichton Memorial Church of 1890-97 at Dumfries and the Thomas Coats Memorial Baptist Church at Paisley of 1894; both preserve their original furnishing virtually intact. Slightly altered but still impressive is the Kelvinside-Hillhead Parish Church of 1875-6 in Glasgow.

Sweden

The church of 1858 at Kristinehamn was designed by C.G. Brunius, who supervised the restoration of Lund Cathedral. Its exterior is strongly influenced by Danish Gothic but the interior is very traditional with box pews and a re-used pulpit and reredos from an earlier church. There are handsome neo-Gothic churches in brick at Luleå (1893), now the cathedral, Sundsvall (1889-94) and Umeå (1887-94), though all have been altered internally. There is also a handsome neo-Gothic church in wood at Videln, north-west of Umeå, built in 1901-3 to a design by F.O. Lindström, but some of the furnishings are either earlier or later. The Gothic revival in Scandinavia generally was heavily constrained by traditional Lutheran concepts of church design and liturgical arrangement.

Wales

There are early ecclesiological buildings, substantially unaltered internally, at Llangorwen (Ceredigion) of 1841 by H.J. Underwood, at Pentrobin (Flintshire) of 1843 by John Buckler and at Llangasty Talyllyn (Powys) of 1848-56 by J.L. Pearson. One of the finest ecclesiological restorations in Wales was that carried out at Hawarden (Flintshire) by Sir G.G. Scott for Sir Stephen Glynne in 1857-9. Although there are a large number of later Victorian churches, most are by local architects and there is comparatively little work by major English architects. Exceptions are the churches by Sir G.G. Scott at Bwlch-y-Cibau (Powys) of 1862-4 and Rhyl (St Thomas) of 1861-9; by William Butterfield at Penarth (St Augustine) of 1865-6 and Elerch (Ceredigion) of 1868; by John Gibson at Bodelwyddan (Denbighshire) of 1858-60; by Alfred Waterhouse at Penmaenmawr (Conwy) of 1868; by G.E. Street at Llandysilio (Powys) of 1867-8; by J.L. Pearson at St Theodore's, Port Talbot, of 1895-7; and by G.F. Bodley at St German's, Roath, of 1882-4. The finest Arts and Crafts church in Wales is that by Sedding and Wilson of 1895-8 at Brithdir (Gwynedd). Welsh nonconformists remained deeply suspicious of the ecclesiological movement and there are no buildings that fully reflect its principles.

Liturgical Renewal and Church Design in the Twentieth Century

Church building in Europe since the First World War has been extensive, partly to meet the growth in population and partly to replace buildings severely damaged or completely destroyed in two world wars. Many other churches, especially Roman Catholic ones, have been extensively reordered to meet the needs of the modern worshipping community and liturgical directives. The range, in architectural terms, has been enormous, from the late phases of neo-Gothic, to new variations of the Classical and Byzantine styles, to the revival of nationalistic styles in parts of

Scandinavia, to the thoroughly contemporary and functional. The examples that follow are, therefore, highly selective and reflect the personal choice of the author.

Belgium

The cathedral at Ieper (Ypres) was almost completely destroyed in the First World War. It was rebuilt as an exact replica of its previous late medieval style afterwards. Also at Ieper, St George's Anglican church is an interesting building of 1927-9, designed by Sir Reginald Blomfield in the Dutch colonial style with neo-Classical furnishings. The church at Waha, built in 1050, has been re-ordered since 1950 in a manner which enhances its original architecture. The modern furnishings include stained glass by Louis-Marie Loudot (1958) and Jean-Michel Folon (2004), the rood over the chancel arch, the crucifix on the east wall of the chancel and the free-standing stone altar.

Channel Islands

The undistinguished church at Millbrook, Jersey, built in 1840, was transformed in 1934 by A.B. Grayson with glass fittings by René Lalique, including the font, reredos to the high altar and side altar, altar rails, screens, windows and door panels, in a style remarkably reminiscent of cinema architecture of the period.

Denmark

The most important modern church in Denmark is undoubtedly Grundtvig's Church in Copenhagen, designed by P.V.J. Klint and built between 1921 and 1940. Though dramatic externally it is very conservatively arranged internally and not well adapted to contemporary liturgical needs. Far more functional are the Lutheran and Roman Catholic churches in Esbjerg. The former was built in 1961 with its altar, font and pulpit on a platform at the east end; it has a tent-like roof, the angles of which are filled with abstract stained glass. The latter was built in 1969 and is a simple square, arranged diagonally inside, with a modest altar, font, benches and organ case in bleached wood, a free-standing tabernacle and a large crucifix suspended over the altar. The twelfth-century church at Jelling, the most important early Christian site in Denmark, has been excellently reordered since 1960, with a new organ case, seating, flooring and sanctuary furnishings.

England

Gothic remained the predominant style for church buildings in England until after the Second World War. An early example of a church to reject ecclesiological principles was the Epiphany, Gipton, Leeds, designed by N.F. Cachemaille-Day in 1938 with a central altar balanced on either side by two ambos serving as lectern and pulpit, and with the choir and organ in transeptal galleries. The Lady chapel formed a separate small church raised sixteen steps behind the main altar. There are four late-twentieth-century cathedrals in England: the Anglican ones at Guildford

(1932-66) and Coventry (1951-62) and the Roman Catholic ones at Liverpool (1960-67) and Clifton (1965-73). Whereas the Anglican ones are still basically ecclesiological in their arrangement, with separate chancels and with the choir stalls between the congregation and the high altar, the Roman Catholic ones are circular with a free-standing central high altar in the middle of the seating. Whereas the furnishings are as conservative as the building at Guildford, those at Coventry are much more modern and include works by major contemporary artists such as John Piper and Graham Sutherland. Another very satisfactory circular Roman Catholic church is that at Leyland (Lancs), designed by the Liverpool firm of Weightman and Bullen, and built in 1959-64. It includes in its decoration ceramics by Adam Kossowski and Stations of the Cross in cast-bronze by Arthur Dooley.

France

Churches were still being designed in the traditional manner in the inter-war period. Good examples are the Ossuary Chapel of 1927-32 at Douaumont, near Verdun, a fine essay in neo-Romanesque with Art Nouveau furnishings, and the neo-Byzantine basilica of St Theresa at Lisieux, begun in 1929 but taking forty years to complete, its interior filled with marble and brightly-coloured mosaics. Among the finest recent churches in France is that of St Joan of Arc, built over the spot on which she was burnt in 1431 in the Grande Place at Rouen. It was designed by Louis Arretche and opened in 1979. It has a central altar with, behind it, a wall of brightly-coloured late medieval stained glass from the former church of St Vincent. It is both a statement of contemporary church design and a vehicle for the conservation and display of important medieval artifacts.

Germany

As noted in Chapter 7, Germany was the birthplace of modern church design in the 1930s. Extensive damage to German churches in the Second World War necessitated major rebuilding and restoration schemes. Good examples are Lübeck cathedral, where the nave has been re-ordered with a central altar and the apsidal choir partitioned off by glass screens, and the Protestant church of Our Saviour in Trier. This is housed in the fourth-century tribunal of the Roman imperial palace and has been used as a Protestant church since 1856. The vast interior, reopened in 1956, has simple modern furnishings with a sunken baptistery at the west end. Also in Trier the Roman Catholic church of Our Lady, built in 1235-60, has been effectively re-ordered with a new circular sanctuary and free-standing altar under the lantern of the central tower.

Ireland

Irish church design remained highly traditional until the 1960s. Good examples are the country's three twentieth-century cathedrals. That at Mullingar, designed by Ralph Byrne and built in 1933-9, is neo-Classical in style with twin west towers and a shallow dome over the crossing. Its interior is a riot of marble and mosaics.

The cathedral at Cavan, designed by W.H. Byrne and built in 1939-42, is also neo-Classical, but without the central dome, and with elaborate neo-Classical furnishings. The cathedral at Galway, designed by J.J. Robinson and built in 1957-65, is similar to Byrne's design for Mullingar cathedral, also with twin west towers and a central dome; its only concession to the liturgical movement is the placing of the high altar centrally under the dome. The earliest 'modern' Roman Catholic church in Ireland, and indeed the only one until well after the Second World War, was Christ the King, Turner's Cross, Cork, designed in 1927 by the Chicago-based architect and pupil of Frank Lloyd Wright, Barry Byrne. Its impressive west front incorporates a statue of Christ over the main doorway and leads one into a vast tent-like interior, though the furnishings are insipid and disappointing. A particularly attractive and successful group of post-1960 churches are those designed by Liam McCormick in County Donegal, of which the best examples are those at Burt (1965-7), Creeslough (1970) and Glenties (1975). Much damage was done to church buildings, notably the cathedrals designed by A.W.N. Pugin at Enniscorthy and Killarney, as a result of poorly-planned and executed reorderings after the Second Vatican Council. That at Enniscorthy was partially restored in 1994 when Pugin's canopied pulpit and episcopal throne were reinstated and much of the original colour scheme restored or replicated.

Luxembourg

The former seventeenth-century Jesuit church was made the cathedral in 1870 and substantially enlarged at the east end between 1935 and 1963. This, though Gothic in style, has a strong Art-Deco ethos and much excellent modern stained glass.

Scotland

There is comparatively little good modern church-building in Scotland and some of the best post-war work has been in the reordering of existing buildings. Three good examples of such reordering schemes in the Church of Scotland are those at the Canongate Kirk in Edinburgh, Bellie Kirk in Fochabers and Daviot Kirk, near Inverness. The Canongate Kirk was a late-seventeenth-century building, remodelled internally in 1946-54 in imitation of an Anglican Laudian interior, with a draped communion table, canopied pulpit and painted box pews. Bellie Kirk was built in 1798; in 1954 it was given a neo-Classical makeover with five blocks of seating facing the new pulpit and communion table. Daviot Kirk was built in 1826 and much altered in 1935 when the galleries were removed; in 1991 the church was returned to something approaching its original appearance when the galleries were reinstated and a new coved plaster ceiling introduced to complement the original pulpit and seating in the body of the church.

Sweden

The churches at Bureå and Skellefteå are good examples of the Swedish national style of the early twentieth century. The former was built in 1917-20 and preserves its original, very traditional fittings, together with a crucifix over the entrance to the chancel, dating from 1957. St Olof's, Skellefteå, was built in 1925-7 and a new organ gallery was fitted in 1964-5. Two Swedish cathedrals also have important modern furnishings. Karlstad Cathedral, built in 1723-7, was reordered in 1967-8 with new seating and light fittings, and a free-standing altar with a cross of Orrefors crystal. A more recent addition is a wrought iron candlestand designed to replicate the branches of a tree. The fifteenth-century cathedral at Vaxjö was remodelled in the late nineteenth century but returned to its original design and plan in 1957-60. The interior is a most agreeable mix of traditional and modern furnishings. The traditional includes the grey-painted box pews and the baroque organ case in the western organ gallery. More contemporary furnishings and works of art include the altar table, canopied pulpit and font by Jan Brazda (1959); the altar triptych by Bertil Vallien (2002); the sanctuary carpet by Ulla Gowenius (1995); a second font in stone and glass by Göran Wärff (1995); the candlestand illustrating the Tree of Life and Knowledge by Erik Höglund (1995); statues by Eva Spångberg and stained glass by Bo Beskow and Jan Brazda.

Wales

There are few good modern churches in Wales. Interesting Roman Catholic ones are at Amlwch, designed by the Italian-Welsh architect, G. Rinvolucci, to resemble an upturned boat, and built in 1932-7, and Machynlleth, an early example of a post-Vatican II building, designed by Sir Percy Thomas, with seating on three sides of a free-standing altar, and opened in 1965. Two important pieces of reconstruction after war damage for the Anglican Church in Wales are Llandaff Cathedral and St Mary's, Swansea. The former is the work of George Pace between 1949 and 1957; the medieval fabric was reinstated but the building given a new chapel, entirely contemporary in design, off the north aisle and the choir was separated from the nave by a new organ loft, the front of which was used to display Sir Jacob Epstein's *Christ in Majesty*. By comparison, St Mary's, Swansea, rebuilt in 1954-9, is a rather old-fashioned Gothic revival building with very insipid furnishings, though it does have some good modern stained glass.

Index